"So often I've been asked to recommend a st
interested in the workings of the mind – no
Kirschner and Hendrick offer alongside each seminai a...
wonderful job of situating the content in the broader scientific context,
and in the classroom".

– **Daniel Willingham**, *Professor of Psychology and Director
of Graduate Studies, University of Virginia*

"As the volume of research into psychology and education grows, it
becomes ever harder for researchers, let alone teachers, to keep up
with the latest findings. Moreover, striking results often turn out to
be difficult, or impossible to replicate. What teachers need, therefore,
is good guidance about research that has stood the test of time, and
practical guidance about how these well-established findings might
be used to inform teaching practice, and this is why this is such an
extraordinary, wonderful and important book. Paul Kirschner and Carl
Hendrick have selected the most important research publications in the
psychology of education, and, for each publication, they have provided a
summary of the research, the main conclusions, and a series of practical
suggestions for how the findings might inform teaching practice. I know
of no other book that provides such a rigorous, accessible and practical
summary of the last fifty years of research in educational psychology, and
anyone who wants to understand how research can improve teaching
needs to read this book. Highly recommended".

– **Dylan Wiliam**, *Emeritus Professor of Educational Assessment,
University College London*

"It's hard to overstate just how fabulous this book is; a book I've wanted
to exist for years and now here it is. A judicious and comprehensive
selection of seminal research papers presented by two expert
communicators, this is absolutely superb – from the mouth-watering
list of contents, and through each of the chapters. I meet teachers
in schools every week who, on hearing about various findings from
research, feel liberated, enlightened with a whole new perspective on the
problems they wrestle with in their classrooms. Teachers are busy – often
overwhelmed – and all too frequently have not yet found the time or had
the opportunity to engage with research that underpins the profession
they've committed their lives to. This book is going to change that for
a lot of people. The format is excellent, presenting the original papers
alongside insightful commentary and key practical recommendations; a
brilliant idea executed with style! Every school should have this book and
every teacher should read it".

– **Tom Sherrington**, *Education Consultant; author of
The Learning Rainforest and Rosenshine's Principles in Action*

"Teachers are rightly encouraged to base their practice on research – but education research is a huge field and it's hard to know where to start. This book provides the answer: it's valuable in its own right as a summary of some key research papers, and it's also a great starting point for further reading and research".

– **Daisy Christodolou**, *Director of Education at No More Marking*

"With the increasing volume of calls for education to become more evidence based, teachers everywhere have shaken their heads and wondered where on earth they're supposed to find the time to locate, read and evaluate the ever-increasing acreage of research papers out there. Worry no more. In *How Learning Happens: Seminal Works in Educational Psychology and What They Mean in Practice*, Kirschner and Hendrick have done the hard work so that you don't have to. The volume you have in your hands has compiled some of the most important and prominent research papers in the field of education and distilled them into a form that is genuinely useful to anyone chipping away at the chalkface. But, not only is this a resource of unparalleled utility, it's also a fascinating and world-enlarging read".

– **David Didau**, *author of Making Kids Cleverer*

"Future historians of education will look back on this period as a Renaissance; a time when dogma and orthodoxy were being challenged, and gatekeepers, priesthoods, and shamans felt the ground shift beneath their feet. The sleep of reason has bred monsters of pedagogy, and they have been fattened and nurtured by the relative ignorance of the teaching profession. Not a general ignorance, but a specific one: ignorance of the evidence bases behind the claims made in education. This Renaissance has been accompanied by an evolution, as teachers and academics reach out to one another and seek sincere, authentic dialogue. But, unless we stand on the shoulders of giants who have gone before us, each generation is doomed to rediscover what their ancestors painstakingly uncovered. For the health of the profession, we need the best of what we know in one place, so that successive generations of educators can carry on from their ancestors, and carry the conversation into the future rather than tread water endlessly.

This book is the perfect resource with which to do so. I can give no higher accolade than to say that every teacher should be familiar with the research it represents, its chapters should be required reading on every teacher induction course, and no teacher should account themselves a professional until they can demonstrate its acquaintance. I wish I had read it in the infancy of my career".

– **Tom Bennett**, *Founder, researchED*

How Learning Happens

How Learning Happens introduces 28 giants of educational research and their findings on how we learn and what we need to learn effectively, efficiently, and enjoyably. Many of these works have inspired researchers and teachers all around the world and have left a mark on how we teach today.

Exploring 28 key works on learning and teaching, chosen from the fields of educational psychology and cognitive psychology, the book offers a roadmap of the most important discoveries in how learning happens. Each chapter examines a different work and explains its significance before describing the research, its implications for practice, how it can be used in the classroom and the key takeaways for teachers. Clearly divided into six sections, the book covers:

- How the brain works and what this means for learning and teaching
- Prerequisites for learning
- How learning can be supported
- Teacher activities
- Learning in context
- Cautionary tales and the ten deadly sins of education.

Written by two leading experts and illustrated by Oliver Caviglioli, this is essential reading for teachers wanting to fully engage with and understand educational research as well as undergraduate students in the fields of education, educational psychology and the learning sciences.

Paul A. Kirschner is Emeritus Professor of Educational Psychology at the Open University of the Netherlands as well as Guest Professor at the Thomas More University of Applied Science in Belgium.

Carl Hendrick teaches at Wellington College, UK, and holds a PhD in Education from King's College London.

How Learning Happens

Seminal Works in Educational Psychology
and What They Mean in Practice

Paul A. Kirschner and Carl Hendrick
Illustrated by Oliver Caviglioli

Routledge
Taylor & Francis Group

LONDON AND NEW YORK

First published 2020
by Routledge
2 Park Square, Milton Park, Abingdon, Oxon OX14 4RN

and by Routledge
52 Vanderbilt Avenue, New York, NY 10017

Routledge is an imprint of the Taylor & Francis Group, an informa business

British Library Cataloguing-in-Publication Data
A catalogue record for this book is available from the British Library

Library of Congress Cataloging-in-Publication Data
Names: Kirschner, Paul A., author. | Hendrick, Carl, author.
Title: How learning happens : seminal works in educational
    psychology and what they mean in practice / Paul A. Kirschner and Carl
    Hendrick.
Description: Abingdon, Oxon ; New York : Routledge, 2020. | Includes
    bibliographical references and index.
Identifiers: LCCN 2019043773 (print) | LCCN 2019043774 (ebook) | ISBN
    9780367184568 (hardback) | ISBN 9780367184575 (paperback) | ISBN
    9780429061523 (ebook)
Subjects: LCSH: Learning, Psychology of. | Educational psychology. |
    Effective teaching.
Classification: LCC LB1060 .K57 2020 (print) | LCC LB1060 (ebook) | DDC
    370.15/23--dc23
LC record available at https://lccn.loc.gov/2019043773
LC ebook record available at https://lccn.loc.gov/2019043774

ISBN: 978-0-367-18456-8 (hbk)
ISBN: 978-0-367-18457-5 (pbk)
ISBN: 978-0-429-06152-3 (ebk)

Typeset in Tisa OT
by Swales & Willis, Exeter, Devon, UK

Contents

Preface: "standing on the shoulders of giants"

Of all the bitter feuds in science, one of the fiercest is the "war of letters" between Robert Hooke and Isaac Newton. One particular dispute between them popularised a phrase which has now become one of the most prominent observations about progress and the way in which true scientific discovery is inherently cumulative in nature. The source of their disagreement was on the nature of diffraction, how light bends around objects. Hooke claimed to have discovered this but Newton claimed that this "discovery" was largely as a result of earlier work by French and Italian scientists who had conducted similar experiments. In a letter to his great rival in 1675, Newton wrote:

> You have added much several ways, & especially in taking the colours of thin plates into philosophical consideration. If I have seen further it is by standing on the shoulders of Giants.

Although widely attributed to Newton, the phrase dates back a lot further. In 1159, John of Salisbury (1955) wrote of Bernard of Chartres that he

> used to compare us to dwarfs perched on the shoulders of giants. He pointed out that we see more and farther than our predecessors, not because we have keener vision or greater height, but because we are lifted up and borne aloft on their gigantic stature.

However, the earliest recorded usage of the phrase dates back to the sixth century with the Latin Grammarian Priscian.

At the time of Newton's use of the phrase, the notion of knowledge as a perpetually changing process that is refined and built upon previous knowledge and discovery was very much a contested one as James Gleick (2004) notes:

> The idea of knowledge as cumulative – a ladder, or a tower of stones, rising higher and higher – existed only as one possibility among

many. For several hundred years, scholars of scholarship had considered that they might be like dwarves seeing farther by standing on the shoulders of giants, but they tended to believe more in rediscovery than in progress.

(p. 29)

Newton's great achievement was to shift our understanding of the world away from philosophical speculation to empirical analysis based on testable hypotheses. A similar process is currently happening in education where, in the last 30 years, findings from cognitive psychology have radically changed our understanding of how we learn. Up until relatively recently, pedagogy, and more specifically instructional design was largely based on theory drawing on tangential fields such as philosophy, politics, sociology, anthropology, and linguistics, often to the exclusion of research on psychology, cognition, and the brain. For example, Vygotsky's theory of the zone of proximal development and the idea that knowledge is socially constructed is a *sine qua non* in most teacher training courses while Baddeley's model of working memory is often omitted. Many teachers could go through their whole training without ever hearing about cognitive load theory despite the fact that Dylan Wiliam (2017) has referred to it as the "single most important thing that teachers need to know".

Research on how we learn should endeavour to stand on the shoulders of giants and aim to move toward a broad consensus where multiple different disciplines converge on a common, agreed set of principles. E. D. Hirsch (2002) refers to this as "the principle of independent convergence" which he claims

has always been the hallmark of dependable science. In the nineteenth century, for example, evidence from many directions converged on the germ theory of disease. Once policymakers accepted that consensus, hospital operating rooms, under penalty of being shut down, had to meet high standards of cleanliness. The case has been very different with schools.

We can see this convergence in some areas. For example, one of the most uncontested areas of research on learning is on the testing effect; the finding that retrieving something from our long-term memory is enhanced when the to-be-remembered information is retrieved through testing with proper feedback. This retrieval practice is possibly the most effective way of retaining knowledge and yet this discovery is often used poorly in schools with testing being used as the final endpoint in a process of learning as opposed to a means of facilitating learning along the journey. Not only is it often used poorly, or not at all in schools, it is apparently also not taught to future teachers in universities and teacher colleges (Pomerance, Greenberg, & Walsh, 2016; Surma, Van Hoyweghen, Camp, & Kirschner, 2018). This neglect is compounded by ideologically based movements that see the testing of children as a form of abuse which is leading to a mental health crisis. This speaks to the problem of resistance to scientific progress and the persistence of dogmatic positions. The case of Ignaz Semmelweis is instructive here in illustrating this.

In 1846 the general hospital in Vienna, Austria, was experiencing a peculiar problem. There were two maternity wards at the hospital, but at the first clinic the puerperal fever mortality rate was around 16% while at the second the rate was much lower, often below 4% (see Figure 0.1). Mysteriously there were no apparent differences between the two clinics to account for this. Part of the mystery was that there was no mystery at all. Almost all of the maternal deaths were due to puerperal fever (a bacterial infection of the uterus following childbirth), a common cause of death in the nineteenth century. This fact was well known outside the hospital and many expectant mothers begged to be taken to the second clinic instead of the first. The stigma around the first clinic was so great that many women preferred to give birth in the street than be taken there.

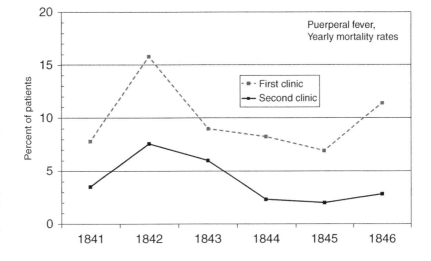

FIGURE 0.1
PUERPERAL FEVER
MORTALITY RATES
FOR THE FIRST
AND SECOND
CLINIC AT THE
VIENNA GENERAL
HOSPITAL
1841–1846.
(SEMMELWEIS,
1983)

Working at the hospital at the time was the Hungarian Ignaz Philipp Semmelweis, a young physician who had risen to the ranks of assistant professor where his duties included the examining of patients before the professor's rounds. Perturbed by the seemingly unsolvable nature of this mystery, young Ignaz recorded that it made him "so miserable that life seemed worthless" and so he dedicated himself to finding a solution. The breakthrough came when his close friend and colleague Jakob Kolletschka died of the same infection after cutting himself with a surgeon's scalpel during an operation.

Semmelweis then noticed that in the first clinic doctors were routinely conducting autopsies while in the second this practice did not occur. He also noticed that doctors were often delivering babies and treating patients with the same unwashed hands they were performing autopsies with and so proposed that doctors were contaminating patients with "cadaverous particles". He then insisted doctors wash their hands in a chlorinated lime solution before dealing with patients. This simple intervention resulted in a drop in deaths from puerperal fever to around 1%.

However, despite this transformative discovery many in the medical community at the time were not only sceptical of his findings but openly mocked them. Charles Meigs (1854), a prominent American obstetrician (and teacher) derided the notion of bacterial infection and antiseptic policy noting that "Doctors are gentlemen, and gentlemen's hands are clean" and that it was morally unacceptable to "contravene the operations of those natural and physiological forces that the Divinity has ordained us to enjoy or to suffer". Even when Semmelweis published his findings, he still came up against intransigence and entrenched partisanship.

This reactionary short-sightedness gave rise to the term "The Semmelweis Reflex", characterised as the reflex-like tendency to reject new evidence or new knowledge because it contradicts established norms, beliefs or paradigms. What Semmelweis discovered was that dogmatic belief often trumps objective evidence despite the transformative change it would bring. His idea of using evidence to solve seemingly intractable problems such as unseen bacteria causing infection would take another few decades to become compulsory in hospitals and would go on to save millions of lives.

If we are to move towards a truly evidence-informed approach to designing and developing the best learning experiences for our students, then we must stand on shoulders of giants and build upon their hard-earned discoveries that have been independently verified and which have achieved consensus in the wider scientific community. A broad recognition that novices learn differently than experts or that learning means a change in long-term memory creates a powerful *lingua franca*, a common language, from which all stakeholders can begin to move towards a proper science of learning, based upon strong research, that allows all learners to maximise their potential.

References

GLIEK, J. (2004) *ISSAC NEWTON*. NEW YORK, NY: HARPER PERRENIAL.

HIRSCH, E. D. (OCTOBER 1, 2002). CLASSROOM RESEARCH AND CARGO CULTS [BLOG POST]. *HOOVER INSTITUTION POLICY REVIEW*. AVAILABLE FROM WWW.HOOVER.ORG/RESEARCH/CLASSROOM-RESEARCH-AND-CARGO-CULTS.

JOHN OF SALISBURY. (1955). *THE METALOGICON: A TWELFTH-CENTURY DEFENSE OF THE VERBAL AND LOGICAL ARTS OF THE TRIVIUM* (P. 167). TRANSLATED BY D. D. MACGARRY. BERKELEY, CA: UNIVERSITY OF CALIFORNIA PRESS.

MEIGS, C. D. (1854). *ON THE NATURE, SIGNS, AND TREATMENT OF CHILDBED FEVERS*. PHILADELPHIA, PA: BLANCHARD AND LEA.

NEWTON, I. (1675). LETTER FROM SIR ISAAC NEWTON TO ROBERT HOOKE. *HISTORICAL SOCIETY OF PENNSYLVANIA*. AVAILABLE FROM HTTPS://DISCOVER.HSP.ORG/RECORD/DC-9792/DESCRIPTION#TABNAV

POMERANCE, L., GREENBERG, J., & WALSH, K. (2016). *LEARNING ABOUT LEARNING: WHAT EVERY NEW TEACHER NEEDS TO KNOW*. WASHINGTON, DC: NATIONAL COUNCIL ON TEACHER QUALITY. AVAILABLE FROM WWW.NCTQ.ORG/DMSVIEW/LEARNING_ABOUT_LEARNING_REPORT

SEMMELWEIS, I. (1983). *THE ETIOLOGY, CONCEPT, AND PROPHYLAXIS OF CHILDBED FEVER*. TRANSLATED AND EDITED WITH AN INTRODUCTION BY K. CODELL CARTER. MADISON, WI: UNIVERSITY OF WISCONSIN PRESS. AVAILABLE FROM HTTPS://GRAPHICS8.NYTIMES.COM/IMAGES/BLOGS/FREAKONOMICS/PDF/THE%20ETIOLOGY,%20CONCEPT%20AND%20PROPHYLAXIS%20OF%20CHILDBED%20FEVER.PDF

SURMA, T., VANHOYWEGHEN, K, CAMP, G., & KIRSCHNER, P. A. (2018). DISTRIBUTED PRACTICE AND RETRIEVAL PRACTICE: THE COVERAGE OF LEARNING STRATEGIES IN FLEMISH AND DUTCH TEACHER EDUCATION TEXTBOOKS. *TEACHING AND TEACHER EDUCATION, 74*, 229–237. AVAILABLE FROM WWW.SCIENCEDIRECT.COM/SCIENCE/ARTICLE/PII/S0742051X17320656

WILIAM, D. [DYLANWILIAM]. (JANUARY 17, 2017). I'VE COME TO THE CONCLUSION SWELLER'S COGNITIVE LOAD THEORY IS THE SINGLE MOST IMPORTANT THING FOR TEACHERS TO KNOW. AVAILABLE FROM HTTPS://TWITTER.COM/DYLANWILIAM/STATUS/824682504602943489?LANG=EN

Acknowledgements

This book is truly an example of collaboration and, as such, a heartfelt acknowledgement is in order here.

In the first place we'd like to thank Sanna Järvelä, Professor of Learning Sciences and Educational Technology and head of the Learning and Educational Technology Research Unit (LET) at the University of Oulu, Finland. It was she who planted the seed that has grown into this book. She asked one of us (Paul) when he was a visiting professor there to come up with a list of ten core articles that all of the researchers and teachers there should have in their baggage. That question was the beginning of this journey.

Next, we'd like to thank the Tweeters and Facebookers who we crowdsourced for input as to what were core articles and/or seminal works in educational and cognitive psychology, the educational sciences, and the learning sciences. Those who responded broadened our ken outside of our own bubbles. In addition to them, there's a whole arena of colleagues who we know personally and/or via social media who have influenced us. This list can never be exhaustive, but we'd like to name a few: Tom Bennett (the man behind researchED), Jan Tishauser, Sara Hjelm and Eva Hartell (people behind local researchED events), Pedro De Bruyckere and Casper Hulshof (Paul's partners in crime in debunking educational myths and exposing eduquacks), Mirjam Neelen (Paul's long-suffering co-author of blogs on their 3-Star Learning Experiences blog site), and international colleagues – in no particular order – like Marcel Schmeier, David Didau, Dylan Wiliam, Dan Willingham, Oliver Caviglioli, Daisy Christodolou, Greg Ashman, Nick Rose, Andrew Old, James Theobald, Martin Robinson, Tom Sherrington, Adam Boxer, Blake Harvard, and Alex Quigley.

Then we have Luce Claessens and Steven Raaijmakers, two exceptional young academics at Utrecht University who assisted Paul in writing a simpler Dutch version of this book for teachers and teachers-in-training in primary education in the Netherlands and Flanders. Many of the texts, ideas, and insights in this book were born in the Dutch book which would never have seen the light of day if it weren't for the hard work and dedication of Monique Marreveld and Bea Ros.

Of course, we want to thank and acknowledge the work of all of the giants upon whose shoulders both this book and our own work and thinking is based. If you read the original articles, which we sincerely hope that you will, you'll see that standing on the shoulders of giants is a recursive process. The giants that we have included here stood on the shoulders of the giants of their day who stood on the shoulders of ... and so forth. We hope that, in the field of education and teaching, you – the readers – will become giants in the eyes of your students by creating more effective, efficient, and enjoyable learning experiences for them than you would have before reading this book.

And last but not least, we'd like to thank those nearest and dearest to us:

Carl would like to thank his wife Lu for the ocean of patience afforded to him in the writing of this book and he would like to dedicate this book to his daughter Ava, who has taught him more in the first year of her life than words can express.

Paul thanks above all Catherine, his muse and the anchor in his life, who makes it possible for him to combine projects like this book with all his other crazy ideas. And a special word for grandchildren Elsa and Benjamin, who are now so small and innocent, but deserve to enjoy good education as they grow up.

---

1 IN DER BESCHRÄNKUNG ZEIGT SICH ERST DER MEISTER (JOHANN WOLFGANG VON GOETHE, DAS SONETT – KAPITEL 1).
2 IN DEFENCE OF OURSELVES: WE CANNOT GUARANTEE THAT ALL OF THE LINKS THAT WORKED WHEN WE WROTE THE BOOK WILL STILL BE WORKING WHEN YOU READ IT. THE INTERNET IS DYNAMIC.

Introduction

Those that know, do. Those that understand, teach.[1]

Quizzing kids on what they remember from the previous lesson, demonstrating and explaining how something should be done, guiding students until they can do it themselves – these are just a few of the things we do as teachers every day. You may not think about it anymore, but many of the things that you do are not in your toolbox by chance. They're based on how children learn and what they need to learn effectively, efficiently, and enjoyably. They are things that have been investigated and described by the giants of educational research.

In this book we will introduce you to some of those giants. Often they are pioneers, creative educational researchers who first shone a light on matters that we hadn't thought about, studied things we didn't really understand, and/or tried to find solid scientific proof for things of which we had no proof. They looked closely at how teachers teach and how children learn and made the often implicit knowledge that we had about our profession explicit. Their work has inspired many researchers and teachers and has left a mark on how we teach today.

With respect to the content, we selected what we considered to be 28 key works on learning and teaching. The oldest article/chapter is from 1960 and the most recent is from 2013. Like every anthology or compilation, ours is far from complete. But that wasn't our goal. We can easily write a second book with another 28 articles and it would still be incomplete. The works chosen come primarily from the fields of educational psychology and cognitive psychology, though we did wet our toes in some social psychology. There was also no scientific

---

[1]   OFTEN ATTRIBUTED TO ARISTOTLE, BUT MOST PROBABLY FROM LEE SHULMAN WHEN HE EXPLAINED ARISTOTELIAN VIEWS ON PROFESSIONAL MASTERY (HTTPS://EN.WIKIQUOTE.ORG/WIKI/ ARISTOTLE).

research done to determine our selection, although we did look beyond our own bookcases and preferences. To do this we chose to make use of the wisdom of the crowd via Twitter and Facebook so as to broaden our ken. But the master (or teacher) shows himself in the limitation.[2]

Each chapter has the same structure. First we explain why the work is so important or ground-breaking (Why you should read this article). We then present the original abstract or paraphrase it (due to rights questions) and describe the research that was carried out and the insights that we've gained from it (The article). Having described the research, we continue by describing the work's implications for both education in general (Conclusions/implications of the work for educational practice) and the classroom teaching in particular (How to use the work in your teaching). We end each chapter with tips and tricks for teachers (Takeaways) and then provide the references used for the chapter followed by "Suggested readings and links" with QR codes that lead you to other, often popular articles or websites.

The chapters are divided into six sections. In the first section we describe how our brains work and what that means for learning and teaching. This is followed by sections on the prerequisites for learning, how learning can be supported, teacher activities, and learning in context. The final chapter is called "Cautionary tales". In this section we discuss three articles on how learning can be hindered rather than facilitated if you do the "wrong" things, and close the book with a chapter on prevalent myths and fables in education ("The ten deadly sins of education"); ideas on or approaches to teaching that sound temptingly logical and good – and for that reason are unfortunately embraced by many – but which actually prevent learning.

This book is not meant as a set of stone tablets to be obeyed but rather as an introduction to a trajectory of thought on a particular area that will hopefully lead to more investigation of that area. It is meant to help you know and understand the theories behind your practice so as to optimise your teaching. Like most things, good teaching is ultimately an art that is informed by science – both anticipates the future and acknowledges the past. Any serious exploration of how learning happens will encompass those early frontiersmen like Albert Bandura and Herbert Simon as much as it will attend to the work of latter-day pioneers such as John Hattie and Dylan Wiliam. The young singer-songwriter who has a strong knowledge of contemporary music but knows little of Bob Dylan and Leonard Cohen is ultimately

---

2   "IN DER BESCHRÄNKUNG ZEIGT SICH ERST DER MEISTER", JOHANN WOLFGANG VON GOETHE, *WAS WIR BRINGEN* (1802).

compromised because they don't really understand what has been achieved, who their heroes' heroes were/are or the boundaries of the terrain they are trying to map. It is our hope that this book will provide a roadmap at least, of the most important discoveries in how learning happens and a set of provocations you can use to make sense of them in your own world.

Paul A. Kirschner and Carl Hendrick
September 2019

PART 1

HOW DOES OUR BRAIN WORK?

RIDDLE

What is a small part of a whole, weighs less than 2% of that whole, uses between 20% and 25% of the available energy, consists of around 190 billion parts, and is mechanical, electrical, chemical, and biological?[1]

What a miracle, our brains! We humans have wonderful bodies. Because of this lump of soft tissue in our heads, weighing – on average – a little more than a kilo, we are able to receive, process and respond to countless signals from our environment through our eyes, ears, skin, noses, and mouths. Almost effortlessly, we ignore a multitude of unimportant signals and respond specifically to the relevant ones. To top it all off, we can also store an infinite amount of information from those signals for later use.

But how do we make proper use of this miracle when it comes to learning and instruction? John Sweller (2017) stated: "[W]ithout an understanding of human cognitive architecture, instruction is blind".[2] In this respect, it could be the case that many of us in the teaching profession are flying blind.

In this part we discuss how our brains work and what that means for learning and teaching. We explain why students learn some things almost effortlessly without instruction, while other things are learnt with great difficulty through instruction, how our memory works and how we can make it work better, how we (learn to) solve problems, how and why images and words together can help us learn better, and why children should not be taught as if they were small adults.

---

1   **ANSWER:** THE BRAIN!
2   **SWELLER, J.** (2017). *WITHOUT AN UNDERSTANDING OF HUMAN COGNITIVE ARCHITECTURE, INSTRUCTION IS BLIND. THE ACE CONFERENCE.* RETRIEVED FROM HTTPS://YOUTU.BE/GOLPFI9LS-W.

A NOVICE IS NOT A LITTLE EXPERT

NOVICES AND EXPERTS

A NOVICE IS NOT A LITTLE EXPERT

PAPER   "Categorization and representation of physics problems by experts and novices"[3]

QUOTE   *"Not only do experts have more knowledge and can work faster than beginners, they also look at or tackle problems differently (i.e. what you know determines what you see)".*

Why you should read this article

HOMUNCULUS
A miniature human

In 1537, a Swiss physician, alchemist, and astrologer named Paracelsus outlined a method for creating homunculi (Latin for *little people*). Short but sweet, a mini-human is created by nourishing a male sperm on human blood in a horse's womb where a small version of a living human child grows. This evolved into what became known as *preformationism*, the theory that animals develop from miniature versions of themselves. Sperm were thought to be complete preformed individuals called animalcules, which developed in the woman's womb into fully formed beings. In 1694, Nicolaas Hartsoecker, in his *Essai de Dioptrique* about what could be seen with the aid of Antoni van Leeuwenhoek's microscope, wrote of and produced an image of a tiny human form curled up inside the sperm (see Figure 1.1), which he called *le petit animal* (animalcule) with the human version being *le petit l'infant* (homunculus). The sperm was a homunculus, identical in all but size to an adult. It is just a matter of growth!

As odd as this may sound today, many people actually think that this same thing is true about the cognitive/intellectual development of a child (and by extension, a novice) into an adult (and by extension, an expert). A good example of this is discovery learning. The thinking behind this form of education is that since the epistemology of the scientist (i.e. an expert) is to discover and create new knowledge through

3   **CHI, M. T. H., FELTOVICH, P. J., & GLASER, R.** (1979). CATEGORIZATION AND REPRESENTATION OF PHYSICS PROBLEMS BY EXPERTS AND NOVICES. *COGNITIVE SCIENCE* 5, 121–152 AVAILABLE FROM: HTTPS://ONLINELIBRARY.WILEY.COM/DOI/EPDF/10.1207/S15516709COG0502_2.

experimentation, many mistaken educators and researchers have chosen to apply this approach to the school as a pedagogy for teaching students (i.e. novices) (Kirschner, 2009). Michelene Chi, Robert Glaser, and Paul Feltovich broke with this myth showing how experts not only know more than novices, but that they also think differently.

FIGURE 1.1
PREFORMATION,
DRAWN BY
NICOLAS
HARTSOECKER

Abstract of the article

This study investigates the differences between how physics problems are represented in novices and experts in relation to the organisation of physics knowledge. Different experiments included; problem categories as a means of representation, category differences used by experts and novices, differences in category knowledge, and aspects of the problems that form problem categorisation and how they're represented. The results from these experiments suggest that experts and novices represent problems differently with particular categorisation of the problems and also that the success in completing the problems depends on domain-specific knowledge. Experts use deep physics principles to categorise and solve problems whereas novices use superficial features.

The article

In their search for differences between experts and beginners in solving problems, Chi and her colleagues focused on the very first step when solving a problem, namely reading and interpreting the problem. When dealing with a new problem, the first question is always: what kind of problem is this? To answer this question, you often try to remember similar problems that you have encountered before. You search for landmarks. Classifying the problem in a specific category of similar

Landmarks help
classify a problem

problems is the first step in solving it. The idea is that experts already interpret or categorise problems when reading in a way that's different from beginners, and therefore they're able to solve them more easily, more quickly, and better.

How people categorise a problem depends on previous experiences with similar problems, which shapes how they determine what the problem is and the quality of their solutions. We know this since 1946 when A. D. de Groot published his PhD thesis (which was later translated into English in 1965) on how chess masters interpret chess problems. He found that the chess masters' knowledge and the way of thinking is essentially different from that of beginners. Not only do experts have more knowledge and can work faster than beginners, they also look at or tackle problems differently (i.e. what you know determines what you see). Masters quickly recognise a particular chess position and then determine subsequent moves based on their prior experiences. In the same way, doctors interpret the history (anamnesis) and charts of a new patient by using their knowledge of similar clinical histories and charts that they have dealt with and then make their diagnoses based on this. Thus, our prior knowledge determines the quality of our problem-solving. As experts have both more knowledge as well as qualitatively better knowledge (this is called deep, conceptual knowledge), the categorisation of problems will give them a head start on beginners.

CONCEPTUAL KNOWLEDGE
Deep understanding of concepts and principles

Prior knowledge about problems and their solutions are built through experience with many different types of problems. In this way, experts have acquired rich knowledge about different types of problems and their solutions which they store in their long-term memory; that is they have rich knowledge schemata.

SCHEMA
Cognitive framework which organises knowledge

THE TERM SCHEMA was first used in psychology by Jean Piaget (1896–1980), a Swiss psychologist who studied cognitive psychological development in children. In his words (1952), a cognitive schema is "a cohesive, repeatable action sequence possessing component actions that are tightly interconnected and governed by a core meaning". See it as a way of organising knowledge; a mental structure of already learnt and available knowledge, skills, and even ideas that is used for organising and perceiving new information.

Novices have simple limited schemata

Such a schema may consist of characterisations of different types of problems, possible solutions, different contexts within which these problems may arise, etc. Beginners also have schemata, but these are less extensive and profound (i.e. they are poor). The use of these schemata is therefore less effective for them and sometimes even counterproductive. Beginners often interpret problems by looking at what is called surface characteristics such as "a previous problem also dealt with a moving object and this problem does too" and thus, use the wrong formula (e.g. velocity instead of acceleration). Experts, however, see the underlying concepts of a problem such as "the first problem was about a constant speed, but this is about acceleration, so it's different". Because of their extensive and qualitatively better schemata, experts know how to quickly and accurately categorise new problems and link them to a correct solution strategy and solution.

Experts can 'see' underlying concepts

In their article Chi, Feltovich, and Glaser study the link between a person's prior knowledge and how (s)he categorises problems. To do this they carried out a series of experiments comparing how first-year physics students (novices) and PhD candidates (experts) divide and classify a series of physics tasks into different types. What they found was that the experts indeed classified the types of tasks differently from the beginners.

Do students with a lot of prior knowledge categorise problems differently than students with little prior knowledge?

The study showed that while experts and beginners both categorised the assignments, they did it in different ways. The beginners categorised the problems based on the characteristics in the description of the assignment (e.g. these problems deal with blocks on an inclined plane). The experts, on the other hand, categorised the problems based on the underlying physical laws (e.g. these problems deal with the law of conservation of energy). Because of their focus on the deeper, underlying physical laws, experts also immediately had a solution strategy that matched the problem while the beginners, due to their focus on surface characteristics, made that link more slowly if at all.

What prior knowledge is actually activated when people encounter a new problem?

In identifying and categorising problems, the researchers mapped the students' knowledge schemata with respect to the problems. Again, the beginners focused on superficial problem characteristics while the experts' focused on physical laws and the circumstances in which they apply.

Which words in the problem description do novices and experts pay attention to when they try to interpret a new problem?

Finally, the researchers asked the students to think aloud and freely associate while reading the problem statements. The goal of this was to find out how the students arrived at their categorisations. It was striking that the beginners based their categorisation specifically on words in the problem

BEGINNERS
Problem-specific
categorisation

EXPERTS
Deeper, generalised
categorisation

statement such as "friction" or "gravity". Experts, on the other hand, gave descriptions of the states and conditions of the physical situation described by the problem and in some instances, based on transformed or derived features, such as a "before and after situation" or "no external forces".

This study shows that the prior knowledge of experts differs from that of beginners (see Table 1.1). When encountering a new problem, experts think in a very solution-oriented way and their prior knowledge is mainly procedural in nature about how to tackle a problem along with a deep conceptual knowledge about the conditions under which the procedures can be applied. The prior knowledge of beginners, on the other hand, consists mainly of descriptions of the physical characteristics of various problems, but does not include the link with possible solutions.

▬▬ NOVICES	▬▬ EXPERTS
■ No access to relevant schemata	■ Possess schemata for encoding elements into a single entity
■ Attempt to remember and process individual elements	■ Skills acquisition without needing to recall the rule
■ Need to apply cognitive capacity to inefficient problem-solving	■ Automation important for complex problem-solving transfer
■ Work backwards (means-end)	■ Work forwards

TABLE 1.1
DIFFERENCES
BETWEEN
EXPERTS AND
NOVICES

Based on: Chi, Glaser, & Rees, 1982; De Groot, 1965; Kalyuga, Kalyuga, Chandler, & Sweller, 1998; Schneider & Shiffrin, 1977; Wilson & Cole, 1991.

Conclusions/implications of the work for educational practice

Research that compares the prior knowledge of beginners with that of experts shows that the difference is not only quantitative (i.e. that experts know more) but also qualitatively (i.e. their knowledge is also organised differently). This insight brings with it three important implications for education: (1) beginners are not empty barrels that have to be filled, (2) beginners are not "small" experts, and (3) teaching/ instruction should take this into account.

For optimal learning, new knowledge must be related to the knowledge that students have already acquired. New knowledge must be integrated into existing schemata.[4] Jean Piaget called this *assimilation* and *accommodation*.

TABULA RASA
The mind as a
blank slate

ASSIMILATION
Incorporating
new knowledge in
existing schemata

ACCOMMODATION
Altering existing
schemata to fit new
knowledge

---

4 YOU'LL READ MORE ABOUT THIS IN CHAPTER 6 WHEN DAVID AUSUBEL AND THE USE OF ADVANCE ORGANISERS IS DISCUSSED.

JEAN PIAGET distinguished two important processes in their development: assimilation and accommodation. *Assimilation* is the process by which new knowledge is inserted into existing knowledge schemata while *accommodation* is the process by which existing knowledge schemata are adapted to the new knowledge. When a child sees a Great Dane or a Chihuahua on a leash in the park for the first time, the dogs will be classified in the child's existing dog-schema (assimilation). However, this schema itself will also change, as dogs can from now on be just as big as a Great Dane or as small as a Chihuahua (accommodation).

Beginners have knowledge schemata which are rudimentary, incomplete, shallow, and often contain misconceptions (e.g. naïve hypotheses such as if you kick a ball, then there are still forces working upon it pushing it forward). New knowledge must be given a place in them, either by hanging the new knowledge in them (assimilation) or by adapting them to the new knowledge (accommodation). If a schema contains errors, as is often the case for beginners, then the teacher must focus her/his attention on changing those existing schemata by either eliminating the misconceptions or by helping the student learn and understand the underlying principles. To do this, the teacher needs to make an effort to gain insight into how the student categorises; to understand the schemata so as to take the proper steps to adjust them step by step. It is, thus, extremely important to keep in mind that the novices' prior knowledge and assumptions are not simply a less extensive version of what the expert knows and assumes, but that they really are different.

MISCONCEPTIONS
Error in an existing schema

As the novice is not a miniature expert, it's extremely important to realise that what may work very well for an expert (e.g. discovery learning, problem-based learning, inquiry learning) usually doesn't work well or is even harmful and counterproductive for the novice (and vice versa). This is known as the expertise reversal effect (Sweller, Ayres, Kalyuga, & Chandler, 2003): a reversal of the effectiveness of instructional techniques on learners with differing levels of prior knowledge. While an expert can be given a problem to be solved after having been taught a certain technique or principle, a novice should be given a more structured approach to using that principle for solving the same problem, for example in the form of a worked example. Kalyuga et al. note here that as the learner advances, a fading procedure whereby steps in the solution procedure are gradually left open for the learner to carry out her-/himself, is superior to an abrupt switch from worked example to problems. This

EXPERTISE REVERSAL EFFECT
What works for experts doesn't work for beginners and vice versa

slow reduction of guidance as learner expertise increases is an example of the *guidance-fading effect*; a direct instructional application that is consistent with the expertise reversal effect.

Epistemology is not pedagogy!

How to use the work in your teaching

DIFFERENTIATION
Tailoring instructional methods for different learners

Differentiation with respect to how one teaches cannot be ignored. This article shows that differentiation is desirable at an early stage in the learning process, including when a learner reads the assignment given to her/him. For example, students who are good at maths may immediately link the assignment to possible solution strategies while weaker students need your guidance to think about the possible solution strategies when categorising the problem. During this supervision it's important to try to make the student's thinking process explicit, so as to try to determine what her/his prior knowledge is, whether or not it's correct, and where it needs to be adapted. Asking students to think aloud and discussing what they have done and why can help you to help them on their way to thinking like an expert.

Takeaways

- Beginners aren't "little" experts; they know less and think differently than experts.
- Children also aren't small adults. They see the world very differently and therefore have to learn differently.
- A teaching approach that works well with an expert will most probably not work well with a beginner and can even be detrimental to their learning.
- Try to differentiate at an early stage.
- The epistemology of the expert is not the proper pedagogy for the learner.
- Beware the "curse of knowledge"[5]: a cognitive bias where instructors who are highly knowledgeable in a domain forget the steps they took to acquire that knowledge and can't understand why novices just don't "get it".

References

CHI, M. T. H., FELTOVICH, P. J., & GLASER, R. (1979). CATEGORIZATION AND REPRESENTATION OF PHYSICS PROBLEMS BY EXPERTS AND NOVICES. *COGNITIVE SCIENCE*, 5, 121–152. DOI: 10.1207/S15516709COG0502_2 AVAILABLE FROM: HTTPS://ONLINELIBRARY.WILEY.COM/DOI/EPDF/10.1207/S15516709COG0502_2.

CHI, M. T. H., GLASER, R., & REES, E. R. (1982). EXPERTISE IN PROBLEM SOLVING. IN R. S. STERNBERG (ED.), *ADVANCES IN THE PSYCHOLOGY OF HUMAN INTELLIGENCE* (VOL. 1, PP. 1–75). HILLSDALE, NJ: ERLBAUM. AVAILABLE FROM WWW.DTIC.MIL/DTIC/TR/FULLTEXT/U2/A100138.PDF.

5   **KENNEDY, J.** (1995). DEBIASING THE CURSE OF KNOWLEDGE IN AUDIT JUDGMENT. *THE ACCOUNTING REVIEW*, 70, 249–273. AVAILABLE FROM: WWW.JSTOR.ORG/STABLE/248305.

DE GROOT, A. D. (1946). *HET DENKEN VAN DEN SCHAKER. [THINKING PROCESSES IN CHESS PLAYERS].* AMSTERDAM, THE NETHERLANDS: NOORD HOLLANDSCHE. AVAILABLE FROM: WWW.DBNL.ORG/ TEKST/GROO004DENK01_01/GROO004DENK01_01.PDF

DE GROOT, A. D. (1965). *THOUGHT AND CHOICE IN CHESS.* DEN HAAG, THE NETHERLANDS: DE GRUYTER MOUTON.

KALYUGA, S., CHANDLER, P., & SWELLER, J. (1998). LEVELS OF EXPERTISE AND INSTRUCTIONAL DESIGN. *HUMAN FACTORS, 40*(1), 1–17. AVAILABLE FROM: WWW.RESEARCHGATE. NET/PUBLICATION/220457696_LEVELS_OF_EXPERTISE_AND_INSTRUCTIONAL_DESIGN.

KENNEDY, J. (1995). DEBIASING THE CURSE OF KNOWLEDGE IN AUDIT JUDGMENT. *THE ACCOUNTING REVIEW,* 70, 249–273. AVAILABLE FROM: WWW.JSTOR.ORG/STABLE/248305.

KIRSCHNER, P. A. (2009). EPISTEMOLOGY OR PEDAGOGY, THAT IS THE QUESTION. IN S. TOBIAS AND T. M. DUFFY, *CONSTRUCTIVIST INSTRUCTION: SUCCESS OR FAILURE?* (PP. 144–157). NEW YORK, NY: ROUTLEDGE. AVAILABLE VIA HTTP://DSPACE.OU.NL/BITSTREAM/1820/2326/1/EPISTEMOLOGY%20 OR%20PEDAGOGY%20-%20THAT%20IS%20THE%20QUESTION.PDF.

PIAGET, J. (1952). *THE ORIGINS OF INTELLIGENCE IN CHILDREN.* NEW YORK, NY: INTERNATIONAL UNIVERSITY PRESS. [LA NAISSANCE DE L'INTELLIGENCE CHEZ L'ENFANT] (1936), ALSO TRANSLATED AS THE ORIGIN OF INTELLIGENCE IN THE CHILD (LONDON: ROUTLEDGE AND KEGAN PAUL, 1953).

SCHNEIDER, W., & SHIFFRIN, R. M. (1977). CONTROLLED AND AUTOMATIC HUMAN INFORMATION PROCESSING: I. DETECTION, SEARCH, AND ATTENTION. *PSYCHOLOGICAL REVIEW,* 84, 1–66. AVAILABLE FROM: HTTP://CITESEERX.IST.PSU.EDU/VIEWDOC/ DOWNLOAD?DOI=10.1.1.470.2718&REP=REP1&TYPE=PDF.

SWELLER, J., AYRES, P. L., KALYUGA, S., & CHANDLER, P. A. (2003). THE EXPERTISE REVERSAL EFFECT. *EDUCATIONAL PSYCHOLOGIST, 38*(1), 23–31. DOI: 10.1207/S15326985EP3801_4 (OPEN ACCESS).

WILSON, B., & COLE, P. (1991). A REVIEW OF COGNITIVE TEACHING MODELS. *EDUCATIONAL TECHNOLOGY RESEARCH AND DEVELOPMENT, 39*(4), 47–64.

Suggested readings and links

HOW EXPERTS DIFFER FROM NOVICES.

AVAILABLE FROM WWW.NAP.EDU/READ/9853/CHAPTER/5.

This chapter in *How people learn: Brain, mind, experience, and school: Expanded Edition* illustrates key scientific findings that have come from the study of people who have developed expertise in areas such as chess, physics, mathematics, electronics, and history. We discuss these examples not because all school children are expected to become experts in these or any other areas, but because the study of expertise shows what the results of successful learning look like.

THE MAKING OF AN EXPERT.

AVAILABLE FROM HTTPS://HBR.ORG/2007/07/THE-MAKING-OF-AN-EXPERT.

This article in the *Harvard Business Review* was written by Anders Ericsson (professor of psychology at Florida State University), Michael Prietula (professor at the Goizueta Business School), and Edward Cokely (research fellow at the Max Planck Institute for Human Development). They discuss how scientific research has shown that true expertise is the product of years of intense practice and dedicated coaching.

TCU PSYCHOLOGY OF THINKING AND LEARNING "EXPERTS VS. NOVICES".

AVAILABLE FROM WWW.YOUTUBE.COM/WATCH?V=JZ_C6MNRYFI&T=80S.

A neuropsychological video on the differences between novices and experts. While interesting, the video does break every rule with respect to the redundancy principle from cognitive load theory.

2 TAKE A LOAD OFF ME

PROBLEM SOLVING

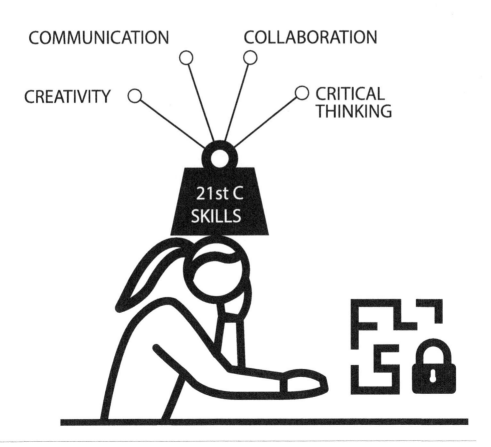

2

TAKE A LOAD OFF ME

PAPER   "Cognitive load during problem solving: Effects on learning"[1]

QUOTE   *"There seems to be no clear evidence that conventional problem solving is an efficient learning device and considerable evidence that it is not".*

Why you should read this article

Cognitive load theory has been described by Dylan Wiliam as "the single most important thing for teachers to know". This theory is based on the limited ability of the working memory to code information. Once learners have built up schemata of knowledge that allow them to work on problems without exceeding their cognitive bandwidth, then they can work independently. Without it, their work might be in vain.

Working memory temporarily holds new information

Why is this important? Solving problems is possibly the hottest topic in education at the moment. It forms the basis of a number of constructivist approaches to teaching and learning such as problem-based learning, inquiry-based learning, discovery learning, experiential learning, and constructivist learning. Also, it's one of the most highly regarded components of what has come to be known as twenty-first century skills. And finally, it has taken centre stage for many people in both education and industry who propagate the notion that the most important thing at the moment is the acquisition of generic, domain-independent skills and that the best way to learn to solve problems is by solving them (e.g. inquiry/discovery learning).

CONSTRUCTIVISM Theory that we construct knowledge from our experiences

What's the problem? Well let's say you're confronted with a problem that you need to solve. If you're well versed in the subject area, that is to say you have a great deal of the knowledge relevant to solving the

1   **SWELLER, J.** (1988). COGNITIVE LOAD DURING PROBLEM SOLVING: EFFECTS ON LEARNING. *COGNITIVE SCIENCE, 12*, 257–285. DOI: 10.1207/S15516709COG1202_4.

problem and you've also solved similar problems, then you follow the necessary steps to define, solve and then evaluate your solution. You might choose to use a problem-solving strategy that you've used before, but only after determining its similarity to the problem at hand and, thus, whether that strategy is relevant. That is to say you make use of the knowledge and strategies you have stored in your long-term memory. Here, we speak of your having domain-specific knowledge, domain-specific procedural knowledge (i.e. knowing what the steps for solution are) and strategies, and the ability (i.e. the skill) to carry out the steps.

LONG-TERM
MEMORY
Permanent store of
knowledge

If, on the other hand, you're not knowledgeable in the area, then you're in trouble. The most often used strategy is a version of what is known as *means–ends analysis*. Here you work backwards, comparing your current state (where you are at the moment) with the goal state (where you need to be; the solution) and you look for moves (steps that you possibly can carry out) that will reduce this distance. All of this requires much mental effort. In that process, you will also need to search for and find problem-relevant information, which is very hard to do if you know little about the area. The process ends up being little more than high mental-effort trial-and-error which is neither effective nor efficient and which often leads to frustration at how long it's taking and the number of dead-ends encountered. In other words, the process is also not very enjoyable.

Means-ends
analysis reduces the
difference between
desired end goal and
current state

Mental effort
depends on task
complexity and level
of expertise

MENTAL EFFORT is about how hard a person tries to actively process presented information. It is a combination of perceived *demand characteristics* (how complex the task is combined with the level of expertise of the person carrying out the task), *perceived self-efficacy* (the extent that one believes that (s)he is capable of performing in a specific manner to attain specific goals), and *level/ depth of information processing* (the degree to which a person encodes/recodes a source) such that the first two influence the last which determines the amount of invested mental effort.

John Sweller's article forms the basis for why domain-specific knowledge is so necessary for solving problems and why domain-independent skills, such as problem-solving, collaborating, writing, communicating, and so forth, don't exist. If only researchers, teachers, administrators, educational policy makers, and politicians had read and applied the content of this article, then we could have saved a lot of wasted time, money, and energy spent chasing those elusive domain-independent skills.

Abstract of the article

There is significant evidence that the main distinguishing factor between experts and novices in problem-solving is domain-specific knowledge. There is also emerging evidence that conventional problem-solving skills are not effective in acquiring schemata. It is suggested that a reason for this is that both of these processes clash and that conventional means-ends analysis uses up a large amount of cognitive bandwidth which in turn is not available for acquiring schemata. This study uses experimental evidence, a computational model and discusses theoretical and practical implications.

The article

According to John Sweller, extensive research on expert–novice distinctions lie at the basis of his article. Experts and novices differ in their memory of problem state configurations, their problem-solving strategies, and the features they use categorising problems. We know that experts and novices differ with respect to their *memory of problem state configurations* since A. D. de Groot (1946, 1978) studied the difference between chess masters and less experienced players. De Groot found that the grandmasters didn't have a superior working memory nor were they more creative or better at problem solving, but rather they remebered more meaningful chess-positions. As Daisy Christodolou (2020) writes,

> These expert chess players have memorised the typical patterns of thousands of chess games. When they see a chess end game and rapidly decide what move to make, they can do so because they can compare the game state to all the board positions they have stored in long-term memory. They aren't reasoning; they're recalling. Or rather, their ability to reason is bound up with recall.

This has been replicated in many fields and is now seen as a given (Chase & Simon, 1973a, 1973b). As regards *problem-solving strategies*, the strategies used by expert and novice problem solvers also differ. As stated, novices use means–ends analysis while experts, in contrast, begin by choosing a strategy that they're familiar with (usually from solving analogous problems) and then work forwards to solve the problem. Experts can work forwards because they recognise each problem and each problem state from previous experience and know which moves are appropriate. They have cognitive schemata in their long-term memory which allow this (Larkin, McDermott, Simon, & Simon, 1980; Simon & Simon, 1978). Finally, regarding the *features used to categorise problems,* experts group problems based on deep structures such as the mode of solution while novices group problems according to surface structures such as how they look (Chi, Glaser, & Rees, 1982; Hinsley, Hayes, & Simon, 1977).

Inquiry-based instruction is demanding on working memory

In addition, inquiry-based instruction requires the learner to search a problem space for problem-relevant information. All problem-based searching makes heavy demands on working memory. Furthermore, that working memory load does not contribute to the accumulation of knowledge in long-term memory because while working memory is being used to search for problem solutions, it is not available and cannot be used to learn. Indeed, it is possible to search for extended periods of time with quite minimal alterations to long-term memory (e.g. see Sweller, Mawer, & Howe, 1982). The goal of instruction is rarely simply to search for or discover information. The goal is to give learners specific guidance about how to cognitively manipulate information in ways that are consistent with a learning goal, and store the result in long-term memory.

EXAMPLE
Categorisation

A SIMPLE EXAMPLE of categorisation based on deep or surface-level structures is how an expert baker may see a problem as opposed to a novice. For the novice, rising is rising and so if (s)he has learned that increasing the baking temperature of soda bread will make it rise better and faster, (s)he will then see a similar problem with getting normal bread to rise more quickly as a question of raising the temperature. Unfortunately for the novice, while the surface structures may be similar (getting bread to rise), the deep structures aren't. The rising process with baking soda is a chemical one; heat catalyses and thus speeds up the chemical process. Yeast, on the other hand, causes dough to rise based on a biological process; yeast digests carbohydrates and produces carbon dioxide and alcohol. This process works optimally at 37° Celsius and temperatures above a certain level kill the yeast (that's why we bake the dough after letting it rise in a warm place!).

In the rest of the article, Sweller shows how conventional problem-solving is inefficient for acquiring problem-solving schemata and how this lies in the demands made upon our cognitive architecture, and primarily the demands made upon our working memory. Based on a theoretical discussion and a number of empirical studies he shows that while solving conventional problems via means–ends analysis used by novices can lead to problem-solution, it doesn't lead to schema acquisition; the cognitive effort expended during conventional problem-solving can lead to the problem goal, but not to learning (an educational goal).

Conclusions/implications of the work for educational practice

Sweller concludes that: (1) conventional problem-solving through means–ends analysis imposes high cognitive load; (2) how we solve problems and how we acquire cognitive schemata differ greatly; (3) the cognitive effort expended by conventional problem-solving doesn't aid schema acquisition; (4) as schema acquisition is a basic component of problem-solving expertise, developing expertise may be stunted by emphasising problem-solving; and (5) you don't learn how to solve problems by solving problems!

Learning through problem-solving induces high cognitive load/ mental effort

In other words if you want your students to learn to solve problems, they first need both the declarative and procedural knowledge within the subject area of the problem in question. This is also true if you want to teach them to communicate, discuss, write, or whatever twenty-first-century skill people are talking about. You can't communicate about something, write about something, discuss or argue about something etc. without first knowing about that something and then also knowing the rules (i.e. the procedures) for doing it.

How to use the work in your teaching

As a teacher, it is imperative that you avoid means–end problem-solving. This approach of working backwards from the goal to the problem and then from the givens to the solution creates too much cognitive load and hinders learning. This means that you need to create situations where learners can work forwards. First, they need the (pre)requisite knowledge. Then, they need to have had multiple exposures to situations where they have employed strategies that may be similar to the strategy needed to solve a specific problem.

INTERLEAVING Mixing up topics to be learned

One of the best ways to do this is to interleave content and problems while teaching as opposed to *blocking* (Van Merriënboer & Kirschner, 2018, call this *variability of practice*). Blocking involves solving one type of problem at a time before the next (for example, "problem A" before "problem B" and so forth. The learning pattern formed looks like this: AAABBBCCC. Interleaving, in contrast, involves solving several related problems mixed up together. The learning pattern here looks like this: ABCBCAACB. This approach helps the learner to choose the correct strategy to solve a problem and helps them see the links, similarities, and differences between problem states. It also leads to increased transfer.

Takeaways

- Acquiring/learning a procedure to solve a problem is not the same as being able to solve a problem. The former is a type of knowledge (procedural knowledge), the latter is a skill.
- If the learner has no relevant concepts or procedures in long-term memory, the only thing to do is blindly search for possible solution steps ... novices can engage in problem-solving for extended periods and learn almost nothing.
- Learning happens best when methods are in line with human cognitive structure.
- While solving problems might lead to solving a problem (i.e. reaching the problem's goal state) in the short term, it doesn't lead to learning how to solve problems (i.e. education's goal state) in the long term.
- Means–end analysis is a bad way to solve a problem. Sometimes the best way to solve a problem is not to "problem solve".

References

CHASE, W., & SIMON, H. (1973A). PERCEPTION IN CHESS. *COGNITIVE PSYCHOLOGY, 4*, 55–81. AVAILABLE FROM WWW.SCIENCEDIRECT.COM/SCIENCE/ARTICLE/PII/0010028573900042.

CHASE, W., & SIMON, H. (1973B). THE MIND'S EYE IN CHESS. IN W. G. CHASE (ED.), *VISUAL INFORMATION PROCESSING* (PP. 215–281). NEW YORK, NY: ACADEMIC PRESS.

CHI, M., GLASER, R., & REES, E. (1982). EXPERTISE IN PROBLEM SOLVING. IN R. STERNBERG (ED.), *ADVANCES IN THE PSYCHOLOGY OF HUMAN INTELLIGENCE* (VOL. 1, PP. 7–75). HILLSDALE, NJ: ERLBAUM. REPORT AVAILABLE FROM HTTPS://FILES.ERIC.ED.GOV/FULLTEXT/ED215899.PDF.

CHRISTODOLOU, D. (2020). *THE UNEXPECTED REVOLUTION.* OXFORD: OXFORD UNIVERSITY PRESS.

DE GROOT, A. D. (1946). *HET DENKEN VAN DEN SCHAKER [THINKING PROCESSES IN CHESS PLAYERS].* AMSTERDAM, THE NETHERLANDS: NOORD HOLLANDSCHE.

DE GROOT, A. D. (1978). *THOUGHT AND CHOICE IN CHESS* (REVISED TRANSLATION OF D. GROOT, 1946; 2ND ED.). THE HAGUE, THE NETHERLANDS: MOUTON PUBLISHERS.

HINSLEY, D., HAYES, J., & SIMON, H. (1977). FROM WORDS TO EQUATIONS: MEANING AND REPRESENTATION IN ALGEBRA WORD PROBLEMS. IN P. CARPENTER AND M. JUST (EDS.), *COGNITIVE PROCESSES IN COMPREHENSION* (PP. 89–106). HILLSDALE, NJ: ERLBAUM. AVAILABLE FROM HTTPS://PDFS.SEMANTICSCHOLAR.ORG/0782/1978CB34A5273C39C98B94F7EDF4EE84BBC5.PDF.

LARKIN, J., MCDERMOTT, J., SIMON, D., & SIMON, H. (1980). MODELS OF COMPETENCE IN SOLVING PHYSICS PROBLEMS. *COGNITIVE SCIENCE, 4*, 317–348. AVAILABLE FROM HTTPS://READER.ELSEVIER.COM/READER/SD/PII/S0364021380800085?TOKEN=75D0E7397526227850713 54BFBC7FD18E8A61202899ABDD0AA1B72CB73F9C5D45989867ABD62EF16E5C8ACDC84DBD525.

SIMON, D., & SIMON, H. (1978). INDIVIDUAL DIFFERENCES IN SOLVING PHYSICS PROBLEMS. IN R. SIEGLER, (ED.), *CHILDREN'S THINKING: WHAT DEVELOPS?* (PP. 215–231). MAHWAH, NJ: ERLBAUM.

SWELLER, J. (1988). COGNITIVE LOAD DURING PROBLEM SOLVING: EFFECTS ON LEARNING. *COGNITIVE SCIENCE, 12*, 257–285. AVAILABLE FROM HTTPS://PDFS.SEMANTICSCHOLAR.ORG/D88C/481743DB95687BF9D2861C16CD006F67A0A1.PDF.

SWELLER, J., MAWER, R., & HOWE, W. (1982). CONSEQUENCES OF HISTORY-CUED AND MEANS-ENDS STRATEGIES IN PROBLEM SOLVING. *AMERICAN JOURNAL OF PSYCHOLOGY, 95*, 455–483.

VAN MERRIËNBOER, J. J. G., & KIRSCHNER, P. A. (2018). *TEN STEPS TO COMPLEX LEARNING (THIRD EDITION).* NEW YORK, NY: ROUTLEDGE.

Suggested readings and links

BADDELEY, A. & HITCH, G. (1974). WORKING MEMORY. IN G. H. BOWER (ED.), *THE PSYCHOLOGY OF LEARNING AND MOTIVATION: ADVANCES IN RESEARCH AND THEORY* (VOL. 8, PP. 47–89). NEW YORK, NY: ACADEMIC PRESS.

SWELLER, J., CLARK, R. E., & KIRSCHNER, P. A. (2010). TEACHING GENERAL PROBLEM-SOLVING SKILLS IS NOT A SUBSTITUTE FOR, OR A VIABLE ADDITION TO, TEACHING MATHEMATICS. *NOTICES OF THE AMERICAN MATHEMATICAL SOCIETY, 57,* 1303–1304.

AVAILABLE FROM WWW.AMS.ORG/NOTICES/201010/RTX101001303P.PDF.

SWELLER, J., CLARK, R. E., & KIRSCHNER, P. A. (2010). MATHEMATICAL ABILITY RELIES ON KNOWLEDGE TOO. *AMERICAN EDUCATOR, 34*(4), 34–35.

AVAILABLE FROM WWW.RESEARCHGATE.NET/PUBLICATION/254913250_ MATHEMATICAL_ABILITY_RELIES_ON_KNOWLEDGE_TOO.

CLARK, R. E., KIRSCHNER, P. A., & SWELLER, J. (2012). PUTTING STUDENTS ON THE PATH TO LEARNING: THE CASE FOR FULLY GUIDED INSTRUCTION. *AMERICAN EDUCATOR, 36*(1), 6–11.

AVAILABLE FROM WWW.AFT.ORG/SITES/DEFAULT/FILES/PERIODICALS/ CLARK.PDF.

A Conversation with John Sweller. In mid-2017 Ollie Lovell met with John Sweller to ask him a few questions that he had about cognitive load theory, and his work. John was gracious enough to let him record the conversation and turn it into a series of blog posts. All together, these posts amount to almost 9000 words of text, so they have been split into nine different sub-posts for the convenience of readers.

AVAILABLE FROM WWW.OLLIELOVELL.COM/PEDAGOGY/JOHNSWELLER.

A DISCUSSION OF WORKING MEMORY FROM *SIMPLY PSYCHOLOGY.*

AVAILABLE FROM WWW.SIMPLYPSYCHOLOGY.ORG/WORKING%20 MEMORY.HTML.

WHAT YOU NEED TO KNOW ABOUT COGNITIVE LOAD: **A CONVERSATION WITH JOHN SWELLER.**

AVAILABLE FROM HTTP://THEELEARNINGCOACH.COM/PODCASTS/55/.

AND HERE'S ANOTHER PRESENTATION BY JOHN SWELLER AT RESEARCHED MELBOURNE IN 2017 ENTITLED *WITHOUT AN UNDERSTANDING OF HUMAN COGNITIVE ARCHITECTURE, INSTRUCTION IS BLIND.*

Our knowledge of human cognition has advanced substantially over the last few decades. That knowledge has considerable implications for instructional design but is almost unknown among instructional designers. Cognitive load theory is an instructional design theory based on our knowledge of human cognition. In this talk John Sweller describes those aspects of human cognition that are relevant to instruction and briefly describes some of the instructional implications that follow.

AVAILABLE FROM HTTPS://YOUTU.BE/GOLPFI9LS-W.

3 HOW DEEP IS YOUR PROCESSING?

DEPTH OF PROCESSING

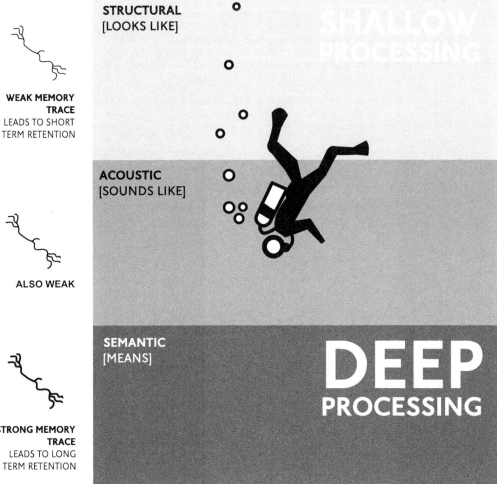

STRUCTURAL
[LOOKS LIKE]

SHALLOW PROCESSING

WEAK MEMORY TRACE
LEADS TO SHORT TERM RETENTION

ACOUSTIC
[SOUNDS LIKE]

ALSO WEAK

SEMANTIC
[MEANS]

DEEP PROCESSING

STRONG MEMORY TRACE
LEADS TO LONG TERM RETENTION

3 HOW DEEP IS YOUR PROCESSING?

PAPER "Levels of processing: A framework for memory research"[1]

QUOTE *"The processing that a student consciously engages in determines what will be encoded into memory and retained".*

Why you should read this article

Ever been introduced to someone and before you know it you're no longer able to remember her or his name? The reason for this is that when you were introduced, you probably didn't process the new information in a deep or meaningful way but rather processed it in a very shallow way and then just took it for granted and went upon your further business. You heard the name and processed it in a shallow phonemic way (i.e. how it sounded) but not in a deeper semantic way (i.e. related it to something you already knew). If you had heard that the person's name was Baker and then related it to the baker around the corner who bakes that delicious bread and pastries as you mentally repeat the name a few times, you would have elaborated on the name by relating it to what you know about bakers in general and that specific baker in particular, making the new information more salient and thus making you more likely to remember it.

EPISODIC
MEMORIES
Consciously recalled
events or facts

This article by Fergus Craik and Robert Lockhart (1972), along with its sister article on the depth of processing and the retention of words in episodic memory by Craik and Endel Tulving (1975), form the basis for almost 50 years of thinking on how we can help learners learn and retain information better. And let's face it, that should be our goal as educators.

---

1 **CRAIK, F. I. M., & LOCKHART, R. S.** (1972). LEVELS OF PROCESSING: A FRAMEWORK FOR MEMORY RESEARCH. *JOURNAL OF VERBAL LEARNING AND VERBAL BEHAVIOR, 11*, 671–684. 10.1016/S0022-5371(72)80001-X (OPEN ACCESS).

Abstract of the article

This paper briefly reviews the evidence for multistore theories of memory and points out some difficulties with the approach. An alternative framework for human memory research is then outlined in terms of depth or levels of processing. Some current data and arguments are re-examined in the light of this alternative framework and implications for further research considered.

The article

Craik and Lockhart wrote their pioneering article as a reaction to what was known as the multistore model of information processing (Atkinson & Shiffrin, 1968; see Figure 3.1). It wasn't that they didn't agree with the fact that a stimulus (a signal) enters our brains through a sensory register (eyes: seeing, ears: hearing, nose: smelling, mouth: tasting, skin: feeling), and that there's a limited short-term store (what we now call short-term memory or working memory) and a virtually unlimited long-term store (long-term memory).

MULTISTORE MODEL
Structural model of memory

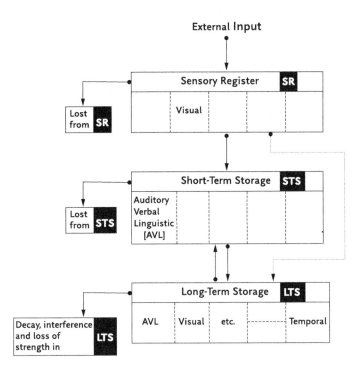

FIGURE 3.1
STRUCTURE OF THE MEMORY SYSTEM (ATKINSON & SHIFFRIN, 1968)

Their problem was that this multistore model of information processing didn't properly explain why some things were learnt and retained better than others. To this end, they proposed a *depth of processing* model based on the idea that perception involves the analysis of stimuli at a number of levels starting with the analysis of physical or sensory features (e.g. lines, angles, brightness, pitch, loudness) while later stages are involved with matching this new input to what is already stored in our memory through processes like pattern recognition and extraction of meaning (Craik & Lockhart, 1972, p. 675). After something is recognised, it then undergoes further mental processing through enrichment and/or elaboration. Craik (1973) defined depth as: "the meaningfulness extracted from the stimulus rather than in terms of the number of analyses performed upon it" (p. 48).

PATTERN
RECOGNITION
To automatically
recognising patterns
and trends

The second part of their theory holds that after perceptual analysis, a memory trace is created. Specifically they

> suggest that trace persistence is a function of depth of analysis, with deeper levels of analysis associated with more elaborate, longer lasting, and stronger traces. Since the organism is normally concerned only with the extraction of meaning from the stimuli, it is advantageous to store the products of such deep analyses, but there is usually no need to store the products of preliminary analyses.
>
> (p. 675)

Deeper analysis/processing, thus, leads to a more persistent trace and in turn better retention and learning.

According to the authors, although levels can be grouped into what can be seen as discrete stages (e.g. sensory analysis, pattern recognition, stimulus elaboration), the levels are better described as an analysis continuum. In extension of this, memory was also viewed by them as a continuum that goes from fleeting memories that decay rapidly based on sensory analyses (e.g. processing based on phonemic and orthographic components) to highly durable products based upon the semantic-associative processing.

In contrast to the multistore model, levels of processing are relatively non-structured; what we remember is what happens as a result of our processing of the information. According to Craik and Lockhart, we can process information in three ways. The first two ways are what can be called *shallow processing*. As their research, as well as the research of Craik with Endel Tulving dealt primarily with learning written words, we'll use this to try to make this clear. You can process a written word in a structural way (*structural processing*). That is to say, you pay attention to its appearance, encoding only its physical qualities or how the letters look (e.g. typeface, size, colour, etc.). A second type of processing that is a little less shallow is what in this case would be called *phonemic processing*, where you encode the sound of the word, or *graphemic processing*, where you encode the letters contained in a word (i.e. spell it).

Shallow processing
focuses on
superficial features

Finally there is *orthographic processing,* where you encode the shape of something. These two forms of shallow processing involve maintenance rehearsal (i.e. you repeat something to hold it in your short-term memory store) which leads to a weak, non-persistent memory trace and, thus, fairly short-term retention. There are also other forms of shallow processing such as highlighting and underlining passages and literally transcribing what the instructor has said as a form of note-taking.

Semantic processing focuses on deeper meaning

Deep processing, on the other hand, involves the *semantic processing* of the information, which is what occurs when you encode the meaning of a word and relate it to similar words with similar meaning. Craik and Lockhart explain it as follows: "after a word is recognized, it may trigger associations, images or stories on the basis of the subject's past experience with the word" (p. 675). This deep processing involves what is known as elaboration rehearsal involving meaningful analysis, for example in the form of giving a word or words a meaning or linking it/them with previous knowledge leading to stronger, more persistent traces and better retention.

Handwriting or keyboard?

TAKING NOTES WITH PEN AND PAPER OR WITH THE LAPTOP?

THERE HAS BEEN MUCH DISCUSSION as to whether laptops should be allowed in the classroom. Typical reasons for banning them are that (1) students use them for things other than taking notes (e.g. Facebook®, Instagram®, email, checking the news, and gaming just to name a few) and (2) even if you don't use a table or laptop, the screens of those using them is distracting. Both of these are very valid. But there's a third reason, namely that most kids today can type as fast as the teacher talks and, thus, the student can type a verbatim transcript. In essence, the words go in their ears and out of their fingers and they process the information only at the phonemic level. If they use pen and paper, then – unless they've taken steno – they are required to paraphrase, abbreviate, and extract the important things that are said (i.e. separate the wheat from the chaff). As such they are more deeply processing what is being said and, thus, they remember and learn better.

By now it should be clear that we, as teachers, should strive to have our students process information as deeply as possible and thus should make use of those techniques and pedagogies that facilitate, stimulate, and even require this to happen.

Conclusions/implications of the work for educational practice

As we can do only one thing at a time (we can't multitask!), processing something at a shallow level disrupts processing at a deeper level. In other words, the processing that a student consciously engages in determines what will be encoded into memory and retained. As Craik & Tulving (2015) showed in their series of ten experiments, it's even so that how the material is processed is more important than the student's intention to learn. What this means is that the fact that a student who deliberately prepares for a test but neglects deep processing of the material won't do as well as one who engages in deep processing, even if (s)he isn't deliberately trying to learn (Marsh & Butler, 2013).

In summary, it's key to consider what type of processing different teaching and learning strategies bring about. For most educational tasks, students will benefit from those strategies that specifically encourage them to extract the meaning of to-be-remembered information. Thus, if you want your students to learn well, and that means here that they not only know things, but they also have to do things with what they've learnt.

How to use the work in your teaching

Making use of the ideas of Craik and Lockhart is relatively easy. Some of you might even say that this is common sense. Be that as it may, below are a number of easy ways to make use of depth of processing in your teaching.

1. Encourage students to explore what is being studied on their own in order to elaborate on it. How does what I have learnt – this concept, principle, strategy – relate to other concepts? This *elaborative encoding* helps learners learn more about a concept and also increase their retention as it helps the learner to construct a richer set of integrated memories relating to what is being studied.

Make it distinct

2. Encourage students to think about the *distinctiveness* of what they have learnt. How is this concept, principle, strategy ... similar to or different from other concepts, principles, strategies (i.e. distinctiveness).

Link it to prior knowledge

3. Relate the new information to *pre-existing knowledge*. As we will see in Chapter 6 on the importance of prior knowledge (via advance organisers) learners retain and recall information better if it's linked to what they already know. They form connections between new information and what they already have in their mental schemata, which allows them to process it on a deeper level.

Apply it

4. Include activities that focus on *application*. How can you apply what you've learnt to a different situation? Can it be applied and if not, why not? When a learner is encouraged to interact with what (s)he is learning by applying it knowledge retention will be enhanced.

TRANSFER
APPROPRIATE
PROCESSING
When encoding
and retrieval of
information is
analogous

5. *Rework* what has been studied. Let students put information in their own words; write a summary or paraphrase what they've learnt. Have them create a concept map of what they've learnt. Have students talk about it with someone else.
6. Make it *personal* for the student. How can what has been learnt relate to the student's own personal experience?
7. Make use of *transfer appropriate processing*, that is that the student processes the information in a way that (s)he either expects to have to use it or in the way that you as teacher will assess it. Encourage students to try to *imagine* what it is that they are expected to do with what they've learnt: by the textbook authors and/or by you as teacher?

Takeaways

- Whether or not a student retains what (s)he has learnt depends upon how deeply the student has processed it.
- The greater the depth of information processing by the learner during learning, the better it will be retained and remembered.
- The more techniques that a learner or teacher uses to stimulate deep learning, the better the information will be retained. In other words, if a learner processes information in a variety of ways (s)he will remember and recall it more effectively.
- Processing will be automatic unless attention is focused on a particular level and this is usually a low level.
- Being able to "just Google it" is not enough. Instruct students to consider the *meaning* of concepts and how they relate to *other* concepts, rather than an isolated definition of them.
- Learning is largely a question of what we pay attention to, so ensure students are paying attention to the right things. For example, making a PowerPoint presentation of the Battle of Hastings might make a student better at using PowerPoint as opposed to knowing more about the Battle of Hastings.

References

ATKINSON, R. C., & SHIFFRIN, R. M. (1968). HUMAN MEMORY: A PROPOSED SYSTEM AND ITS CONTROL PROCESSES. IN K. W. SPENCE AND J. T. SPENCE (EDS.), *THE PSYCHOLOGY OF LEARNING AND MOTIVATION* (VOL. 2, PP. 89–195). NEW YORK, NY: ACADEMIC PRESS. AVAILABLE FROM: HTTPS://PDFS. SEMANTICSCHOLAR.ORG/5E32/B224224IDE92D6F20FD315C2BEBCIF251CB7.PDF.

CRAIK, F. I. M. (1973). A "LEVEL OF ANALYSIS" VIEW OF MEMORY. IN P. PLINER, L. KRAMES AND T. ALLOWAY (EDS.), *COMMUNICATION AND AFFECT: THOUGHT AND LANGUAGE.* NEW YORK, NY: ACADEMIC PRESS.

CRAIK, F. I. M., & LOCKHART, R. S. (1972). LEVELS OF PROCESSING: A FRAMEWORK FOR MEMORY RESEARCH. *JOURNAL OF VERBAL LEARNING AND VERBAL BEHAVIOR, 11,* 671–684. 10.1016/ S0022-5371(72)80001-X (OPEN ACCESS).

CRAIK, F. I. M., & TULVING, E. (1975). DEPTH OF PROCESSING AND THE RETENTION OF WORDS IN EPISODIC MEMORY. *JOURNAL OF EXPERIMENTAL PSYCHOLOGY: GENERAL, 104*, 268–294. AVAILABLE FROM: HTTP://ALICEKIM.CA/CRAIKTULVING1975.PDF.

MARSH & BUTLER (2013). MEMORY IN EDUCATIONAL SETTINGS. IN D. REISBERG (ED.). *THE OXFORD HANDBOOK OF COGNITIVE PSYCHOLOGY* (PP. 299–317). OXFORD/NEW YORK, NY: OXFORD UNIVERSITY PRESS.

Suggested readings and links

MARSH & BUTLER (2013). MEMORY IN EDUCATIONAL SETTINGS. IN D. REISBERG (ED.). *THE OXFORD HANDBOOK OF COGNITIVE PSYCHOLOGY* (PP. 299–317). OXFORD/NEW YORK, NY: OXFORD UNIVERSITY PRESS.

The authors describe three theoretical principles from cognitive science that have implications for educational practice: introducing desirable difficulties during learning, processing information to extract meaning, and the importance of a match between the processing that occurs during initial learning and the processing required by the criterial task.

Simply Psychology: Levels of Processing written by Saul Mcleod, psychology tutor and researcher for The University of Manchester, Division of Neuroscience & Experimental Psychology, *Simply Psychology* is an online study guide for psychology students, educators and enthusiasts. Here you can find psychology articles, study notes and learn about the theories and perspectives that have shaped the discipline.

AVAILABLE FROM WWW.SIMPLYPSYCHOLOGY.ORG/LEVELSOFPROCESSING. HTML.

LEVELS OF PROCESSING MODEL: A DISCUSSION OF THE THREE LEVELS OF PROCESSING OF CRAIK AND LOCKHART (AUGUST 11, 2014).

AVAILABLE FROM WWW.YOUTUBE.COM/WATCH?V=NV2RE427FDI.

LEVELS OF PROCESSING THEORY INCLUDING A DISCUSSION OF SOME OF THE STUDIES CARRIED OUT BY CRAIK AND TULVING (1975) INCLUDING TRANSFER APPROPRIATE PROCESSING, AND ENCODING SPECIFICITY.

AVAILABLE FROM WWW.YOUTUBE.COM/WATCH?V=WLWSC7VM6NM.

COGNITIVE PRINCIPLES FOR OPTIMIZING LEARNING: VIDEO BY PROFESSOR STEPHEN CHEW WHICH OPERATIONALISES THE CONCEPT OF LEVEL OF PROCESSING INTO FOUR PRINCIPLES THAT STUDENTS CAN USE TO DEVELOP EFFECTIVE STUDY STRATEGIES.

AVAILABLE FROM WWW.YOUTUBE.COM/WATCH?V=1XEHH5DNCIW.

 PUTTING THE PRINCIPLES FOR OPTIMIZING LEARNING INTO PRACTICE: VIDEO BY PROFESSOR STEPHEN CHEW WHICH APPLIES THE PRINCIPLES OF DEEP PROCESSING TO COMMON STUDY SITUATIONS, INCLUDING NOTE-TAKING AND HIGHLIGHTING WHILE READING.

AVAILABLE FROM WWW.YOUTUBE.COM/WATCH?V=E9GROXHYZDQ.

4 AN EVOLUTIONARY VIEW OF LEARNING

EVOLUTIONARY PSYCHOLOGY

BIOLOGICALLY PRIMARY LEARNING

MOVING
SPEAKING
RELATING
FOLK PSYCHOLOGY
FOLK BIOLOGY
FOLK PHYSICS

BIOLOGICALLY SECONDARY LEARNING

CULTURAL KNOWLEDGE:
SCHOOL CURRICULUM
READING
WRITING
MATHEMATICS

4 AN EVOLUTIONARY VIEW OF LEARNING

PAPER "An evolutionarily informed education science"[1]

QUOTE *Evolutionary educational psychology is the study of the relation between folk knowledge and abilities and accompanying inferential and attributional biases as these influence academic learning in evolutionarily novel cultural contexts, especially schools.*

Why you should read this article

A baby is born. Almost immediately they communicate with the parents. They let them know when they are happy, hungry, and uncomfortable. They smile at mum and dad within six to eight weeks, who smile back, and they begin to make sounds that are echoed back and forth with the parents. A little later they begin speaking their first words and learn to live and play with others. How is it that babies and toddlers learn and can do these things? How is it that they learn to speak seemingly effortlessly, but a few years later learn to read and write that same language with great pain and difficulty? And why do children in a class have more attention for each other than for school work? In his article David Geary answers these and other questions by looking at children's learning through an evolutionary lens. Viewing and studying learning from such an evolutionary point of view leads to refreshing insights. It can offer us an explanation for why children are endlessly motivated for some things and for others much less or not at all, and why certain ways of learning are so popular.

Abstract of the article

Schools are a central interface between evolution and culture. They are the contexts in which children learn the evolutionarily novel abilities and knowledge needed to function as adults in modern societies.

---

1   **GEARY, D. C.** (2008). AN EVOLUTIONARILY INFORMED EDUCATION SCIENCE. *EDUCATIONAL PSYCHOLOGIST, 43*(4), 179–195. HTTP://DOI.ORG/10.1080/00461520802392133S.

Evolutionary educational psychology is the study of how an evolved bias in children's learning and motivational systems influences their ability and motivation to learn evolutionarily novel academic abilities and information in school. I provide an overview of evolved domains of mind, corresponding learning and motivational biases, and the evolved systems that allow humans to learn about and cope with variation and change within lifetimes. The latter enable the creation of cultural and academic innovations and support the learning of evolutionarily novel information in school. These mechanisms and the premises and principles of evolutionary educational psychology are described. Their utility is illustrated by discussion of the relation between evolved motivational dispositions and children's academic motivation and by the relation between evolved social-cognitive systems and mechanisms that support children's learning to read.

The article

We learn many things "automatically" without having to make any noticeable effort. The reason for this is simple, namely that learning certain things are genetically programmed into us as a result of natural selection; certain types of learning are, so to speak, hardwired into us by way of our evolution. This way we learn to recognise faces by looking and comparing, we learn to talk by listening and we learn to walk through trial and error. They are all forms of learning that, we, as a species, have specifically evolved to acquire over many generations. We also call it biological or evolutionary primary learning. Primary skills, such as learning general problem-solving strategies, imitation, recognising faces, communicating through listening and speaking a native language, and social relations including our ability to communicate with each other, have evolved via evolution. Geary speaks of "[H]umans' brain and cognitive systems that have evolved to attend to, process, and guide behavioural response to evolutionarily significant information compose 'biologically primary' or core domains of human cognition, and coalesce around folk psychology, folk biology, and folk physics" (p. 180). Folk psychology (i.e. common sense psychology) deals with awareness of the self, other individuals, and group dynamics; our innate capacity to explain and predict the behaviour and mental state of others so as to deal and form relationships with them (e.g. (s)he's nice or I can depend on her/him). Folk biology deals with how we classify and reason about the organic world around and develop taxonomies about their behaviour and their "essence" (e.g. heuristics we use to make sense of the natural world around us). Folk physics is the untrained human perception of basic physical phenomena that support navigation, forming mental

BIOLOGICALLY
PRIMARY
KNOWLEDGE
Evolutionary skills/
knowledge we
acquire naturally like
speaking

representations of phenomena (e.g. what goes up must come down), and tool construction. Evolutionarily speaking, Geary states that we also have biological biases towards social play and exploration of our surroundings. We acquire such primary knowledge easily, unconsciously, and without explicit instruction merely by membership in a group and as such, do not need to be taught. We also store biological primary knowledge directly in our long-term memory without conscious processing in working memory.

THOUGH ATTRIBUTED TO CHARLES DARWIN, the phrase *survival of the fittest* was actually coined by Herbert Spencer, an all-around scientist in Victorian England. In everyday language, people understand the term to mean that a stronger animal will defeat a weaker one and, thus, survive. But this is true only in a very specific sense. Survival of the fittest is about evolution to describe the mechanism of *natural selection*, the term that Darwin used. Natural selection is a biological concept and only relates to reproductive strength (i.e. success). In other words it is actually the survival of any form of life that will have the greatest chance of living long enough to both reproduce and, if necessary, care for as many of their offspring long enough so that they too are eventually able to reproduce. In other words the fittest plant or animal is one that is fitter than others, and fit to leave as many copies of itself as possible in successive generations. If we look at primary knowledge like communicating (both orally and physically), recognising others, and forming social bonds with parents and others necessary for survival, then it's clear that without these skills a baby will not survive very long, not reproducing and not perpetuating this non-ability.

NATURAL
SELECTION
Traits which lead to
survival of a species

As societies became more complicated, more than just this primary knowledge was needed. In addition to staying physically afloat, people need to acquire a different kind of knowledge in order to be able to participate in society. This involves acquiring cultural knowledge – in the broadest sense of the word; knowledge that we consciously and not evolutionarily acquire and transfer to following generations such as reading, writing, doing mathematics, working with a computer, or searching the internet. We are no longer solely dependent on information that is immediately available in the here and now, but can make accessible information for many people through information carriers such as teachers and then books. This cultural or secondary

BIOLOGICALLY SECONDARY KNOWLEDGE
Cultural knowledge we don't acquire naturally like reading/writing

knowledge is often separate from the three aforementioned domains and is often taught in schools. We call this type of learning "biologically secondary" and such knowledge and skills are acquired consciously, often requiring considerable effort. Also, unlike the biologically primary generic-cognitive skills, biologically secondary skills tend to be domain-specific (Sweller, 2015; Tricot & Sweller, 2014). In other words, they are the skills we learn in school.

SYSTEMATIC PROBLEM SOLVING
Using both primary and secondary biological knowledge

PROBLEM-SOLVING 101

AT A CERTAIN POINT in our development as homo sapiens, the automatic processes involved in primary learning fell short. To survive in rapidly changing social and ecological conditions, people developed a systematic problem-solving capacity. With this they were able to suppress the innate tendencies to naively explore and to learn in a more systematic way and to solve problems. For example, the tendency to run away from a wolf could be suppressed when the wolf was an affectionate specimen. This possibility for systematic problem-solving is one of the most important characteristics of the human brain. Together with the automatic cognitive processes, this forms the core of the human brain. This enables both primary and secondary learning. Our ability for secondary learning is, however, from an evolutionary point of view, much younger and not as well developed as our predisposition to primary learning. According to Geary, this cognitive architecture has consequences for learning in school and how that should take shape.

How we learn in school

Evolution plays a role not only in what we want to learn, but also in how we prefer to learn. In everyday situations we can lean on heuristics, handy rules of thumb and mnemonics in our brain. In this way we can give meaning to the world around us quickly and automatically. If you meet someone, your brain usually knows immediately whether it is a friend or a stranger and you can tell by the state of the mouth and eyes if s(he) is happy, angry, or sad. These automatic cognitive processes help us to successfully interact with others. We have mastered these processes by observing, discovering, and playing; a kind of unconscious learning. It would be nice if we could acquire secondary knowledge with the same ease, but that is not the case. We learn to speak and listen on autopilot, but need explicit instruction to learn to spell and write (see also

Chapter 21, Learning techniques that really work and Chapter 17, Why discovery learning is a bad way to discover things/Why inquiry learning isn't). In contrast to the primary knowledge, the acquisition of knowledge at school does not happen automatically. It takes effort, is conscious, and takes place in the working memory.

Conclusions/implications of the work for educational practice

Evolutionary psychology helps us understand why students learn certain things easily and with a lot of motivation (primary learning) and why other assignments cost them more effort (secondary learning). As Geary says,

PHONETIC
DECODING
The identification of
word sounds

> [I]f our goal is universal education that encompasses a variety of evo-lutionarily novel academic domains (e.g. mathematics) and abilities (e.g. phonetic decoding as related to reading), then we cannot assume that an inherent curiosity or motivation to learn will be sufficient for most children and adolescents.
>
> (p. 187).

ROMANTICISM
Cultural movement
celebrating the
natural state of man

> Children's natural interest in novelty and their motivation to learn their culture will get them started but is not predicted to maintain long-term academic learning, contra Rousseau (1979) and other "romantic" approaches to education
>
> (see Hirsch, 1996, p. 190).

To properly learn in school, you have to take students by the hand and motivate them to learn in a different way because:

- children will have to suppress their natural tendencies, which itself takes effort;
- children will have to learn in a different way than they do in primary learning; and
- direct instruction by someone with expertise is preferable for second-ary learning

To stimulate motivation for evolutionarily secondary learning in schools, Geary states that teachers can best seek out the grey area between primary and secondary learning. An example that he gives is a parent (or it could be a teacher) who "reads" a picture book to a child. The child is interested, because (s)he likes to focus on the parent (or teacher) and wants to learn the language (primary focus). At the same time, the pictures in the book are abstract versions of the things in the world around them and the communication is not direct in colloquial language, but via a written story (both secondary knowledge). If pupils experience such learning situations often enough and find that they learn something from them, they'll also become motivated to learn other, increasingly abstract, schoolwork. Success leads to motivation and not the other way around.

How to use the work in your teaching

Learning at school takes effort; sometimes a lot of effort. That is not only good to realise, but it also contributes to how students function. Make them aware that you are learning some things by themselves and that you only learn other things if you make an effort. Direct instruction by someone who already controls the substance – you – is a good way to guide students in secondary learning.

As explained above, you can motivate students by connecting school secondary learning to natural, primary learning. This can be done by linking teaching material to issues that pupils are already focused on. For example, the direct environment or the social processes. Nowadays we already pay a lot of attention here in schools, such as authentic learning or meaningful learning (see also Chapter 23 on The culture of learning). Here too, the connection between the material to be learned and the pupils' world of life is sought.

Takeaways

- People have a natural focus on things that are important for our survival, learning about this is effortless.
- Learning at school requires effort and active use of the working memory.
- Everyone learns to talk and listen without school, learning to read and write is only possible with explicit instruction.
- Students need to be helped to balance or "manage" their own interests alongside the interests of the classroom.
- Students are "naturally" able to develop social skills (biologically primary (folk) knowledge) but must learn appropriate domain-specific application of these skills (biologically secondary knowledge).
- You can motivate pupils by connecting with their natural way of learning.

References

GEARY, D. C. (2008). AN EVOLUTIONARILY INFORMED EDUCATION SCIENCE. *EDUCATIONAL PSYCHOLOGIST, 43*(4), 179–195.

HIRSCH, E. D., JR. (1996). *THE SCHOOLS WE NEED AND WHY WE DON'T HAVE THEM.* NEW YORK, NY: DOUBLEDAY.

ROUSSEAU, -J.-J. (1979). *EMILE: OR, ON EDUCATION* (A. BLOOM, TRANS.). NEW YORK, NY: BASIC BOOKS. (ORIGINAL WORK PUBLISHED 1762).

SWELLER, J. (2015). IN ACADEME, WHAT IS LEARNED AND HOW IS IT LEARNED? *CURRENT DIRECTIONS IN PSYCHOLOGICAL SCIENCE, 24*, 190–194. DOI: 10.1177/0963721415569570.

TRICOT, A., & SWELLER, J. (2014). DOMAIN-SPECIFIC KNOWLEDGE AND WHY TEACHING GENERIC SKILLS DOES NOT WORK. *EDUCATIONAL PSYCHOLOGY REVIEW, 26*, 265–283.

Suggested readings and links

GEARY, D. (2002). PRINCIPLES OF EVOLUTIONARY EDUCATIONAL PSYCHOLOGY. *LEARNING AND INDIVIDUAL DIFFERENCES, 12*, 317–345.

KAHNEMAN, D. (2011). *THINKING FAST AND SLOW.* NEW YORK, NY: FARRAR, STRAUS AND GIROUX.

Why do we assess the same situation before and after lunch? Why do we think that handsome people are more competent than others? Daniel Kahneman shows in this book that we are much more irrational than we think. He explains that we have two systems of thought: a quick, intuitive way and a slow, well-considered way. Both are extremely practical, but we are often wrong because we use the wrong way of thinking – without our being aware of it.

SWELLER, J. (2016). WORKING MEMORY, LONG-TERM MEMORY, AND INSTRUCTIONAL DESIGN. *JOURNAL OF APPLIED RESEARCH IN MEMORY AND COGNITION, 5*, 360–367.

AVAILABLE FROM HTTPS://READER.ELSEVIER.COM/READER/SD/PII/ S2211368115000935?TOKEN=EF48F65D8FD2D1EDE0353F210 1862506EB5EB11D757A203BE1EC1AC1BAA800E31BE29C17B7505807000 F52FE27FC2B03.

EVOLUTIONARY EDUCATIONAL PSYCHOLOGY AS A BASE FOR INSTRUCTIONAL DESIGN.

AVAILABLE FROM WWW.YOUTUBE.COM/WATCH?V=ZD33ZREJ0D4.

A "video", actually more a podcast with John Sweller, explaining how evolutionary educational psychology relates to teaching and learning.

EVOLUTIONARY EDUCATIONAL PSYCHOLOGY – A POWERPOINT ON THE THEORY.

AVAILABLE FROM HTTPS://ACHEMICALORTHODOXY.FILES.WORDPRESS. COM/2017/06/EVOLUTIONARY-EDUCATIONAL-PSYCHOLOGY.PPTX

5 ONE PICTURE AND ONE THOUSAND WORDS

DUAL CODING

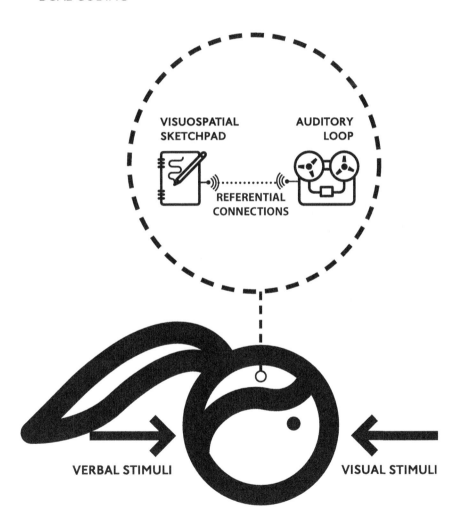

5 ONE PICTURE AND ONE THOUSAND WORDS

PAPER   "Dual coding theory and education"[1]

QUOTE   *"Human cognition is unique in that it has become specialized for dealing simultaneously with language and with nonverbal objects and events".*[2]

Why you should read this article

You know the saying: *A picture is worth a thousand words*. While there is a basis of truth to it, there are two problems. The first is that this is the case only when the concept represented is concrete and/or unequivocal. An example of the first case is *Lady Justice* (the Roman goddess of justice). To most of us, it is as clear as the nose on our faces but justice is a very abstract concept and without the necessary prior knowledge and cultural history, the statue doesn't explain anything. Or take the term *mammal*. It would take countless pictures to get someone to understand/ deduce what this term entails ranging from bumblebee bats, through tree shrews, to cows, people, elephants, and blue whales plus all their distinguishing features. The second problem is that it ignores the fact that the two can be/are cumulative.

Going back to the first case, combining a picture of Lady Justice with an explanation of the purpose of the blindfold (symbol of impartiality without regard to wealth, power, or other status), scales (symbol of measuring the strength of a case's support and opposition), sword (symbol of swift and final authority), and toga (symbol of status) makes the term, and its understanding, both possible and stronger. The same is true for the concept "mammal", which can be determined based upon five simple principles, namely: females that bear live young and nurse them,

---

1   **CLARK, J. M., & PAIVIO, A**. (1991). DUAL CODING THEORY AND EDUCATION. *EDUCATIONAL PSYCHOLOGY REVIEW, 3*(3), 149–210. HTTPS://DOI.ORG/10.1007/BF01320076
2   **PAIVIO, A**. (1986). *MENTAL REPRESENTATIONS*. NEW YORK, NY: OXFORD UNIVERSITY PRESS.

being warm-blooded, having body hair, having a neocortex, and having three ear bones. It is questionable whether someone could deduce these things and successfully classify animals as mammals without a verbal (either textual or oral) explanation.

The second problem, ignoring the fact that pictures and words can be additive in their impact, is the basis of Allan Paivio's *dual coding theory*, the subject of this chapter.

Abstract of the articles

Dual coding theory explains human behaviour and experience in terms of dynamic associative processes that operate on a rich network of verbal and non-verbal (or imagery) representations that are specific to a certain modality. We first describe the underlying premises of the theory and then show how the basic dual coding theory mechanisms can be used to model diverse educational phenomena. The research demonstrates that concreteness, imagery, and verbal associative processes play major roles in various educational domains: the representation and comprehension of knowledge, learning and memory of school material, effective instruction, individual differences, achievement motivation and test anxiety, and the learning of motor skills. Dual coding theory also has important implications for the science and practice of educational psychology – specifically, for educational research and teacher education. We show not only that dual coding theory provides a unified explanation for diverse topics in education, but also that its mechanistic framework accommodates theories cast in terms of strategies and other high-level psychological processes. Although much additional research needs to be done, the concrete models that dual coding theory offers for the behaviour and experience of students, teachers, and educational psychologists further our understanding of educational phenomena and strengthen related pedagogical practices.

The article

In 1969, Allan Paivio published the article "Mental imagery in associative learning and memory" (Pavio, 1969). In that article, he posited that non-verbal imagery and verbal symbolic processes are operationally distinguishable from each other and are differentially available to a learner as associative mediators or memory codes.

The verbal system processes information in the form of words; Paivio refers to these forms as *logogens*. The non-verbal system processes information in the form of the properties that occur in the real world, and this form is called *imagens*. For example, when we think of a tennis ball, we can recall the word (the logogens) for it, but we can also summon

ASSOCIATIVE
PROCESSES
Creating connections between pieces of information

NONVERBAL
IMAGERY
Visual representation associated with particular words.

LOGOGENS
Word

IMAGENS
Image associated with a word

up how it feels to hold a tennis ball and how it looks and smells (the imagens). These imagens are directly related to the outside world, while the logogens are an abstraction, a symbol for something in the outside world.

Furthermore, dual coding theory states that connections can arise within each system (i.e. *associations*). For example, you can associate a word like "school" with other words such as reading, writing, arithmetic, teacher, or classroom. And you can associate the image of a school with the smell of the gym or the instructional materials hanging on the classroom wall. Also, connections can also arise between the two systems (i.e. *references*). For example, the word "school" can evoke an image of your own school and the image of a school building can evoke words such as "class" and "learning" (and of course "school"). Paivio illustrated (see Figure 5.1) these systems and their relationships as follows:

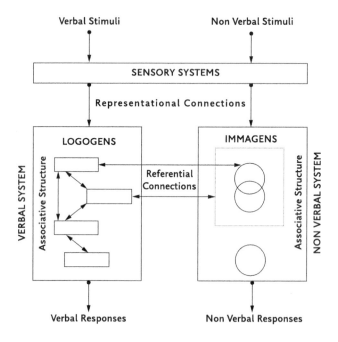

FIGURE 5.1
DUAL CODING
MODEL FOR
PROCESSING
WORDS AND
IMAGES

One of the most important predictions from dual coding theory is that the logogens and the imagens have additive effects on memory. In other words, you remember information better if you use both systems at the same time than if you use only one system. This, though today seen as common sense, was a watershed idea at the time. And what's more, research clearly shows that this prediction is correct.

Dual coding theory as basis for cognitive theory of multimedia learning

DCT AS BASIS FOR CLT AND CTMML

DUAL CODING THEORY can be seen as part of the basis for a number of later theories. For example, John Sweller's *cognitive load theory* (1988, see Chapter 3) and Richard Mayer's *cognitive theory of multimedia learning* (2003) both build on Paivio's work. Both theories hold that you remember information better if you process it both verbally and non-verbally. In CLT and CTMML at least three principles are directly related to Paivio's work, namely the (1) *modality* or *multimedia principle* which states that words and graphics are more conducive to learning than just text or graphics alone; (2) *redundancy principle* which states that we learn better with animation and narration and that when visual text information is presented simultaneously with verbal information (e.g., when you read your slides to a class) this is redundant and impedes learning; and (3) *spatial contiguity* or *split-attention principle* which holds that we learn better when corresponding words and pictures are presented near rather than far from each other on a page or screen. An example of this can be seen in Figure 5.2.

Example A

Example B

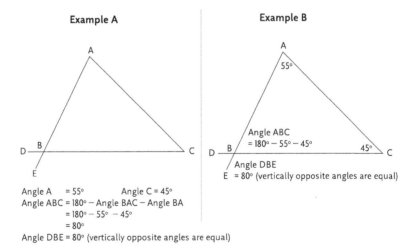

Angle A = 55°   Angle C = 45°
Angle ABC = 180° − Angle BAC − Angle BA
= 180° − 55° − 45°
= 80°
Angle DBE = 80° (vertically opposite angles are equal)

FIGURE 5.2
SPLIT-ATTENTION PRINCIPLE WHERE CORRESPONDING TEXT AND PICTURES ARE EITHER SPLIT (LEFT) OR SPATIALLY CONTIGUOUS (RIGHT)

Concrete examples are easier to process than abstract concepts.

Dual coding theory also explains why providing concrete things (e.g. examples, information, concepts) to a learner is important. Concrete things are easier to process because they're more "appealing to the imagination"; they evoke images more quickly and more easily than abstract ones. Think about the difference between processing the concepts "tree" (concrete) versus "freedom" (abstract). For "tree", images are more likely to pop up in your head than for "freedom". To aid in the processing of abstract concepts, you can work with examples. For example, you can explain "freedom" by pointing out the difference between following a lesson in the classroom and playing in the break in the schoolyard.

Also in mathematical education, examples prove their services. Many teaching methods begin by making use of real materials (such as marbles or buttons) and then proceeding to the numbers and numerals (just like words and symbols that refer to the imagens). Slowly you remove the support with the marbles and teach the students to count via symbols. Other examples are pies and slices of pizza to explain percentages or fractions. By making things concrete and using the non-verbal system well, we connect better to how our cognitive architecture works.

Conclusions/implications of the work for educational practice

Looking at teaching and learning through the dual coding lens is useful for educational practice, even if it's only for choosing between the different methods that we have at our disposal: A method that properly combines both systems and uses examples is – from a dual coding theory perspective – preferred. A method that only caters to one system, either verbally or non-verbally, is less useful. And remember, nobody thinks or learns best (i.e. has a visual or a verbal learning style) in an environment that only makes use of one system. These so-called learning styles have been exposed as nonsense in research time after time. There are no "image thinkers" or "language thinkers". Everyone thinks with both systems and everyone benefits from using both. The more often you use the two systems together, the stronger the trace in your memory and the better you will remember and thus will learn.

LEARNING STYLES
Bogus theory
claiming learners
learn best in a
preferred style. (see
Chapter 29)

How to use the work in your teaching

The first way to make use of dual coding is to make proper use of images and words when teaching. One of the major mistakes made by teachers (but also by academics presenting at conferences) is that they fill their PowerPoint® slides with words and then proceed to read what's on those slides to their students (audience). The mistake is understandable. You have the idea that by repeating orally what you have written on the slide (i.e. a form of redundancy in the 'common' meaning of the word) will strengthen the message. Unfortunately, this has been shown to be a misconception. Also, when explaining a diagram for example, do it verbally and not through text in or around the diagram. Try using signalling (e.g. animations or highlighting) when you talk a class through a diagram or a formula. Don't explain it in writing on the slide!

When using dual coding theory, it's extremely important to properly mix what you present in words (either orally or textually) with images that can illustrate, explain, and concretise the textual concept. A good example of this is when you try to explain a fairly complex and abstract idea like *affordances*[3], which are the reciprocal relationships between artefacts and agents, and how designers neglect this in their design is to show someone trying to pull open a door with its handle while the door needs to be pushed open, which is completely obvious if there is a push-plate instead of a handle. In Figure 5.3 below, everyone knows instinctively to push and not pull on the left-hand side and vice versa on the right.

AFFORDANCES
The options an object offers the user

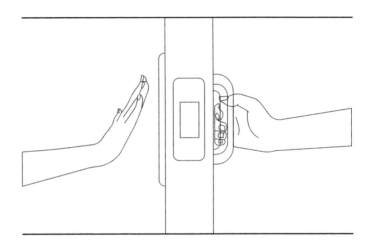

FIGURE 5.3
AN IMAGE THAT MAKES THE CONCEPT OF AFFORDANCES IMMEDIATELY CLEAR (HTTPS:// MRJOE.UK/ FLAT-DESIGN-AFFORDANCE-AND-USABILITY/)

Or if you're trying to make clear the concept that technology sometimes fails miserably (technology bites back), tell the class about how an escalator was expected to move people more quickly because the stairs move and you climb them too and then let them see an image of people

---

3   AFFORDANCES ARE THE PERCEIVED PROPERTIES OF A THING IN REFERENCE TO A USER THAT INFLUENCES HOW IT IS USED. SOME DOOR HANDLES LOOK LIKE THEY SHOULD BE PULLED. THEIR SHAPE LEADS OUR BRAINS TO BELIEVE THAT IS THE BEST WAY TO USE THEM. OTHER HANDLES LOOK LIKE THEY SHOULD BE PUSHED, A FEATURE OFTEN INDICATED BY A BAR SPANNING THE WIDTH OF THE DOOR OR EVEN A FLAT PLATE ON THE SIDE. ORIGINALLY PROPOSED BY JAMES GIBSON IN 1977 (AND REFINED IN 1979), THE TERM AFFORDANCE REFERS TO THE RELATIONSHIP BETWEEN AN OBJECT'S PHYSICAL PROPERTIES (ARTEFACTS) AND THE CHARACTERISTICS OF AN AGENT (USER) THAT ENABLES PARTICULAR INTERACTIONS BETWEEN AGENT AND OBJECT. GIBSON DEFINED THAT "THE AFFORDANCE OF ANYTHING IS A SPECIFIC COMBINATION OF THE PROPERTIES OF ITS SUBSTANCE AND ITS SURFACES WITH REFERENCE TO AN ANIMAL" (GIBSON, 1977, P. 67). A POND, DUE TO THE SURFACE TENSION OF THE WATER, AFFORDS A SURFACE TO WALK ON FOR CERTAIN SPECIES OF FLIES WHILE ALSO AFFORDING A LIVING ENVIRONMENT FOR CERTAIN TYPES OF FISH. KNOBS ARE FOR TURNING AND SLOTS ARE FOR INSERTING THINGS. THESE PROPERTIES/ARTEFACTS INTERACT WITH POTENTIAL USERS AND PROVIDE STRONG CLUES AS TO THEIR OPERATION (THINK OF YOUR CHILD, HIS/HER PEANUT BUTTER SANDWICH AND THE SLOT IN YOUR VIDEO RECORDER!).

crowding around the bottom of the escalator because everyone stands still once they set foot on the escalator (see Figure 5.4).

FIGURE 5.4
AN IMAGE THAT
MAKES THE
CONCEPT OF
TECHNOLOGY
BITING BACK
IMMEDIATELY
CLEAR. (PHOTO BY
PAVEL LOSEVSKY/
ADOBE STOCK)

EXAMPLES
Encourage learners
to create mental
images of abstract
concepts.

You can also use this by appealing to your students' imagination (picture something in their mind's eye). There are many ways to interweave this in educational practice. Examples are asking students to create a mental image of something that has just been discussed, especially if it is an abstract concept. These evoke images with the students more easily and help them to better understand abstract concepts and to remember them. For example, if teaching a play by Shakespeare with a large number of characters and related themes, you could ask them to create a mental image of those characters by focusing on their particular personality traits and how they link up with the thematic concerns of the play. Shakespeare does this quite well himself in fact and the keen reader will be able to conjure up the image of a 'green-eyed monster'[4] when considering the character of Iago and the significance of jealousy in the play. Another way is to have them make a diagram of a concept with its sub-concepts in a concept-map. Finally, you can ask students to either illustrate written content or to write descriptions of visual content. In this way you help them on the one hand

---

4   **SHAKESPEARE, W.** (1603). *OTHELLO* (ACT III, SCENE 3, LINE 169). AVAILABLE FROM HTTP://SHAKESPEARE.MIT.EDU/OTHELLO/FULL.HTML.

to create extra memory traces which strengthen the memory. On the other hand, you are asking them to retrieve information that they have already stored (i.e. retrieval practice) which also strengthens the memory.

Takeaways

- Everyone has two cooperating memory systems, a non-verbal and a verbal system.
- Both systems are active during learning. Image thinkers or language thinkers do not exist.
- The use of both systems is more effective in remembering things than using one system.
- Use examples to explain abstract concepts.
- Extensive experience with objects and environments is a rich basis for later verbal development.
- Offer images and text at the same time so that the learner doesn't have to remember the one part while processing the other, like the image below.

References

CLARK, J. M., & PAIVIO, A. (1991). DUAL CODING THEORY AND EDUCATION. *EDUCATIONAL PSYCHOLOGY REVIEW, 3*(3), 149–210.

GIBSON, J. J. (1977). THE THEORY OF AFFORDANCES. IN R. SHAW & J. BRANSFORD (EDS.), *PERCEIVING, ACTING AND KNOWING* (PP. 67–82). HILLSDALE, NJ: ERLBAUM.

GIBSON, J. J. (1979). *THE ECOLOGICAL APPROACH TO VISUAL PERCEPTION.* NEW YORK, NY: HOUGHTON MIFFLIN.

PAIVIO, A. (1969). MENTAL IMAGERY IN ASSOCIATIVE LEARNING AND MEMORY. *PSYCHOLOGICAL REVIEW, 76,* 241–263.

PAIVIO, A. (1986). *MENTAL REPRESENTATIONS: A DUAL-CODING APPROACH.* NEW YORK, NY: OXFORD UNIVERSITY PRESS.

Suggested readings and links

MAYER, R.E., (2014). *THE CAMBRIDGE HANDBOOK OF MULTIMEDIA LEARNING.* CAMBRIDGE, MA: CAMBRIDGE UNIVERSITY PRESS.

MAYER, R. E. & MORENO, R. (2003) NINE WAYS TO REDUCE COGNITIVE LOAD IN MULTIMEDIA LEARNING, *EDUCATIONAL PSYCHOLOGIST,* **38, 43–52. DOI: 10.1207/S15326985EP3801_6**

AVAILABLE FROM WWW.THEURBANCLIMATOLOGIST. COM/UPLOADS/4/4/2/5/44250401/ MAYERMORENO2003REDUCINGCOGNITIVEOVERLOAD.PDF.

THE LEARNING SCIENTISTS HAVE POSTED A VIDEO DISCUSSING HOW TO USE DUAL CODING AS A STUDY STRATEGY.

AVAILABLE FROM WWW.YOUTUBE.COM/WATCH?V=6XCZ4XNKPCC.

DUAL CODING THEORY & MULTIMEDIA LEARNING FROM CIAN MAC MAHON.

AVAILABLE FROM HTTP://BLOGS.ONLINEEDUCATION.TOURO.EDU/THE-DUAL-CODING-THEORY-MULTIMEDIA-LEARNING/.

LEARN MORE ABOUT DUAL CODING THEORY FROM SCIENCE DIRECT, WHICH CONTAINS A WEALTH OF INFORMATION RELATING TO THE THEORY ALONG WITH LINKS TO THE ORIGINAL SOURCES.

AVAILABLE FROM WWW.SCIENCEDIRECT.COM/TOPICS/NEUROSCIENCE/DUAL-CODING-THEORY.

DOUBLE-BARRELLED LEARNING FOR YOUNG & OLD BY PAUL ALONG WITH MIRJAM NEELEN.

AVAILABLE FROM HTTPS://3STARLEARNINGEXPERIENCES.WORDPRESS.COM/2017/05/30/DOUBLE-BARRELLED-LEARNING-FOR-YOUNG-OLD/.

DUAL CODING – WHAT, WHY AND HOW BY VICKI BARNETT (RESEARCH LEAD AT NOTRE DAME HIGH SCHOOL).

AVAILABLE FROM HTTPS://NORWICH.RESEARCHSCHOOL.ORG.UK/2017/10/16/DUAL-CODING-A-USERS-GUIDE/.

IF YOU WANT TO READ MORE ABOUT AFFORDANCES, ESPECIALLY AFFORDANCES WITH RESPECT TO EDUCATION, READ PAUL'S INAUGURAL ADDRESS AT THE OPEN UNIVERSITY.

AVAILABLE FROM HTTPS://DSPACE.OU.NL/BITSTREAM/1820/1618/1/THREE%20WORLDS%20OF%20CSCL%20CAN%20WE%20SUPPORT%20CSCL.PDF.

PART II

PREREQUISITES FOR LEARNING

"You can lead a horse to the water, but the only water that gets into his stomach is what he drinks". This famous quote which comes from Ernst Rothkopf's article on mathemagenic activities[1] should be a wake-up call for all teachers: How do you help make sure that students start drinking and make use of what we offer them in the lessons?

For students to learn effectively, efficiently and preferably also enjoyably, our instruction must try to meet certain conditions. At the risk of sounding trite, it often helps to have an enclosed space (though sometimes a museum or a walk in nature is also good), paper and pen/pencil (or computers or tablets when applicable), a teacher/instructor, learning materials, and so on. But there are also conditions in which students themselves play a role. These conditions are primarily psychological. For example, students must know and understand what they're doing, have the feeling that they can handle what's coming, be motivated to begin, want to learn or achieve, and feel that they themselves are the masters of their fates and captains of their souls. If students start working on something thinking that they won't succeed, don't understand what they're doing, aren't motivated to begin with, and think that their success is not up to them but that their fate lies in the hands of others, then chances are that they won't learn very well.

These and other conditions for learning that lie within the grasp of the student are discussed in this part.

---

[1]   **ROTHKOPF, E. Z.** (1970). THE CONCEPT OF MATHEMAGENIC ACTIVITIES. *REVIEW OF EDUCATIONAL RESEARCH, 40,* 325–336.

6 WHAT YOU KNOW DETERMINES WHAT YOU LEARN

ADVANCE ORGANISERS

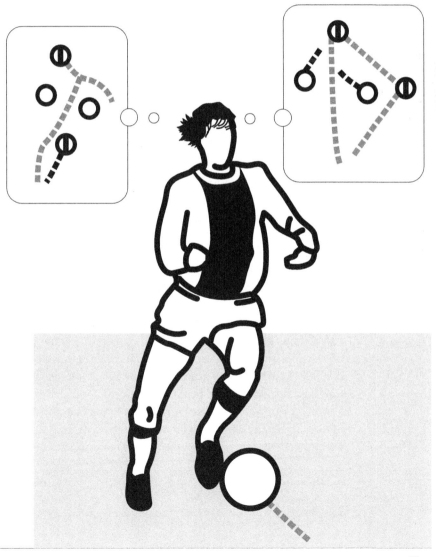

6 WHAT YOU KNOW DETERMINES WHAT YOU LEARN

PAPER "The use of advance organizers in the learning and retention of meaningful verbal material"[2]

QUOTE *"The most important single factor influencing learning is what the learner already knows. Ascertain this and teach him accordingly".*[3]

Why you should read this article

Imagine the following. You're walking around a school or a company and you see a setup with lots of glassware, plastic and glass tubes, bubbling liquids, and so forth. If you've never taken a chemistry course, then you probably have no idea what's going on. If you took chemistry in high school, chances are that you remember that this has something to do with distillation. Maybe you even remember that when you distil something (like gin, whisky, or gasoline) you separate two different things that are present together in a liquid. If, however, you studied chemistry at college, then you see that the distillation setup is being put to a specific use, as you see on the water bath instead of a Bunsen burner that the temperature has to be carefully limited to a temperature under 100° Celsius (212 Fahrenheit) and the temperature gauge gives a reading of 78.33° Celsius (173 Fahrenheit), which tells you that ethanol is being distilled. In other words, what you know determines what you see and not the other way around (Kirschner, 2009).

Johan Cruijff (for Brits and Americans Johan Cruyff), who is for one of the authors the greatest football player (soccer for Americans) that ever graced the pitch, was famous for his maxims such as "If I wanted

---

2   **AUSUBEL, D. P.** (1960). THE USE OF ADVANCE ORGANIZERS IN THE LEARNING AND RETENTION OF MEANINGFUL VERBAL MATERIAL. *JOURNAL OF EDUCATIONAL PSYCHOLOGY*, 51, 267–272. HTTP://DX.DOI.ORG/10.1037/H0046669.
3   **AUSUBEL, D. P.** (1968). *EDUCATIONAL PSYCHOLOGY. A COGNITIVE VIEW*. NEW YORK, NY: HOLT, RINEHART AND WINSTON, INC.

you to understand it I would have explained it better", "If you can't win, make sure you don't lose", or "Playing football is very simple, but playing simple football is the hardest thing there is", but also said "You will only see it when you get it". And that's basically what David P. Ausubel was all about. In his mind, and as reflected in his research and writings, prior knowledge is the most important influence on what is learnt. To ensure that learners have the necessary basis for what they're supposed to learn, even when studying something new, he introduced the concept of the *advance organiser*; a text or presentation at a higher level of *generality*, *inclusiveness* and *abstraction*, which is presented before the learning event and which forms a conceptual framework for learning the new information (see Figure 6.1).

ADVANCE ORGANISER
General, inclusive, and abstract framework presented prior to learning

FIGURE 6.1
SIMPLE REPRESENTATION OF ADVANCE ORGANISERS WITH RESPECT TO LEARNING

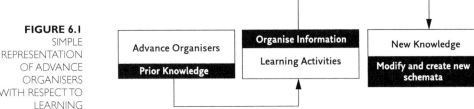

Abstract of the article

The purpose of this study is to test the hypothesis that the learning and retention of unfamiliar but meaningful verbal material can be facilitated by the advance introduction of relevant subsuming concepts (organisers). This hypothesis is based on the assumption that cognitive structure is hierarchically organised in terms of highly inclusive concepts under which are subsumed less inclusive subconcepts and informational data. If this organisational principle of progressive differentiation of an internalised sphere of knowledge does in fact prevail, it is reasonable to suppose that new meaningful material becomes incorporated into cognitive structure in so far as it is subsumable under relevant existing concepts. It follows, therefore, that the availability in cognitive structure of appropriate and stable subsumers should enhance the incorporability of such material. If it is also true that "meaningful forgetting" reflects a process of memorial reduction, in which the identity of new learning material is assimilated by the more inclusive meaning of its subsumers, the same availability should also enhance retention by decelerating the rate of obliterative subsumption. In the present study, appropriate and relevant subsuming concepts (organisers) are deliberately introduced prior to the learning of unfamiliar academic material, in order to ascertain whether learning and retention are enhanced thereby in accordance with the theoretical premises advanced above.

The article

The experiment that Ausubel carried out was designed to determine if and how well learners would learn from a 2500-word article about something the learners knew little or nothing about. The article dealt with the metallurgical properties of carbon steel and the participants were students of educational psychology. Before reading the article, the participants were presented with an introductory passage (500 words) which was either an advance organiser (i.e. the experimental intervention condition) or historically relevant background information (i.e. the control condition). The former contained background information at a higher level of abstraction, generality, and inclusiveness; information that could be used as an *ideational framework* for organising the more detailed ideas, facts, and relationships in the to-be-learnt text. The latter contained background information on the evolution of iron and steel processing methods; interesting but not relevant for learning what was in the article. The results show clearly that the group that received an advance organiser scored significantly better on a 36-item examination – taken three days after reading – covering facts, principles, and application of what they had read. Ausubel concluded that the advance organiser (1) facilitated the uptake and retention of meaningful verbal material by drawing upon and mobilising any relevant subsuming (higher-order) concepts already in memory so as to incorporate the new material and (2) provided optimal anchorage for the new material promoting both initial incorporation and later resistance to *obliterative subsumption* (where meaningfully learnt information can't be recalled in the precise form in which it was learnt due to its subsumption/incorporation into a larger concept). He concluded:

> Even though this principle seems rather self-evident it is rarely followed in actual teaching procedures or in the organization of most textbooks ... in most instances, students are required to learn the details of new and unfamiliar disciplines before they have acquired an adequate body of relevant subsumers at an appropriate level of inclusiveness.

What does all this mean? To understand this we must look at Ausubel's ground-breaking book *The psychology of meaningful verbal learning* (1963). The reason why we consider the book ground-breaking is that it broke with the prevalent behaviourist thinking about learning that assumed that learners are essentially passive, and that learning is a response to environmental stimuli. As such, behaviourist learning theory didn't take internal mental states or consciousness into account. In the book, Ausubel speaks of "reception learning", but this term, today, might be

IDEATIONAL FRAMEWORK
Conceptual scaffold that incorporates more detailed knowledge

OBLITERATIVE SUBSUMPTION
When a more specific idea becomes indistinguishable from its subsumer until it's forgotten

BEHAVIOURISM
Theory that all behaviours are acquired through conditioning; as a response to a stimulus

a bit misleading. A better term, and one that characterises his theory, is *subsumptive* learning. In plain English, subsumption theory holds that learning is a process in which new, to-be-learnt information is related by learners to what is already present in their existing cognitive structures (i.e. the schemata in their long-term memory). This is similar to another pioneer in cognition, Jean Piaget (1952; see also Wadsworth, 1996), who spoke of learning as a process of assimilation and accommodation. Ausubel's major hypothesis was that learning and retention are facilitated when the learner has acquired a meaningful cognitive framework that allows new information to be organised, assimilated, and subsumed in what is already known.

SUBSUMPTION THEORY
Another name for Ausubel's theory of advance organisers

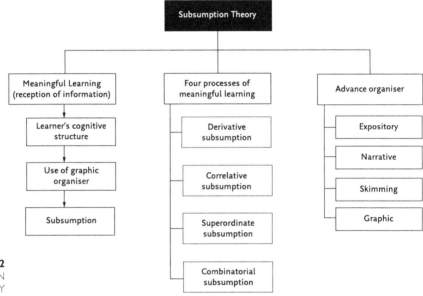

FIGURE 6.2
SUBSUMPTION THEORY

TYPES OF SUBSUMPTION:
- Derivative: Linking new things to old
- Correlative: Adding details
- Superordinate: Introducing a higher-level concept
- Combinatorial: Linking higher-level concepts

IF WE LOOK AT FIGURE 6.2 we can see that there are actually four types of subsumption, namely derivative, correlative, superordinate, and combinatorial subsumption. Each of these processes plays a role in the working of an advance organiser. *Derivative subsumption* is when you add new things to existing cognitive structures, linking them to concepts already known. For example, if you already have the concept of "mammal" you can add the characteristics of "bat", "whale", and "cow" to it without making any change in the concept "mammal". *Correlative subsumption* is when you add new details to what

(Continued)

(Continued)

you already know, usually a higher-order concept. This occurs, for example, when you add to the concept of "mammal" that they can fly (bat) or swim (whale). *Superordinate subsumption* introduces a new higher-level concept into which already existing categories can be integrated. This occurs, for example, when the concept of "vertebrate" is added to include "mammals", "reptiles", and "birds". Finally, *combinatorial subsumption* is when ideas are linked (combined) between higher-level concepts such as when one knows form physics, for example, the fact that stationary air-spaces insulate helps to better understand the function of hair or feathers in keeping certain animals warm.

> Even though this principle [subsumption] seems rather self-evident it is rarely followed in actual teaching procedures or in the organization of most textbooks ... in most instances, students are required to learn the details of new and unfamiliar disciplines before they have acquired an adequate body of relevant subsumers at an appropriate level of inclusiveness.

TYPES OF
ORGANISERS:
• Expository:
  Describes
• Narrative:
  Tells a story
• Skimming:
  Presents an
  overview
• Graphic: Visual
  representation

Also, there are four types of advance organisers that can be used prior to instruction, namely expository, narrative, skimming, and graphic organisers. An *expository organiser* provides a description of new knowledge that learners will need to understand what follows and is often used when the new learning material is relatively unknown to the learner. It usually relates the new information to what is already known. A *narrative organiser* presents new information in a story format to the learners. It uses stories to activate background knowledge so that learners can make connections to what they know, often creating a personal connection to inspire learning. For example, at the beginning of a lesson you might tell a story that relates to important concepts in the lesson. A *skimming organiser* is an organiser that gives a helicopter overview of the new learning material. It involves focusing on and noting what stands out in the new material such as headings, subheadings, and highlighted information. This acquaints them with the material before they read it more carefully. *Graphic organisers* include different types of visuals such as concept maps, pictographs, Venn diagrams, and so forth. These organisers capitalise on both linguistic and non-linguistic information storage, as discussed in Chapter 5 on the dual coding theory.

TROUBLE IN ADVANCE ORGANISER PARADISE?

BARNES AND CLAWSON published an article in the *Review of Educational Research* (RER; 1975) with the title "Do advance organizers facilitate learning?" They concluded that "[T]he efficacy of advance organizers has not been established" (p. 651) for a number of reasons. Their major criticism was that "Ausubel has not operationally defined the advance organizer" and that he "made logical but not operational distinctions between organizers and overviews" (p. 653). This article was followed up by Lawton and Wanska in the RER (1977) in which they criticised Barnes and Clawson. In that article, they support the basic premises of Ausubel, but conclude that more study is needed on how to construct (again the operationalisation question) and use organisers. These two reviews were met with a scathing rebuke by Ausubel himself (1978) again in the RER of all criticism, and primarily with respect to his lack of operationalisation.

> If these critics had read my books on meaningful verbal learning and on educational psychology (1963, 1968) [as well] as my research articles, they would have found precise operational criteria for an advance organizer and a discussion of how to construct one
>
> (p. 251).

Finally, Richard Mayer wrote in the RER (1979) that there is clear evidence for "an assimilation encoding theory" and that there is "consistent evidence that advance organizers can influence the outcome of learning if used in appropriate situations and measured properly" (p. 371).

Whatever the school of thought is with respect to advance organisers, no one refutes that the availability and presentation of prior knowledge, especially incorporating references to super- and subordinate concepts and their critical relationships, facilitate meaningful learning.

Conclusions/implications of the work for educational practice

New knowledge must be incorporated into existing structures

Research on prior knowledge and its effects on learning give us directions for how best to organise education. In order to create rich and coherent knowledge schemes, students must actively insert new information into existing knowledge structures. Making students' prior knowledge explicit is a first step in learning and can help you to recognise weaker learners, determine the level of your lesson, or group students into different level groups. Barak Rosenshine (2010, 2012) suggests, for example, that the teacher should begin each lesson with a short recapitulation – 3 to 5 minutes – of what was previously learnt and relevant to what is to come. This can be in expository form, but can also take the form of a quiz or a discussion.

Rosenshine's principles of instruction

In order to get a grip on this prior knowledge, or lack of it, you can have students take a small test or quiz before introducing new material. This can be a multiple-choice test, matching, an open question test or even a test where the students have to indicate which things they recognise and what they entail. Based upon this you can present an advance organiser and/or tailor the instruction to student knowledge. Give students feedback on the results of the prior knowledge test, so that they get insight into what they know and how the new material fits. Taking such a prior knowledge test also helps students see that learning new material requires effort, since they must link the new knowledge to their own personal knowledge structures.

How to use the work in your teaching

RETRIEVAL PRACTICE
A learning strategy which brings already learnt things to mind to boost learning

Retrieval of prior knowledge or framing new knowledge is something that most teachers are familiar with. This is logical in some subject areas because procedures, for example, become progressively more complex. For example, calculating with dozens is difficult if learners have not yet mastered arithmetic with units as well as the concept of a dozen as a unit of 12. You will therefore need to know whether students have already mastered previous steps and/or concepts and help them where this isn't the case.

But also in more thematic subjects such as language, history, or geography, it's important to determine the learners' prior knowledge and/or frame new knowledge. In these subject areas, learners also acquire a lot of their knowledge outside of the school. Complicating this is that this also often differs with the socioeconomic status (SES) of the children. Children from families with a higher SES often have more "world knowledge" and a better vocabulary than children from families with a lower SES (Hart & Risley, 1995). If a child already knows a lot about the subject you want to deal with, you can enrich the content through expository organisers. If, however, there's little prior knowledge, it's a good idea to first pay attention to presenting necessary anchor concepts and their mutual relationships (e.g. through correlative subsumption) and, in that way, offer ideational scaffolding where they can frame the new knowledge.

EXAMPLE
Comparative
organiser

A well-known example of this can be found in research by Ausubel with Donald Fitzgerald (1961). Students who were supposed to learn about Buddhism were first given a short text on Christianity comparing these two religions. This comparative organizer in Ausubel and Fitzgerald's own words "pointed out explicitly the principal similarities and differences between Buddhist and Christian doctrines. This comparison was presented at a much higher level of abstraction, generality, and inclusiveness than the Buddhism passage itself, and was deliberately designed to increase discriminability between the two sets of concepts" (p. 268). The frame of Christianity led to better learning and retention of the text than a historical text prior to reading, and also than an expository organiser that "explained principal Buddhist doctrines at a high level of abstraction, generality, and inclusiveness, without making any reference whatsoever to Christianity".

(p. 268)

Takeaways

- Learning involves building on what you already know, so pay attention to the prior knowledge of your pupils.
- The role of the teacher is to bridge the gap between what's already known and what's about to be learnt.
- Activate prior knowledge regularly, for example, by starting the lesson with a short quiz or test.
- If students know very little about a subject, "create" prior knowledge by providing them with a framework (ideational scaffolding) in which they can place new knowledge.
- Present learners first with the most general concepts (more general, abstract, inclusive) and then become more specific (see also Chapter 16 on Reigeluth's elaboration theory).
- Instructional materials should include both new and previously acquired information whereby comparisons between old and new concepts are essential.

References

AUSUBEL, D. P. (1960). THE USE OF ADVANCE ORGANIZERS IN THE LEARNING AND RETENTION OF MEANINGFUL VERBAL MATERIAL. *JOURNAL OF EDUCATIONAL PSYCHOLOGY, 51*, 267–272. AVAILABLE FROM: WWW.COLORADO.EDU/FTEP/NODE/504/ATTACHMENT.

AUSUBEL, D. P. (1963). *THE PSYCHOLOGY OF MEANINGFUL VERBAL LEARNING.* OXFORD: GRUNE & STRATTON.

AUSUBEL, D. P. (1978). IN DEFENSE OF ADVANCE ORGANIZERS: A REPLY TO THE CRITICS. *REVIEW OF EDUCATIONAL RESEARCH, 48*, 251–257.

AUSUBEL, D. P., & FITZGERALD, D. (1961). THE ROLE OF DISCRIMINABILITY IN MEANINGFUL VERBAL LEARNING AND RETENTION. *JOURNAL OF EDUCATIONAL PSYCHOLOGY, 55*, 266–274.

BARNES, B. R., & CLAWSON, E. U. (1975). DO ADVANCE ORGANIZERS FACILITATE LEARNING? RECOMMENDATIONS FOR FURTHER RESEARCH BASED ON AN ANALYSIS OF 32 STUDIES. *REVIEW OF EDUCATIONAL RESEARCH, 45*, 637–659. READ ONLINE HERE: WWW.JSTOR.ORG/STABLE/1170068?SEQ=1#PAGE_SCAN_TAB_CONTENTS.

HART, B., & RISLEY, T. R. (1995). *MEANINGFUL DIFFERENCES IN THE EVERYDAY EXPERIENCE OF YOUNG AMERICAN CHILDREN.* BALTIMORE, MD: PAUL H. BROOKES PUBLISHING COMPANY.

KIRSCHNER, P. A. (2009). EPISTEMOLOGY OR PEDAGOGY, THAT IS THE QUESTION. IN S. TOBIAS AND T. M. DUFFY (EDS.). *CONSTRUCTIVIST INSTRUCTION: SUCCESS OR FAILURE?* (PP. 144–157). NEW YORK, NY: ROUTLEDGE.

LAWTON, J. T., & WANSKA, S. K. (1977). ADVANCE ORGANIZERS AS A TEACHING STRATEGY: A REPLY TO BARNES & CLAWSON. *REVIEW OF EDUCATIONAL RESEARCH, 47*, 233–244.

MAYER, R. E. (1979). CAN ADVANCE ORGANIZERS INFLUENCE MEANINGFUL LEARNING? *REVIEW OF EDUCATIONAL RESEARCH, 49*, 371–383.

PIAGET, J. (1952). *THE ORIGINS OF INTELLIGENCE IN CHILDREN.* NEW YORK, NY: INTERNATIONAL UNIVERSITY PRESS. AVAILABLE FROM WWW.PITT.EDU/~STRAUSS/ORIGINS_R.PDF.

ROSENSHINE, B. (2010). *PRINCIPLES OF INSTRUCTION.* GENEVA, SWITZERLAND: INTERNATIONAL BUREAU OF EDUCATION. AVAILABLE FROM WWW.IBE.UNESCO.ORG/FILEADMIN/USER_UPLOAD/PUBLICATIONS/EDUCATIONAL_PRACTICE S/EDPRACTICES_21.PDF

ROSENSHINE, B. (2012, SPRING). PRINCIPLES OF INSTRUCTION: RESEARCH BASED PRINCIPLES THAT ALL TEACHERS SHOULD KNOW. *AMERICAN EDUCATOR, 12–19, 39.* AVAILABLE FROM WWW.AFT.ORG/PDFS/AMERICANEDUCATOR/SPRING2012/ROSENSHINE.PDF.

WADSWORTH, B. J. (199619961). *PIAGET'S THEORY OF COGNITIVE AND AFFECTIVE DEVELOPMENT: FOUNDATIONS OF CONSTRUCTIVISM.* WHITE PLAINS, NY: LONGMAN PUBLISHING.

Suggested readings and links

HAILIKARI, T., KATAJAVUORI, N., & LINDBLOM-YLANNE, S. (2008). THE RELEVANCE OF PRIOR KNOWLEDGE IN LEARNING AND INSTRUCTIONAL DESIGN. *AMERICAN JOURNAL OF PHARMACEUTICAL EDUCATION, 72(5),* **ARTICLE 113.**

AVAILABLE FROM HTTPS://WWW.NCBI.NLM.NIH.GOV/PMC/ARTICLES/PMC2630138/PDF/AJPE113.PDF.

HEWSON, M. G., & HEWSON, P. W. (1983). EFFECT OF INSTRUCTION USING STUDENTS' PRIOR KNOWLEDGE AND CONCEPTUAL CHANGE STRATEGIES ON SCIENCE LEARNING. *JOURNAL OF RESEARCH IN SCIENCE TEACHING, 20,* **731–743.**

AVAILABLE FROM HTTPS://ONLINELIBRARY.WILEY.COM/DOI/PDF/10.1002/TEA.3660200804.

THIS VIDEO (MCREL – CLASSROOM INSTRUCTION THAT WORKS) HIGHLIGHTS THREE DIFFERENT TYPES OF ADVANCE ORGANISERS.

AVAILABLE FROM HTTPS://YOUTU.BE/ARFKDV8AUIK.

DIFFERENT TYPES OF GRAPHIC ORGANISERS AND THEIR PURPOSES.

AVAILABLE FROM HTTPS://YOUTU.BE/_LTLQVKV3YI.

THIS PRESENTATION BY SUSIE GRONSETH FOCUSES ON MEANINGFUL RECEPTION LEARNING AND SCHEMA THEORIES TO UNDERSTAND HOW LEARNERS ACQUIRE, REMEMBER, AND APPLY LEARNT INFORMATION. A TRANSCRIPT IS

AVAILABLE FROM HTTPS://GOO.GL/VQBIMW.

 COLLEGE STAR (SUPPORTING TRANSITION ACCESS AND RETENTION) PROVIDES RESOURCES TO HELP ALL DIFFERENT TYPES OF STUDENTS LEARN BETTER.

AVAILABLE FROM WWW.COLLEGESTAR.ORG/MODULES/ADVANCE-ORGANIZERS.

 COMMON ADVANCE ORGANIZERS AND WHY THEY WORK.

AVAILABLE FROM WWW.UNDERSTOOD.ORG/EN/SCHOOL-LEARNING/PARTNERING-WITH-CHILDS-SCHOOL/INSTRUCTIONAL-STRATEGIES/COMMON-ADVANCE-ORGANIZERS-AND-WHY-THEY-WORK.

7

WHY INDEPENDENT LEARNING IS NOT A GOOD WAY TO BECOME AN INDEPENDENT LEARNER

SELF REGULATION

7 WHY INDEPENDENT LEARNING IS NOT A GOOD WAY TO BECOME AN INDEPENDENT LEARNER

PAPER "A social cognitive view of self-regulated academic learning"[1]

QUOTE *"Student's self-efficacy perceptions depend in part on each of four other types of personal influence, students' knowledge, metacognitive processes, goals, and affect".*

Why you should read this article

When we think of a "self-regulated person", we imagine a highly confident individual planning their day meticulously and executing every task like a machine. This person's motivational energy is often imagined as an *internal* force: they are "driven" in some way by some interior engine that propels them towards success. Motivational posters and inspirational quotes put forward the idea that if you "look inside and just believe in yourself" then anything is possible, but what about the importance of *external* factors on motivation, achievement, and the ability to self-regulate? We all want students to be self-regulated people who are able to regulate their own learning. But what can teachers actually do about it?

SELF-REGULATION
Ability to manage
one's emotions and
behaviour

In this article, Zimmerman's social cognitive approach to self-regulation is significant because he moves the debate away from such theoretical approaches that view self-regulation as an *internal* state that is personally discovered, to one that is strongly influenced by *external* factors such as environmental conditions, teacher instruction and modelling and peer/parental influence.

1   **ZIMMERMAN, B. J.** (1989). A SOCIAL COGNITIVE VIEW OF SELF-REGULATED ACADEMIC LEARNING. *JOURNAL OF EDUCATIONAL PSYCHOLOGY, 81*, 329–339.

What does that mean specifically? Well, Zimmerman offers a model of self-regulation that has a symbiotic relationship between three key factors: personal, behavioural, and environmental. These three elements form what he calls a "triadic reciprocality" in which they work together to affect students' self-regulatory states. He builds upon the work of Alfred Bandura (1986, p. 454) who noted that how students perform is a product of exterior forces just as much as interior ones: "Behavior is, therefore, a product of both self-generated and external sources of influence".

SELF-REGULATED
LEARNING
Triadic reciprocality

SELF-REGULATED LEARNING STRATEGIES are actions and processes directed at acquiring information or skill that involve agency, purpose, and instrumentality perceptions by learners. They include such methods as organizing and transforming information, self-consequating, seeking information, and rehearsing or using memory aids".

Why is this important? Well one of the most common aims in education is to create so called independent learners, however allowing students to work independently is paradoxically probably a bad way to achieve this end. The widely held constructivist view that students need minimal guidance and that instructors should be seen and not heard (first vocally aired by Jerome Bruner in 1961) is probably not the most effective way of affecting student self-regulation (at least not in the long run). Rather, providing clear instruction and explicit modelling of solutions and strategies and changing environmental conditions can have a dramatic impact on student achievement (Kirschner, Sweller, & Clark, 2006; Rosenshine, 2012).

A key facet of self-regulation is what Bandura (1982) called "self-efficacy" which is related to two key elements; the knowledge and use of specific learning strategies and self-monitoring of performance.

SELF-EFFICACY

SELF-EFFICACY is an individual's belief in his or her innate ability to achieve goals. In Bandura's words it's a personal judgement of "how well one can execute courses of action required to deal with prospective situations". In other words, it's whether you think that you can do what is asked of you.

It is important to note that self-efficacy is not a general skill but rather is something very much domain specific. For example, a student may have high self-efficacy in history but low self-efficacy in mathematics. It may be the case that their subject knowledge of history means they can break down bigger tasks into smaller, more achievable ones and will have good internal models of what success looks like in that subject, whereas their lack of mathematical knowledge means they don't even know where to start.

A big question facing all educators is how exactly do you create more self-regulated learners? Zimmerman's paper is significant because he emphasises the importance of wider socialising agents on this process such as teachers, parents and peers. He also offers a useful table of 14 self-regulated learning strategies that were highly correlated with student academic success such as goal-setting, environmental structuring and seeking social assistance.

Original abstract of the article

Researchers interested in academic self-regulated learning have begun to study processes that students use to initiate and direct their efforts to acquire knowledge and skill. The social cognitive conception of self-regulated learning presented here involves a triadic analysis of component processes and an assumption of reciprocal causality among personal, behavioural, and environmental triadic influences. This theoretical account also posits a central role for the construct of academic self-efficacy beliefs and three self-regulatory processes: self-observation, self-judgement, and self-reactions. Research support for this social cognitive formulation is discussed, as is its usefulness for improving student learning and academic achievement.

The article

Zimmerman defines self-regulated learning as "the degree to which students are metacognitively, motivationally, and behaviorally active participants in their own learning processes" (p. 337). A vital element here is that students have knowledge of specific knowledge, skills, and strategies to achieve specific outcomes whereby self-efficacy – the perceptions one has about one's ability to organise and execute skills to achieve those outcomes – plays an important role.

METACOGNITION
Awareness and understanding of one's own thought processes

"METACOGNITION" means cognition about cognition, or to put it more simply; thinking about thinking. If a student realises that they are not learning in an optimum way and change their practice by adopting more productive strategies, then they are thinking metacognitively.

Now there is a lot of "self" going here and a lot of this might sound like everything is going on solely within the head of the student, but Zimmerman offers the following model (see Figure 7.1) based on the work of Bandura (1986) as a way of showing that many exterior forces also affect the learner:

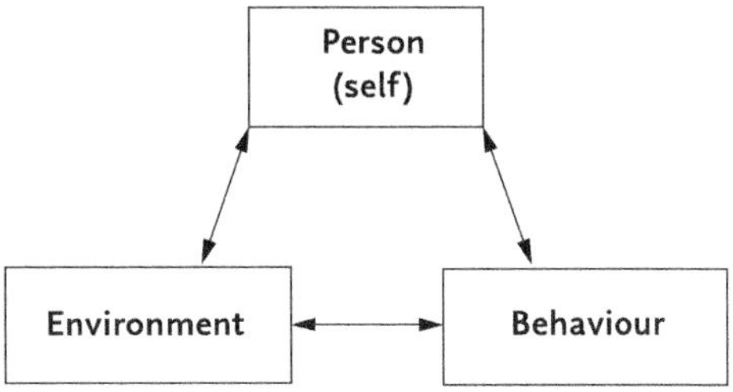

FIGURE 7.1
A TRIADIC ANALYSIS OF SELF-REGULATED FUNCTIONING

Students with high self-efficacy have two specific characteristics. First, they have more effective learning strategies (Kurtz & Borkowski, 1984) and second, they have better self-monitoring of their learning outcomes (Diener & Dweck, 1978; Kuhl, 1985; Pearl, Bryan, & Herzog, 1983) than students displaying low self-efficacy. In other words, student self-efficacy is directly related to what students *know* they can do in a particular area to modify their behaviour. However, when an instructor models how to solve problems explicitly, this can also greatly affect student self-efficacy. Schunk (1981) found that an adult modelling mathematics problem solving to fourth graders resulted in significantly higher self-efficacy (and better division accuracy) than comparable fourth graders in a control group where here was no modelling.

An important point to make is that self-regulated learning is not an absolute state but is highly variable in time and dependent on context (Thoresen & Mahoney, 1974) and so the idea that you can teach generic independent learning skills that will transfer to a wide range of situations is highly problematic. A key element in whether a student is self-regulated or not will be the level of subject knowledge they will have in that particular domain. For example, a student with an extensive knowledge of "Macbeth" and the broader social and historical context around the play will easily be able to identify a set of revision tasks that will consolidate their knowledge and understanding. Furthermore, they will be able to quickly identify what they *don't* know and try to relate any new knowledge to what they already know. As Zimmerman writes, "students' general knowledge of mathematics will contribute to their ability to divide the week's assignment into manageable daily tasks" (p. 332).

Skills are domain specific

Furthermore, self-regulation has a lot to do with effective planning and a lot of the metacognitive decision making that students make will depend on their goals. One way of achieving this is to set intermediate goals with very specific actions in time and difficulty level (Bandura, 1982). Without any specificity, long-term goals rarely work as they learner has nothing to "grip onto" as it were. This is why the often given advice of "do your best" has little effect on motivation or learning (Locke, Shaw, Saari, & Latham, 1981) which again underlines the fact that many attempts to motivate students are of little use.

Goal-setting should be specific in time, action, and difficulty

So what are the environmental factors that can influence student self-regulation? Zimmerman gives special mention to five factors: modelling, verbal persuasion, direct assistance from teachers, and finally the structure of the learning context. Modelling can be particularly effective with low achieving learners as Bandura (1986) points out: "effective coping strategies can boost the self-efficacy of individuals who have undergone many experiences confirming their inefficacy" (p. 400). If learners identify with the coping strategy, that is to say if they feel it *looks like them trying to solve the problem*, then they are far more likely to benefit. For example, showing students an errorless mastery model is far less effective than showing them a coping model requiring high concentration, persistence, and increased effort (Schunk, Hanson, & Cox, 1987). Additionally, students experiencing verbal persuasion during a task have been shown to have increased self-efficacy (Zimmerman & Rocha, 1984).

MODELLING Demonstrating and explaining specific strategies

Conclusions/implications of the work for educational practice

So instead of thinking about self-regulation as a purely internal process, we can think about the behavioural and social experiences that affect student self-regulation. Why is this important and what exactly are the strategies students can use? Well first, it means that teachers can actually help students to better self-regulate through modelling, verbal persuasion, and explicitly teaching specific strategies and second, this paper has a very useful table (see Table 7.1) of 14 self-reported strategies that high school students use. Interestingly, these were very similar to strategies that had been studied in laboratory research (Zimmerman & Martinez-Pons, 1988); 13 out of 14 of these strategies discriminated between student achievement on higher and lower tracks and were also highly correlated with teacher predictions of student self-regulation during class and subsequent test scores.

Categories/ Strategies	Definitions: Statements indicating …
1 Self-evaluating	student-initiated evaluations of the quality or progress of their work; e.g. "I check over my work to make sure I did it right".
2 Organising and transforming	student-initiated overt or covert rearrangement of instructional materials to improve learning; e.g. "I make an outline before I write my paper".
3 Goal-setting and planning	students' setting of educational goals or subgoals and planning for sequencing, timing, and completing activities related to those goals; e.g. "First, I start studying two weeks before exams, and I pace myself".
4 Seeking information	student-initiated efforts to secure further task information from non-social sources when undertaking an assignment; e.g. "Before beginning to write the paper, I go to the library to get as much information as possible concerning the topic".
5 Keeping records and monitoring	student-initiated efforts to record events or results; e.g. "I took notes of the class discussions"; "I kept a list of the words I got wrong".
6 Environmental structuring	student-initiated efforts to select or arrange the physical setting to make learning easier; e.g. "I isolate myself from anything that distracts me"; "I turned off the radio so I can concentrate on what I am doing".
7 Self-consequating	student arrangement or imagination of rewards or punishment for success or failure; e.g. "If I do well on a test, I treat myself to a movie".
8 Rehearsing and memorising	student-initiated efforts to memorise material by overt or covert practice; e.g. "In preparing for a math test, I keep writing the formula down until I remember it".
9 11 Seeking social assistance	student-initiated efforts to solicit help from peers (9), teachers (10), and adults (11); e.g. "If I have problems with math assignments, I ask a friend to help".
12 14 Reviewing records	student-initiated efforts to reread notes (12), tests (13), or textbooks (14) to prepare for class or further testing; e.g. "When preparing for a test, I review my notes".
15 Other	learning behaviour that is initiated by other persons such as teachers or parents, and all unclear verbal responses; e.g. "I just do what the teacher says".

TABLE 7.1
SELF-REGULATED LEARNING STRATEGIES (ADAPTED FROM EFFENEY, CARROLL, & BARR, 2013).

How to use the work in your teaching

One way to approach student self-regulation is to "reverse-engineer" what successful self-regulation looks like. Explicitly teaching these above strategies to students and asking them to think about them on three levels: their own beliefs, their actual behaviour, and their environment will help them to feel they have more control over their own progress.

First, ask students to read through Zimmerman's 14 self-regulated learning strategies and ask them to rate themselves on a scale of 1 to 10 on how effectively they use each strategy in their own practice. In doing this, you are encouraging students to think metacognitively about their own learning. Second, ask them to apply these strategies to a specific domain of a particular subject in which they could improve.

Learners are usually novices and should be taught accordingly (see Chapter 1)

Finally, self-regulation is not a state which learners achieve just by working on their own. When students are novices (and almost all students are novices) it can be counterproductive to think students can regulate their own learning. By modelling successful solutions to problems and giving clear guidance and persuasion at the outset, teachers can have a big impact on student self-efficacy. By presenting material in such a way that students feel "OK, I can do this" you are helping them on the way to becoming a self-regulated learner.

Takeaways

- Self-regulated learning is not just an internal process but rather a combination of personal, behavioural, and environmental factors.
- Independent learning is probably a bad way for a novice to become an independent learner.
- Telling learners to "do your best" is not effective. Long-term goals should be broken down into intermediate goals and most importantly, they should be specific.
- Teacher modelling and verbal persuasion can have a big impact on student self-efficacy.
- Students who know more in a particular domain are better able to think metacognitively about their learning in that domain.
- Make sure that learners have the knowledge and skills necessary for self-regulating their learning.

References

BANDURA, A. (1982). SELF-EFFICACY MECHANISM IN HUMAN AGENCY. *AMERICAN PSYCHOLOGIST, 37*, 122–147.

BANDURA, A. (1986). *SOCIAL FOUNDATIONS OF THOUGHT AND ACTION: A SOCIAL COGNITIVE THEORY.* ENGLEWOOD CLIFFS, NJ: PRENTICE-HALL.

BRUNER, J. S. (1961). THE ART OF DISCOVERY. *HARVARD EDUCATIONAL REVIEW, 31*, 21–32.

DIENER, C. L., & DWECK, C. S. (1978). AN ANALYSIS OF LEARNED HELPLESSNESS: CONTINUOUS CHANGES IN PERFORMANCE STRATEGY AND ACHIEVEMENT COGNITIONS FOLLOWING FAILURE. *JOURNAL OF PERSONALITY AND SOCIAL PSYCHOLOGY, 36*, 451–462.

EFFENEY, G., CARROLL, A., & BAHR, N. (2013). SELF-REGULATED LEARNING: KEY STRATEGIES AND THEIR SOURCES IN A SAMPLE OF ADOLESCENT MALES1. *AUSTRALIAN JOURNAL OF EDUCATIONAL AND DEVELOPMENTAL PSYCHOLOGY, 13*, 58E74.

KIRSCHNER, P. A., SWELLER, J., & CLARK, R. E. (2006). WHY MINIMAL GUIDANCE DURING INSTRUCTION DOES NOT WORK: AN ANALYSIS OF THE FAILURE OF CONSTRUCTIVIST, DISCOVERY, PROBLEM-BASED, EXPERIENTIAL, AND INQUIRY-BASED TEACHING. *EDUCATIONAL PSYCHOLOGIST, 46*(2), 75–86. 10.1207/S15326985EP4102_1 (OPEN ACCESS).

KUHL, J. (1985). VOLITIONAL MEDIATORS OF COGNITIVE-BEHAVIOR CONSISTENCY: SELF-REGULATORY PROCESSES AND ACTION VERSUS STATE ORIENTATION. IN J. KUHLV AND J. BEXKMAN (EDS.), *ACTION CONTROL* (PP. 101–128). NEW YORK, NY: SPRINGER.

KURTZ, B. E., & BORKOWSKI, J. G. (1984). CHILDREN'S METACOGNITION: EXPLORING RELATIONS AMONG KNOWLEDGE, PROCESS, AND MOTIVATIONAL VARIABLES. *JOURNAL OF EXPERIMENTAL CHILD PSYCHOLOGY, 37,* 335–354.

LOCKE, E. A., SHAW, K. N., SAARI, L. M., & LATHAM, G. P. (1981). GOAL SETTING AND TASK PERFORMANCE: 1969–1980. *PSYCHOLOGICAL BULLETIN, 90,* 125–152.

PEARL, R., BRYAN, T., & HERZOG, A. (1983). LEARNING DISABLED CHILDREN'S STRATEGY ANALYSES UNDER HIGH AND LOW SUCCESS CONDITIONS. *LEARNING DISABILITY QUARTERLY, 6,* 67–74.

ROSENSHINE, B. (2012). PRINCIPLES OF INSTRUCTION: RESEARCH-BASED STRATEGIES THAT ALL TEACHERS SHOULD KNOW. *AMERICAN EDUCATOR, 36*(1), 12–19. AVAILABLE FROM WWW.AFT.ORG/SITES/DEFAULT/FILES/PERIODICALS/ROSENSHINE.PDF.

SCHUNK, D. H. (1981). MODELING AND ATTRIBUTION EFFECTS ON CHILDREN'S DEVELOPMENT: A SELF-EFFICACY ANALYSIS. *JOURNAL OF EDUCATIONAL PSYCHOLOGY. 75,* 93–105.

SCHUNK, D. H., HANSON, A. R., & COX, P. D. (1987). STRATEGY SELF-VERBALIZATION DURING REMEDIAL LISTENING COMPREHENSION INSTRUCTION. *JOURNAL OF EDUCATIONAL PSYCHOLOGY, 53,* 54–61.

THORESEN, C. E., & MAHONEY, M. J. (1974). *BEHAVIORAL SELF-CONTROL.* NEW YORK, NY: HOLT, RINEHART & WINSTON.

ZIMMERMAN, B. J. (1989). A SOCIAL COGNITIVE VIEW OF SELF-REGULATED ACADEMIC LEARNING. *JOURNAL OF EDUCATIONAL PSYCHOLOGY, 81,* 329–339. AVAILABLE FROM HTTPS://PDFS.SEMANTICSCHOLAR.ORG/E1FF/53E710437E009F06BC264B093A2BA9523879.PDF.

ZIMMERMAN, B. J., & MARTINEZ-PONS, M. (1988). CONSTRUCT VALIDATION OF A STRATEGY MODEL OF STUDENT SELF-REGULATED LEARNING. *JOURNAL OF EDUCATIONAL PSYCHOLOGY, 80,* 284–290.

ZIMMERMAN, B. J., & ROCHA, J. (1984). INFLUENCE OF A MODEL'S VERBAL DESCRIPTION OF TOY INTERACTIONS ON KINDERGARTEN CHILDREN'S ASSOCIATIVE LEARNING. *JOURNAL OF APPLIED DEVELOPMENTAL PSYCHOLOGY, 5,* 281–291.

Suggested readings and links

BARRY ZIMMERMAN: LEARNING AND THE ADOLESCENT MIND. CONCISE OVERVIEW OF ZIMMERMAN'S WORK.

AVAILABLE FROM HTTP://LEARNINGANDTHEADOLESCENTMIND.ORG/PEOPLE_04.HTML.

BARRY J. ZIMMERMAN, AN EDUCATOR WITH PASSION FOR DEVELOPING SELF-REGULATION OF LEARNING THROUGH SOCIAL LEARNING. PAPER PRESENTED AT AERA.

AVAILABLE FROM HTTPS://FILES.ERIC.ED.GOV/FULLTEXT/ED518491.PDF.

BANDURA, A. (1986). *SOCIAL FOUNDATIONS OF THOUGHT AND ACTION: A SOCIAL COGNITIVE THEORY.* ENGLEWOOD CLIFFS, NJ: PRENTICE HALL.

BROWN, A. L. (1978). KNOWING WHEN, WHERE, AND HOW TO REMEMBER: A PROBLEM OF METACOGNITION. IN R. GLASER (ED.), *ADVANCES IN INSTRUCTIONAL PSYCHOLOGY* (VOL. 7, PP. 55–111). NEW YORK, NY: ACADEMIC PRESS.

BUTLER, D. L., & WINNE, P. H. (1995). FEEDBACK AND SELF-REGULATED LEARNING: A THEORETICAL SYNTHESIS. *REVIEW OF EDUCATIONAL RESEARCH, 65*(3), 245–281.

FLAVELL, J. H. (1979) METACOGNITION AND COGNITIVE MONITORING: A NEW AREA OF COGNITIVE-DEVELOPMENTAL INQUIRY. *AMERICAN PSYCHOLOGIST, 34,* 906–911.

8 BELIEFS ABOUT INTELLIGENCE CAN AFFECT INTELLIGENCE

MINDSET

8 BELIEFS ABOUT INTELLIGENCE CAN AFFECT INTELLIGENCE

PAPER   "A social-cognitive approach to motivation and personality"[1]

QUOTE   *"Implicit beliefs about ability predict whether individuals will be oriented toward developing their ability or towards documenting the adequacy of their ability".*

Why you should read this article

When you see someone push a door that says "pull" on it, do you view that person as stupid or rather do you see them as someone of otherwise normal intelligence, merely doing an unintelligent thing in that moment? According to this article, your response to that question might reveal a lot more than you think about your self-concept, self-esteem, and your view of the external world.

Carol Dweck's work on motivation over the last 40 years has been hugely influential in education. It's impossible to meet someone in education today who isn't familiar with the term "growth mindset", however her work is also one of the most misunderstood, with many schools reducing her work to cheesy motivational posters and assemblies and the misguided idea that innate ability doesn't matter but effort does. Before the terms "growth mindset" and "fixed mindset" came along, there were the less catchy terms "entity theorist" and "incremental theorist" and a set of ideas which can be crudely summarised in the following sentence: *The extent to which an individual believes change is possible, largely determines their ability to affect change.*

Although her work yielded promising results in the lab, more recent attempts to replicate her findings in the field have led to dubious results (Sisk et al., 2018), and suggest that attempts to change pupils' intrinsic

GROWTH MINDSET
The belief that intelligence is malleable

FIXED MINDSET
The belief that intelligence is fixed

---

[1]   **DWECK, C. S., & LEGGETT, E. L.** (1988) A SOCIAL-COGNITIVE APPROACH TO MOTIVATION AND PERSONALITY. *PSYCHOLOGICAL REVIEW, 95,* 256–273.

beliefs about the nature of intelligence may not be as malleable as once thought. Despite this, her work in the 1980s is a hugely important contribution to the field of motivation and remains an important consideration for teachers today. If a student believes that they just can't learn the material you're teaching them then why would they bother? There's something liberating about the belief in the basic mutability of the world around us and that we are not prisoners of our DNA. The notion that intelligence is not fixed but rather something that can be refined and improved through effort and embracing challenge is an important starting point for anyone standing in front of a class trying to motivate students to learn.

Abstract of the article

Past work has documented and described major patterns of adaptive and maladaptive behaviour: the mastery-oriented and the helpless patterns. In this article, we present a research-based model that accounts for these patterns in terms of underlying psychological processes. The model specifies how individuals' implicit theories orient them towards particular goals and how these goals set up the different patterns. Indeed, we show how each feature (cognitive, affective, and behavioural) of the adaptive and maladaptive patterns can be seen to follow directly from different goals. We then examine the generality of the model and use it to illuminate phenomena in a wide variety of domains. Finally, we place the model in its broadest context and examine its implications for our understanding of motivational and personality processes.

The article

This article begins by outlining two patterns of behaviour in which individuals display adaptive (mastery-oriented) and maladaptive (helpless) dispositions. The helpless pattern of behaviour is characterised by "an avoidance of challenge and a deterioration of performance in the face of obstacles" (p. 256). In direct contrast to this, the mastery-oriented pattern of behaviour incorporates "the seeking of challenging tasks and the maintenance of effective striving under failure" (p. 259). Carol Dweck and Ellen Leggett then claim that this difference is not accounted for in terms of raw ability (with some of the brightest and most skilled individuals showing the helpless pattern of behaviour) but rather in the way in which both of these types set out to complete a task.

LEARNED
HELPLESSNESS
Not trying after
experiencing
repeated failures

In attempting to explain this phenomenon, they cite research which claims that both of these types of student might be pursuing very different types of *goals* (Dweck & Elliott, 1983). Researchers identified two types of goals: *performance* goals in which pupils are mostly concerned with measurable results such as exam scores and then *learning* goals (these are now referred to as mastery goals) in which pupils are more interested in improving their general competence and mastering the topic. As the authors neatly put it: "in challenging situations, helpless children might be pursuing the performance goal of *proving* their ability, whereas the mastery-oriented children might be pursuing the learning goal of *improving* their ability" (Dweck & Leggett, 1998, p. 259).

In other words, if you want students to become proficient in a specific domain of knowledge then describing the desired outcome in terms of a target grade or exam score might actually be a poor way of achieving mastery in that domain. Why is this? Well the authors claim that it all comes down to implicit theories about the nature of intelligence and whether or not you think it is something that can be changed or is a static entity.

Exam scores (performance) are not the same as learning

To test this, researchers set up tasks where the stated goals at the outset were either mastery-oriented or performance-oriented. When children were given goals that were about the acquisition of skill over evaluation, their assessment of their current ability was irrelevant and they chose a task displaying a mastery-oriented pattern. However when children were given a goal-based evaluation, they chose tasks that they felt were consistent with their *perceived* ability. In short, if students believe that their ability is low and then ask them to do a test that will reveal that perceived ability, they will invariably shut down. Why would you take a test if you think you are going to fail it?

Performance versus mastery

TWO DIFFERENT INFERENCE RULES

INTERESTINGLY, students with a *performance goal* have a perception of effort which is inversely related to ability. Their inverse rule states that if you need to put a lot of effort into something, then it must mean you aren't very good at it. However students with a *learning (mastery) goal* tend to use a positive rule where effort and ability were positively related. They agreed with statements such as "when something comes easy to you, you don't know how good you are at it". (Jagacinski & Nicholls, 1983; Surber, 1984)

The big question at this point then is, why do certain students favour performance goals which focus on measuring their ability whereas other students choose behaviours focused on the increasing of their ability? For the researchers, this is accounted for by individual beliefs

ENTITY THEORY
OF INTELLIGENCE
Fixed mindset

INCREMENTAL
THEORY OF
INTELLIGENCE
Growth mindset

about intelligence. Students with an *entity* theory of intelligence believe that intelligence is fixed and something you cannot control. In contrast, students with an *incremental* theory of intelligence believe that intelligence is something which is malleable and can be improved through effort. In other words, they have what is more commonly known today as a *growth mindset*. The way in which an individual conceives of their own intelligence as being a fixed entity was associated with the *performance orientation* whereas a conception of intelligence as being malleable in nature was associated with a *learning orientation*.

SELF-CONCEPT
Core beliefs about
oneself

SELF-ESTEEM
How happy you are
with yourself

The authors then go on to generalise these claims and suggest that the two theories (entity and incremental) have an important part to play in terms of self-concept and self-esteem. For the student with an entity theory of intelligence (a fixed mindset), the self is conceptualised as a "collection of fixed traits that can be measured and evaluated" whereas for the incremental theorist (a growth mindset), the self is seen as a "system of malleable qualities that is evolving over time through the individual's efforts" (p. 266). As a result of these two different self-concepts, the ways in which self-esteem is generated is different. Broadly speaking, *self-concept* is the beliefs you hold about yourself such as whether you are male or female or whether you are good at golf or not, whereas *self-esteem* is the level of satisfaction you have with these attributes. (If you don't care about golf then you won't care if you aren't very good at it.)

Earlier data collected by the researchers is offered to provide support for this assertion. After assessing their theories of intelligence, children were asked to describe when they felt smart in school, in other words when they felt high self-esteem. As predicted by the researchers, children with an entity (fixed) theory of intelligence reported that they felt smart when their work had no errors or mistakes or when the work was easy. In contrast, the children with an incremental (growth) theory of intelligence reported that they felt smart when they mastered difficult challenges such as when they overcame a task they were previously unable to do or when they were reading a difficult book.

Alfred Binet's growth
mindset

WHAT ABOUT IQ?

BUT ISN'T THE IDEA of a growth mindset at odds with the notion of IQ? Well perhaps not. Dweck and Leggett claim that Alfred Binet, the grand architect of intelligence testing, was "clearly an incremental theorist" who believed that intelligence

(Continued)

(Continued)

and general capacities for learning were improvable through his own training programme:

> It is in this practical sense, the only one accessible to us, that we say that the intelligence of these children has been increased. We have increased what constitutes the intelligence of a pupil: the capacity to learn and to assimilate instruction.
>
> (Binet, 1909/1973, p. 104)

The authors go on to point out the irony that the assessment tool he developed is now widely associated with an entity theory of intelligence and a performance goal paradigm in which intelligence is measured as a largely stable entity. However, these two positions should not be polarised as Dweck & Elliott (1983) point out that one can recognise that there are individual differences in ability but still emphasise the potential for growth within those individuals.

The authors then attempt to generalise the model beyond the self and consider the ways in which entity and incremental theorists view the external world. They suggest that fixed and uncontrollable things tend to be measured and judged whereas things viewed as malleable or controllable tend to be acted upon or developed. The authors posit the idea that individuals with an entity theory of their own intelligence based on test scores or a few mistakes might also judge others as being intrinsically untrustworthy or incompetent based on isolated factors and limited evidence without consideration of contextual factors or the perspective of the individual concerned. An entity theorist with a fixed view of the world might judge a person who makes a mistake as *always* being like that, whereas an individual with an incremental theory might view that person as a fallible individual whose mistake is a necessary stepping-stone to eventual success.

Conclusions/implications of the work for educational practice

It's important to state here that motivational approaches which seek to deny the significance of inborn ability are destined to fail, because they're not true. If you are trying to convince students that innate ability accounts for 0% of success and effort accounts for 100% of

EFFORT
Can have an
exponential effect

success then you are misleading them. Instead of saying to students "talent doesn't matter, only effort matters", what we should be saying to students is "yes, talent and natural ability play a big part in success but effort matters on the margins, and the marginal gains can go on to yield significant gains".

Furthermore, what is crucial to also understand is that these dispositions really only come into play in the face of struggle or failure. Both entity and incremental theorists show the same behaviours when the work is easy, but when effort is required, then these differences in behaviour become apparent and it is here that the authors suggest that students' innate beliefs about intelligence can yield marginal gains.

How to use the work in your teaching

A key claim in this paper, and indeed this field, is that the adoption of an incremental theory of intelligence (growth mindset) is positively correlated with goal choice, and here is where teachers can have a big impact. If the objective or outcome of a lesson or unit of study is heavily performance based, that is to say one which leans heavily on target grades for example, then it is possible that many students might adopt an entity view of intelligence and choose performance goals over learning/mastery goals. Students who are set *performance* goals in the form of target grades will invariably ask the question, is my ability adequate? Whereas students who are set *learning* goals might ask the question, how can I improve my performance and ability? So instead of telling the class that success can be determined by an exam score, the teacher might define success in terms of specific knowledge-based targets such as understanding what certain vocabulary means or being able to perform a particular experiment or understanding a tricky philosophical concept.

As stated earlier, the efforts to replicate growth mindset interventions in the field have often been patchy and so we might pause to consider if *motivating* students is the best way to motivate them? Is showing them "inspirational" videos or teaching them about the plasticity of the brain the best way to achieve a growth mindset or do students feel motivated when they achieve something? As Graham Nuthall (2007) reminds us: "Learning requires motivation, but motivation does not necessarily lead to learning" (p. 35). What if a growth mindset is viewed as more of a philosophy as opposed to an intervention? All teachers should believe at some level that their students' intelligence is malleable and that they can help them improve it, otherwise why bother? It might be the case that recognising that

Motivation through achievement ≠ achievement through motivation

GROWTH MINDSET
Philosophy or intervention?

novices and experts learn in different ways for example (as discussed in Chapter 1, A novice is not a little expert), and that novices in particular need highly scaffolded learning environments (as detailed in Chapter 7, Why independent learning is not a good way to become an independent learner) might be the best way to motivate them. It may be that we have the causal arrow the wrong way round. To put it another way, motivation doesn't always lead to achievement, but achievement often leads to motivation.

Takeaways

- An entity theory of intelligence is one that believes intelligence is largely fixed.
- An incremental theory of intelligence is one that believes that intelligence is changeable.
- A performance goal can lead to students adopting an entity theory (fixed mindset).
- A learning (mastery) goal can lead to students adopting an incremental theory (growth mindset).
- Mastery-oriented children see difficult or unsolved problems as challenges to be mastered through effort and not as failures.
- Innate ability does matter but effort can yield marginal gains.

References

BINET, A. (1973). *LES IDEES MODERNES SUR LES ENFANTS [MODERN IDEAS ON CHILDREN]*, PARIS, FRANCE: FLAMARION. (ORIGINAL WORK PUBLISHED 1909).

DWECK, C. S., & ELLIOTT, E. S. (1983). ACHIEVEMENT MOTIVATION. IN P. H. MUSSEN AND E. M. HETHERINGTON (EDS.), *HANDBOOK OF CHILD PSYCHOLOGY: VOL. IV. SOCIAL AND PERSONALITY DEVELOPMENT* (PP. 643–691). NEW YORK, NY: WILEY.

DWECK, C. S., & LEGGETT, E. L. (1988) A SOCIAL-COGNITIVE APPROACH TO MOTIVATION AND PERSONALITY. *PSYCHOLOGICAL REVIEW, 95*, 256–273.

JAGACINSKI, C., & NICHOLLS, J. (MARCH, 1983). CONCEPTS OF ABILITY. PAPER PRESENTED AT THE ANNUAL MEETING OF THE AMERICAN EDUCATIONAL RESEARCH ASSOCIATION, NEW YORK, NY.

NUTHALL, G. (2007). *THE HIDDEN LIVES OF LEARNERS.* WELLINGTON, NEW ZEALAND: NEW ZEALAND COUNCIL FOR EDUCATIONAL RESEARCH PRESS.

SISK, V. F., BURGOYNE, A. P., SUN, J., BUTLER, J. L., & MACNAMARA, B. N. (2018). TO WHAT EXTENT AND UNDER WHICH CIRCUMSTANCES ARE GROWTH MIND-SETS IMPORTANT TO ACADEMIC ACHIEVEMENT? TWO META-ANALYSES. *PSYCHOLOGICAL SCIENCE, 29*, 549–571.

SURBER, C. F. (1984). INFERENCES OF ABILITY AND EFFORT: EVIDENCE FOR TWO DIFFERENT PROCESSES. *JOURNAL OF PERSONALITY AND SOCIAL PSYCHOLOGY, 46*, 249–268.

Suggested readings and links

ELLIOT, A. J. (1999). APPROACH AND AVOIDANCE MOTIVATION AND ACHIEVEMENT GOALS. *EDUCATIONAL PSYCHOLOGIST, 34*, 149–169.

AVAILABLE FROM WWW.COMMUNICATIONCACHE.COM/ UPLOADS/1/0/8/8/10887248/APPROACH_AND_AVOIDANCE_MOTIVATION_ AND_ACHIEVEMENT_GOALS.PDF.

ELLIOT, A. J., & MCGREGOR, H. M. (2001). A 2×2 ACHIEVEMENT GOAL FRAMEWORK. *JOURNAL OF PERSONALITY AND SOCIAL PSYCHOLOGY, 80*, 501–519.

AVAILABLE FROM HTTP://ACADEMIC.UDAYTON.EDU/JACKBAUER/ READINGS%20361/ELLIOT%2001%20ACH%2GOAL%202X2.PDF.

AN INTERESTING TABLE DELINEATING THE CHARACTERISTICS OF LEARNERS WITH MASTERY VS. PERFORMANCE GOALS IS

AVAILABLE FROM WWW.WOU.EDU/~GIRODM/100/MASTERY_VS_ PERFORMANCE_GOALS.PDF.

A VIDEO ON ACHIEVEMENT GOAL THEORY IS

AVAILABLE FROM WWW.YOUTUBE.COM/WATCH?V=R1CZ5K8NPSM.

9 ... THINKING MAKES IT SO

SELF EFFICACY

There is nothing either good or bad, but thinking makes it so.

9 ... THINKING MAKES IT SO

PAPER "Self-efficacy: Toward a unifying theory of behavioral change"[1]

QUOTE *"Perceived threats activate defensive behavior because of their predictive value rather than their aversive quality. That is, when formerly neutral stimuli are associated with painful experiences, it is not that the stimuli have become aversive but that individuals have learned to anticipate aversive consequences".*

Why you should read this article

Why is it that some people feel tremendous fear when encountering a dog in the street? Why do some professional sporting figures perform at a high level in training but underperform on the big stage? And more importantly for our discussion, why is it that some students of near equal ability and experiences perform very differently in certain domains and in certain situations? One explanation might be self-efficacy or "judgements of how well one can execute courses of action required to deal with prospective situations" (Bandura, 1982 p. 122). The person who is terrified of dogs may understand at a logical level that most dogs are not going to attack them but if they *believe* that they are likely to experience severe anxiety in that situation then they are likely to exhibit that behaviour when encountering their neighbour's dog.

SELF-EFFICACY
How well you think you can deal with a specific challenge

The central idea in this article is that it is not so much the situation itself which initiates one's behaviour towards it but rather the way in which one *anticipates* the situation. Many students, for example, can perform at a high level in class discussion and assessments but then experience high levels of anxiety in the exam hall during their finals. In many cases, this has little to do with their ability but rather with their perception of how they can handle

1   **BANDURA, A.** (1977). SELF-EFFICACY: TOWARD A UNIFYING THEORY OF BEHAVIORAL CHANGE. *PSYCHOLOGICAL REVIEW*, 84(2), 191–215.
2   **SHAKESPEARE, W.,** & GILL, R. (2002). *HAMLET*. OXFORD, UK: OXFORD UNIVERSITY PRESS. P. 259.

the situation. As noted in the quote from Shakespeare's *Hamlet*, "there is nothing either good or bad, but thinking makes it so".[2] Self-efficacy refers to the extent to which an individual believes they are capable of successfully completing a task. In that sense, self-efficacy is really a domain specific trait and is strengthened by positive experiences within that domain as discussed below.

Abstract of the articles

The present article presents an integrative theoretical framework to explain and to predict psychological changes achieved by different modes of treatment. This theory states that psychological procedures, whatever their form, alter the level and strength of self-efficacy. It is hypothesised that expectations of personal efficacy determine whether coping behaviour will be initiated, how much effort will be expended, and how long it will be sustained in the face of obstacles and aversive experiences. Persistence in activities that are subjectively threatening but in fact relatively safe produces, through experiences of mastery, further enhancement of self-efficacy and corresponding reductions in defensive behavior. In the proposed model, expectations of personal efficacy are derived from 4 principal sources of information: performance accomplishments, vicarious experience, verbal persuasion, and physiological states. Factors influencing the cognitive processing of efficacy information arise from enactive, vicarious, exhortative, and emotive sources. The differential power of diverse therapeutic procedures is analysed in terms of the postulated cognitive mechanism of operation. Findings are reported from microanalyses of enactive, vicarious, and emotive modes of treatment that support the hypothesised relationship between perceived self-efficacy and behavioral changes.

EXPECTATIONS OF SELF-EFFICACY Accomplishments, experience, verbal persuasion, physiological states

The article

Learners expect a link between their ability and the result

I JUST BELIEVE IN ME[3]

IN THE 1960s, educational researchers moving from a behaviourist to a cognitivist view of learning were particularly interested in what goes on in our brain. They compared our brains with computers that worked with input and output based

(continued)

3   **LENNON, J.** (1970). GOD (RECORDED BY THE JOHN LENNON AND THE PLASTIC ONO BAND) ON *JOHN LENNON/PLASTIC ONO BAND* [VINYL]. LONDON, UK: APPLE RECORDS (SEPTEMBER 26–OCTOBER 9, 1970).

(continued)

on rational models and steps. The challenge was understanding how people process and store knowledge in the brain. In the 1970s and 1980s we began to also pay attention to the learning process itself and the learner's role in it. Learners don't always work rationally like computers; they make choices, choose a task (or don't), start on it, give up or persevere, and so on. All of these choices determine what someone ultimately learns. One of the most influential things in this regard is the belief in one's own abilities. Learners often choose a task or an approach that they think will give them the best results. Bandura added that students also expect a link between their own ability – or their belief in their own ability – and the result. They choose a task that they think they can complete or a strategy that they think will work.

In this article, Bandura offers a theoretical framework based on the claim that psychological procedures "serve as a means of creating and strengthening expectations of personal efficacy" p. 193). He examines changes in behaviour specifically looking at cognitive processes such as decision-making or through procedures such as the completion of actions. He argues that both of these approaches work in tandem to produce change but that completing tasks oneself as opposed to watching others complete them was more effective in increasing self-efficacy.

An *outcome expectancy* is one where an individual will estimate that a certain behaviour will lead to certain outcomes whereas an *efficacy expectation* is the belief that an individual can carry out the behaviour that is needed to achieve the outcome. In other words, people avoid threatening situations that they believe are beyond their coping capabilities yet they will more readily get involved in situations that they believe they can handle. For example, you might know and *believe* that you need to eat well and exercise to lose weight but you may lack the motivation to carry out the required action of eating healthy food and regularly going for a run.

Bandura outlines four main sources of information (see Figure 9.1) in which an individual's self-efficacy is fostered: performance accomplishments, vicarious experience, verbal persuasion, and physiological states.

Performance accomplishments refer to experiences where individuals take on a task and master it, thus giving a sense of accomplishment and greater confidence when encountering a similar task in the future. Interestingly, Bandura makes the claim that self-efficacy through mastery

Difference in outcome expectancy and efficacy expectation

PERFORMANCE
ACCOMPLISHMENTS
Self-efficacy through
task mastery

can generalise to other situations such as overcoming a phobia of animals, leading to better coping skills in social situations and reducing fear of other animals. However he stresses that the effects occur most prominently with activities which are more similar to the original mastery activity.

Vicarious experience refers to the fact that it is not only personal mastery that can lead to increased self-efficacy. When we see other people experience threatening situations and overcome them, this can improve our own sense that we will improve and complete a task if we persevere and sustain our efforts. In other words: "if they can do it, so can I".

Verbal persuasion is an easier intervention to achieve in the sense that it's relatively easy to talk to someone and suggest that they can achieve something if they make the effort. However, as you would expect, this approach is not as effective at increasing self-efficacy as ones where the individual experiences mastery themselves. In many cases verbal persuasion "is aimed mainly at raising outcome expectations rather than at enhancing self-efficacy" (p. 198). A key point here is that it's not just enough to persuade people that they can do something, you have to provide "provisional aids for effective action" (p. 198). In other words, it is not enough to tell someone they *can* do it, you also have to show them *how* to do it.

Physiological states, or "emotional arousal" as Bandura puts it, refers to the fact that high levels of anxiety usually impair an individual's ability to complete a task regardless of their ability to complete the task. For example, a football player who never misses a penalty in training can be overcome by fear in a real match situation and miss the penalty due to anxiety rather than ability. In this situation you often hear the phrase "The pressure got to him" or "He choked". In education we often see this with students who experience severe anxiety about studying or tests despite the fact that they're able to do them. Put simply, the fear of the experience is worse than the actual experience. As Bandura notes: "By conjuring up fear-provoking thoughts about their ineptitude, individuals can rouse themselves to elevated levels of anxiety that far exceed the fear experienced during the actual threatening situation" (p. 199). The anticipation of the task is far worse than actually doing the task.

However, there is a distinction to be made between these four levels of information as environmental events and how they are processed by the individual on a subjective level. In certain situations, individuals will

attribute success to external factors such as luck or the degree of difficulty of a task as opposed to their own effort or ability (see Chapter 10, How you think about achievement is more important than the achievement itself). This is particularly problematic when certain aids are used in an attempt to boost self-efficacy such as tasks which are too simple. As Bandura puts

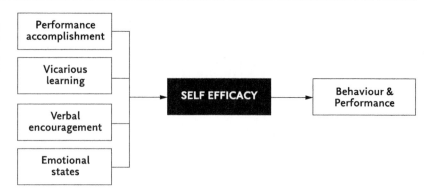

FIGURE 9.1
COMPONENTS OF
SELF-EFFICACY
(Source: Bandura,
1997)

it. "To succeed at easy tasks provides no new information for altering one's sense of self-efficacy, whereas mastery of challenging tasks conveys salient evidence of enhanced competence" (p. 201).

It's claimed that it's possible to create generalised, long lasting changes in self-efficacy. This involves initial induction activities such as clear instruction and modelling, removing the external aids (i.e. support, guidance, scaffolding) to confirm personal efficacy, and then finally allowing for independent practice and mastery will strengthen and generalise expectations of efficacy (see Chapter 18 on Direct instruction).

In addition, self-efficacy is highly contextual. Certain situations or tasks require more skill than others and carry a higher risk of negative consequences. Expectations will vary accordingly: "Thus, for example, the level and strength of perceived self-efficacy in public speaking will differ depending on the subject matter, the format of the presentation, and the types of audiences that will be addressed" (p. 203). This phenomenon would explain why teachers are usually highly confident speaking to their teenage or undergraduate students about a topic on which they know a great deal, yet may feel anxiety speaking about the same topic to their peers, where there is a greater threat to their professional standing and where the audience is far more knowledgeable than their students. All situations are not equal.

EXAMPLE
Exposure as a
means of increasing
self-efficacy

To test this theoretical model, ophidiophobics (i.e. people with a fear of snakes) were tested on their ability to confront their fear of snakes through two different therapeutic interventions. One group watched a facilitator engage in increasingly more threatening interactions with a boa constrictor and the other group actually performed those tasks themselves, becoming more and more exposed to handling the snake. A control group had neither treatment. The results were that the individuals who confronted their fear of snakes through direct handling had more self-efficacy in subsequent tests when confronted with a snake and were able to generalise this self-efficacy to different breeds of snakes.

THE INSIDIOUS MINDSET?

Issues with growth mindset interventions

IN HER STUDY ON MOTIVATION, Carol Dweck (Dweck & Leggett, 1988) saw that students differ in how they think about competence and intelligence. She made a distinction between two different ways or mindsets: a static (fixed) and a growth-oriented (growth) mindset. Students with a fixed way of thinking saw competence as something that must manifest itself immediately and otherwise not. They dropped out or stopped doing something if they couldn't do it right away. On the other hand, students who had a growth-oriented way of thinking believed that ability could grow through hard work and practice. They persisted, even when it was difficult or when they encountered problems.

Today, researchers question the reliability of Dweck's original studies. Later studies showed different results, including that growth-oriented thinking doesn't lead to better learning (Sisk et al., 2018). Dweck's research is also based on a very unreliable method of self-report by students. That students think differently about competence and intelligence is true, but the influence of these ways of thinking on learning performance has never been well demonstrated. Despite all of the recent scientific proof and refutations, this theory has become widely accepted and innovation processes have even been designed based on it.

Conclusions/implications of the work for educational practice

Bandura (2006) later argued that self-efficacy measures should be subject-specific as opposed to generalised and there is a lot of evidence that these subject-specific measures are a strong predictor of attainment (Meece, Wigfield, & Eccles, 1990). For example, measures of writing self-efficacy proved to significantly predict writing achievement as scored by student essays (McCarthy, Meier, & Rinderer, 1985). This has two serious implications for educators: first self-efficacy is largely domain specific and educators should be wary of approaches aimed at boosting self-efficacy that are based on inspirational quotes or motivational posters. There does not appear to be a *global* self-efficacy where individuals can improve self-efficacy in a general sense. Second, self-efficacy is a strong predictor of success in a particular domain and so instruction should be tailored to allowing students to experience success in that domain to affect self-efficacy.

Self-efficacy is domain-specific and predicts success

A central claim in this article is that self-efficacy affects the choice of action that an individual makes, particularly in terms of persistence and effort. Individuals who have low self-efficacy in a particular domain are unlikely to expend much effort to complete a particular task, whereas those with high self-efficacy are more likely to readily take on a task and see failure as a means to eventual success. However, how do educators harness this theoretical model to help their students?

First, returning to Bandura's four components, we can think about the conditions which teachers can create to bolster self-efficacy and it's clear that when students experience success vicariously and then personally, they're likely to experience increased self-efficacy. Clear instruction and modelling of material to be learned is something teachers can do.

SHOW HOW IT'S DONE

Modeled behavior with clear outcomes conveys more efficacy information than if the effects of the modeled actions remain ambiguous. In investigations of vicarious processes, observing one perform activities that meet with success does, indeed, produce greater behavioral improvements than witnessing the same performances modeled without any evident consequences.

(Bandura, 1977, p.197).

In addition to a teacher modelling success, another element to consider with vicarious experience is to allow students to see their peers being successful in a specific task. For example, when students complete an essay on a literature assignment, instead of marking their work and handing it back, a teacher might show the class three examples of students doing that task at a high level and then ask the student to talk the class through how they constructed the essay, what ideas and concepts they used and the ways in which they phrased their ideas.

Vague advice is ineffective, be specific

The key thing here is that there are clear outcomes modelled for the given behaviour, so telling students in general terms that "hard work achieves results" might be true in a general sense but it's unlikely to lead to changes in behaviour, whereas showing students the specific steps required to solve an algebraic equation for example, and then giving them the time and space to independently practice and achieve success doing it is more likely to lead to improved self-efficacy.

Finally, let students work (i.e. make assignments) at their own level, with goals that are within their reach. Bandura himself mentions a number of factors within learning environments that guarantee or increase the self-efficacy of students, such as:

- Focusing on "learning" instead of "knowing": students will then see that they can grow and that knowledge and skills are not innate traits.
- Discouraging mutual competition and emphasising personal progress and achievement.
- Focusing feedback on progress and not on mistakes (see also Chapters 19, Assessment *for*, not *of* learning, and Chapter 20, Feed up, feedback, feed forward).

How to use the work in your teaching

Self-efficacy is a complex cognitive capacity and one which is often formed and consolidated over many years, but one thing that teachers should be aware of is exam or performance anxiety. As Bandura states: "It is often the case that fears and deficits are interdependent. Avoidance of stressful activities impedes development of coping skills, and the resulting lack of competency provides a realistic basis for fear" (p. 199). As stated previously, emotional reactions to performance can cause anxiety, which can initiate avoidance behaviours and seriously impair one's ability to carry out the task. In other words, the anticipation of the task is far worse than *actually doing the task*. To address this, Bandura suggests modelling as a way of alleviating potentially negative emotional states and teaching coping skills by demonstrating effective ways of dealing with threatening situations. So when dealing with students who encounter anxiety around academic writing or exam situations, teachers can break down the component elements of writing an essay and model how to write an introduction and develop an argument for example, and then "expose" students to exam situations by creating the kinds of situations they will encounter in the real situation such as a timed exam in class. Like the penalty taker who is near perfect in training but overcome in a real match, you are never going to be able to properly recreate the kinds of pressure a real life exam will create, but it will go some way to prepare students to cope with their anxiety through mastering simulated versions of the real thing.

In addition, when giving advice to students or in on-on-one discussions, it is important to not use vague, nebulous language or instructions. It might seem like the right thing to do to say "you can achieve anything if you just believe" but advice like this might have an adverse effect. Instead, it's more effective to provide very clear

WHY MOTIVATIONAL POSTERS DON'T WORK

"THE IMPACT of verbal persuasion on self-efficacy may vary substantially depending on the perceived credibility of the persuaders, their prestige, trustworthiness, expertise, and assuredness. The more believable the source of the information, the more likely are efficacy expectations to change". (Bandura, 1977 p. 202)

instructions on what is required to achieve a particular task, then model how to do it and finally allow the student some independent practice to boost self-efficacy.

EXAMPLE
Low self-efficacy

In the classroom, low levels of self-efficacy usually means that a student has a distorted view of a task they are faced with and believes that it is much harder than it actually is. In some situations, low self-efficacy is justified. For example if you had to run 100 metres in less than 10 seconds you would be right to think you can't do it (unless you're Usain Bolt) but in educational settings, tasks are usually within the competence level of the students being asked to do them. Low self-efficacy can also lead to avoidance behaviours and poor planning, and so another approach can be to alleviate this by careful sequencing of instruction and tasks and removal of guidance when appropriate, to ultimately lead them to the mastery of a particular task and the feeling of accomplishment, which is really the most powerful determinant of self-efficacy.

Takeaways

- Self-efficacy refers to the relative belief one has about their ability to complete a task.
- Self-efficacy is boosted by having successful experiences and mastering a task or topic.
- It can also be boosted through seeing others succeed and through persuasion, though this is less strong.
- Emotional states when anticipating a task, such as anxiety, can make a task seem much harder than it actually is.
- Anxiety can be addressed through teacher modelling and exposure to simulated pressurised situations.
- Give students the chance for success experiences by giving them tasks they can handle.

- Focus on "learning" instead of "knowing"; in this way students discover that they can grow.
- Discourage mutual competition and emphasise personal progress.

References

BANDURA, A. (1977). SELF-EFFICACY: TOWARD A UNIFYING THEORY OF BEHAVIORAL CHANGE. *PSYCHOLOGICAL REVIEW, 84,* 191–205.

BANDURA, A. (1982). SELF-EFFICACY MECHANISM IN HUMAN AGENCY. *AMERICAN PSYCHOLOGIST, 37*(2), 122–147.

BANDURA, A. (2006). GUIDE FOR CONSTRUCTING SELF-EFFICACY SCALES. IN F. PAJARES AND T. URDAN (EDS.). *SELF-EFFICACY BELIEFS OF ADOLESCENTS* (VOL. 5, PP. 307–337). GREENWICH, CT: INFORMATION AGE.

DWECK, C. S., & LEGGETT, E. L. (1988). A SOCIAL-COGNITIVE APPROACH TO MOTIVATION AND PERSONALITY. *PSYCHOLOGICAL REVIEW, 95,* 256–273.

MCCARTHY, P., MEIER, S., & RINDERER, R. (1985). SELF-EFFICACY AND WRITING: A DIFFERENT VIEW OF SELF EVALUATION. *COLLEGE COMPOSITION AND COMMUNICATION. 36,* 465–471.

MEECE, J. L., WIGFIELD, A., & ECCLES, J. S. (1990). PREDICTORS OF MATH ANXIETY AND ITS INFLUENCE ON YOUNG ADOLESCENTS' COURSE ENROLLMENT AND PERFORMANCE IN MATHEMATICS. *JOURNAL OF EDUCATIONAL PSYCHOLOGY, 82,* 60–70.

SHAKESPEARE, W., & GILL, R. (2002). *HAMLET.* OXFORD, UK: OXFORD UNIVERSITY PRESS.

SISK, V. F., BURGOYNE, A. P., SUN, J., BUTLER, J. L., & MACNAMARA, B. N. (2018), TO WHAT EXTENT AND UNDER WHICH CIRCUMSTANCES ARE GROWTH MIND-SETS IMPORTANT TO ACADEMIC ACHIEVEMENT? TWO META-ANALYSES. *PSYCHOLOGICAL SCIENCE, 29,* 549–571.

Suggested Readings and Links

BANDURA, A. (1986). *SOCIAL FOUNDATIONS OF THOUGHT AND ACTION: A SOCIAL COGNITIVE THEORY.* ENGLEWOOD CLIFFS, NJ: PRENTICE-HALL.

BANDURA, A. (1997). *SELF-EFFICACY: THE EXERCISE OF CONTROL.* NEW YORK, NY: W. H. FREEMAN.

A FASCINATING INTERVIEW WITH BANDURA ABOUT HIS LIFE AND WORK IS

AVAILABLE FROM HTTPS://YOUTU.BE/-_U-PSZWHY8.

SELF-EFFICACY. AN ACCESSIBLE VIDEO ABOUT SELF-EFFICACY BY RAINA BURDITT.

AVAILABLE FROM WWW.YOUTUBE.COM/WATCH?V=OFSBNQMCLZM.

A USEFUL TIP-SHEET FROM THE APA ON HOW TO TEACH FOR SELF-EFFICACY IS

AVAILABLE FROM WWW.APA.ORG/PI/AIDS/RESOURCES/EDUCATION/ SELF-EFFICACY.

THE NAIL IN GROWTH MINDSET'S COFFIN? A BLOG FROM DAVID DIDAU.

AVAILABLE FROM HTTPS://LEARNINGSPY.CO.UK/PSYCHOLOGY/ NAIL-GROWTH-MINDSETS-COFFIN-2/.

A VIDEO OF SNAKE EXPOSURE THERAPY IS

AVAILABLE FROM HTTPS://YOUTU.BE/ZKTPECOOIEC.

10 HOW YOU THINK ABOUT ACHIEVEMENT IS MORE IMPORTANT THAN THE ACHIEVEMENT ITSELF

ATTRIBUTION THEORY

10 HOW YOU THINK ABOUT ACHIEVEMENT IS MORE IMPORTANT THAN THE ACHIEVEMENT ITSELF

PAPER "An attributional theory of achievement motivation and emotion"[1]

QUOTE *"A virtually infinite number of causal ascriptions are available in memory. However, within the achievement domain, a relatively small number from the vast array tend to be salient. The most dominant of these causes are ability and effort. That is, success is ascribed to high ability and hard work, and failure is attributed to low ability and the absence of trying".*

Why you should read this article

When a football team loses a game, the coach is usually interviewed afterwards and you tend to get two types of response. The first coach will blame the referee, the opponents' unambitious tactics (they parked the bus in front of the goal), or just plain bad luck. In some cases, they will even blame the pitch. The second type of coach will not blame external factors and instead look inwards and blame the team themselves, claiming, "we just didn't work hard enough today" or "the strikers didn't get the passes they should have gotten". Both of these responses are an attempt to not only make sense of a particular performance, but also to ensure any future performance will still be under their control. The coach who blames the referee allows his team to retain a degree of agency in the future, as they will not always have the same referee. (However, the coach is also missing a vital opportunity for the team to learn from

I **WEINER, B.** (1985). AN ATTRIBUTIONAL THEORY OF ACHIEVEMENT MOTIVATION AND EMOTION. *PSYCHOLOGICAL REVIEW*, 92(4), 548–573.

their mistakes in the match.) Similarly, the coach who assigns blame on internal factors like effort is not saying his team are *perpetually* not good enough. After all, many teams with "inferior" players can beat "superior" teams with the right tactics and application. (S)he is saying that they can increase their effort in the future and perform better. One thing you'll almost never hear a coach say is "they have better players than we do and so are a much better team" despite the fact that often this is the most obvious factor to anyone watching the game.

ATTRIBUTION
THEORY
What we think
causes our successes
or failures

Attribution theory is essentially the causes that individuals attribute to their own successes or failures. Weiner's work looks more closely at how those perceptions affect their emotional state and crucially, how that process affects their subsequent motivation for future tasks. A hugely important factor is that the *perceived* cause is more significant that the *actual* cause. For example, a student's emotional response to a bad test score is more important than the score itself because it can establish a pattern of future behaviour that can prove to be self-defeating. As Hamlet said to Rosencrantz, "there is nothing either good or bad, but thinking makes it so". If a student feels that their poor score in a mathematics test is down to a fundamental lack of ability that they have no control over, then their negative emotional response is likely to result in a lack of effort in the future despite the fact that this might not be true. However, if a student blames poor performance on a lack of effort, they may feel an initial degree of shame but there is still the possibility that they can change this behaviour in the future to achieve success.

EXAMPLE
Perceived vs.
actual cause

This article by Bernard Weiner (1985) seeks to systematise how students in achievement-related contexts attribute causes to academic outcomes, and how those attributions affect future motivation and performance. As Heider noted in 1958, we are all "naïve psychologists" seeking to make sense of an uncertain world and understanding how students respond to academic performance and how this affects their future motivation is an important string to any teacher's bow (Heider, 1958).

Abstract of the article

A theory of motivation and emotion is proposed in which causal ascriptions play a key role. It is first documented that in achievement-related contexts there are a few dominant causal perceptions. The perceived causes of success and failure share three common properties: locus, stability, and controllability, with intentionality and globality as other possible causal structures. The perceived stability of causes influences changes in expectancy of success; all three dimensions of causality affect a variety of common emotional experiences, including anger, gratitude, guilt, hopelessness, pity, pride, and shame. Expectancy and affect, in turn, are presumed to guide motivated behavior. The theory therefore relates the structure of thinking to the dynamics of feeling and action. Analysis of a created motivational episode involving achievement strivings is offered, and numerous empirical observations are examined from this theoretical position. The strength of the empirical evidence, the capability of this theory to address prevalent human emotions, and the potential generality of the conception are stressed.

The article

Building on the pioneering work of Fritz Heider in the 1950s, Bernard Weiner establishes the fact that causes within achievement contexts are broadly ascribed to a set of internal and external factors. For example, a student might ascribe poor performance on a test to an internal cause such as lack of effort or ability or they might ascribe it to an external one such as test difficulty or teacher bias. Weiner developed this idea in the 1970s when he noted that within both of these domains, some causes are stable whereas some are prone to fluctuation. Furthermore, students tend to attribute academic outcomes to one of the following four causes: ability, effort, task difficulty, or luck. Of these four, ability and effort were cited as the most common.

CAUSES OF
ACADEMIC
OUTCOMES:
• Ability
• Effort
• Difficulty
• Luck

In addition to the locus dimension, Weiner added another to this dynamic: stability, which describes how stable these specific causes are over time – something which becomes crucial when considering how much control one has and as a result, how motivated one is in the future. In this dimension, elements such as ability or aptitude are seen as relatively stable causes whereas mood and effort are seen as more variable.

TABLE 10.1
LOCUS OF
CONTROL
DIMENSION 1
(ADAPTED FROM
WEINER, 1985)

	Internal	External
Stable	Ability	Task Difficulty
Unstable	Effort	Luck

However, it was realised that this did not quite capture the problem as to the "naïve attributor", effort might be perceived as a stable characteristic and tasks can be changed to become easy or difficult. Although effort is an unstable cause in the sense that we can expend more or less effort in a given situation, there is also the belief that a person can be just simply lazy, which is seen as a far more stable construct. As Rosenbaum (1972) notes, mood, fatigue, and effort are all internal and unstable causes but effort is different in the sense that it can be manipulated in a way that mood or fatigue cannot. Therefore, a third dimension of "controllability" (Weiner, 1979) was added to account for this. So for example, a cause of success or failure might be internal *yet uncontrollable,* such as mathematics aptitude. It's not uncommon to hear students, or indeed many adults, say "I'm just not good with numbers".

	Internal		External	
	Controllable	**Uncontrollable**	**Controllable**	**Uncontrollable**
Stable	Effort	Ability	Teacher bias	Difficulty of test
Unstable	Domain	Mood	Lack of help Luck knowledge	

TABLE 10.2
LOCUS
DIMENSION 2.
(ADAPTED FROM
WEINER, 1985)

Link between
experience and
expectation

Crucially, when students experience success or failure and ascribe causes to those outcomes, those attributions affect their *expectations* of future failure or success. There is also the question of incentive – a student may feel confidence and expect success but their motivation to work for a test may depend on whether that test counts towards their final grade or whether it is just a one-off test. Weiner then details the emotional response to attributing different causes to performance. Following the outcome of an event, individuals will experience an initial positive or negative reaction or what is described as a "primitive" emotion. The next thing to happen is to ascribe a cause to that outcome and this is where emotions such as anger, shame and guilt can have a devastating impact on future performance.

So students who experience failure and attribute that to internal, stable causes such as personality or ability are likely to experience a lack of self-esteem and will often shut down and give up, saying "I'm just no good at this". Conversely, students who attribute failure to external, unstable causes are likely to blame it on other people or outside factors and so miss an opportunity for growth and reflection that might lead to future improvement.

Conclusions/implications of the work for educational practice

Causes of success
or failure are not
often clear

When students experience academic success, the behaviour that led to that success is positively reinforced and they are likely to engage in that behaviour again. Conversely, when a student experiences failure, their evaluation of that failure is critical in determining future behaviours. By attributing their failure to an internal and stable cause such as ability, their emotional response can be shame, guilt, and frustration and can lead to a negative cycle of underachievement. However, in many cases, the factors determining success or failure are not so set in stone. The combination of unstable causes such as effort, persistence, and specific subject knowledge go a very long way in most academic environments and are malleable, that is to say, students can do something about it.

The other important factor is to remember to always be honest with students in terms of their effort and level of attainment. It is one thing to inspire students but another to give them a false picture of where they are that can have potentially damaging effects. For example as Weiner (1980) notes:

PRIZES FOR ALL
Not good for long-
term motivation

Causal attributions determine affective reactions to success and failure. For example, one is not likely to experience pride in success, or feelings of competence, when receiving an "A" from a teacher who gives only that grade, or when defeating a tennis player who always loses.

(p. 362)

The teacher who only says positive things to their students is a little bit like the boy who cried wolf. Praise is a potent tool to use in motivating students, but if it becomes the default, then students develop a resistance to it and disregard it. However, the teacher who can cultivate a culture where success is linked to effort and not latent ability is likely to contribute to student success.

How to use the work in your teaching

Attribution theory is probably most useful when working with students who have experienced repeated academic failure and have low motivation. Those types of students can often become trapped in a negative cycle where learned helplessness takes over and their behaviour becomes a self-fulfilling prophecy. With students like this, it is crucial to address fundamental beliefs about their performance in order to improve future performance, and so a coaching approach where they're asked a series of questions with a period of reflection can yield positive results. The kinds of questions teachers might ask are:

Five key questions
for demotivated
students

1. What happened in that test?
2. How did you feel about it? (primitive emotion)
3. Is this something to do with you or something else? (internal/external)
4. Is this reason fixed or does it change over time? (stable/unstable)
5. Can you change this and if so, how? (controllability)

It may be the case that there are genuine external/uncontrollable factors which have affected student performance such as the difficulty of a particular test or just plain bad luck, but the crucial point is that their *perception* of the cause is more significant than the *actual* cause. The more a student feels that they have no control over a situation, the less they are likely to respond positively to that situation. The vast majority of students are doing tasks that are within their capability given a relatively constructive set of personal conditions, proper instruction, and the requisite amount of effort.

OWNERSHIP
Students need to feel they have control

A vital aspect of attribution theory is the extent to which individuals feel they have *ownership* over a situation. If a student has a misconception about their academic performance, citing internal causes such as a lack of ability or external ones like teacher bias as a reason for underachievement, it can be transformative to shift their thinking towards variables that they can do something about such as increased effort, skills, and knowledge; all of which they can change with the right approach.

Takeaways

- When attributing academic success or failure to particular causes, there are three common properties: locus, stability, and controllability.
- The *perceived* cause of academic performance is as significant as the *actual* cause.
- The relative stability of a cause affects how students will "expect" success in the future.
- Student's emotional response to performance can profoundly affect future motivation.
- It is important to shift student thinking away from uncontrollable factors to controllable ones.
- Constant positive praise can dilute the effect of that praise over time.

References

HEIDER, F. (1958). *THE PSYCHOLOGY OF INTERPERSONAL RELATIONS.* NEW YORK, NY: JOHN WILEY & SONS.

ROSENBAUM, R. M. (1972). *A DIMENSIONAL ANALYSIS OF THE PERCEIVED CAUSES OF SUCCESS AND FAILURE.* UNPUBLISHED DOCTORAL DISSERTATION, UNIVERSITY OF CALIFORNIA, LOS ANGELES, 1972.

WEINER, B. (1979). *A THEORY OF MOTIVATION FOR SOME CLASSROOM EXPERIENCES. JOURNAL OF EDUCATIONAL PSYCHOLOGY, 71,* 3–25.

WEINER, B. (1980). *HUMAN MOTIVATION.* NEW YORK, NY: HOLT, RINEHART & WINSTON.

WEINER, B. (1985). *AN ATTRIBUTIONAL THEORY OF ACHIEVEMENT MOTIVATION AND EMOTION. PSYCHOLOGICAL REVIEW, 92*(4), 548–573. AVAILABLE FROM HTTPS://PDFS.SEMANTICSCHOLAR. ORG/23DB/126E3C39983E1F72964544636103C6C313C2.PDF.

Suggested readings and links

USEFUL PRIMER OF ATTRIBUTION THEORY WITH POSSIBLE APPLICATIONS: WWW.INSTRUCTIONALDESIGN.ORG/THEORIES/ATTRIBUTION-THEORY/

MCLEOD, S. A. (2012). ATTRIBUTION THEORY.

AVAILABLE FROM WWW.SIMPLYPSYCHOLOGY.ORG/ATTRIBUTION-THEORY.HTML.

ATTRIBUTION THEORY – BASIC COVARIATION (VIDEO FROM KHAN ACADEMY): WWW.KHANACADEMY.ORG/TEST-PREP/MCAT/INDIVIDUALS-AND-SOCIETY/PERCEPTION-PREJUDICE-AND-BIAS/V/ATTRIBUTION-THEORY-BASIC-COVARIATION

11 WHERE ARE WE GOING AND HOW DO WE GET THERE?

GOAL ORIENTATION

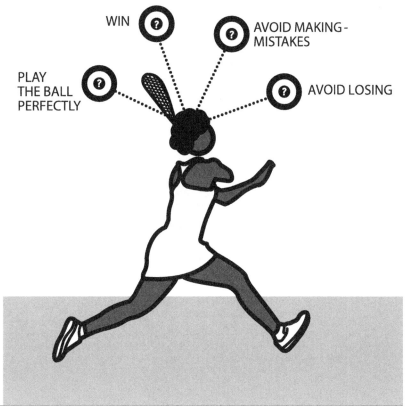

WHERE ARE WE GOING AND HOW DO WE GET THERE?

PAPER "Multiple goals, multiple pathways: The role of goal orientation in learning and achievement"[1]

QUOTE *"Future research on achievement goals needs to move beyond a simplistic mastery goals (good) versus performance goals (bad) characterization to consider multiple goals, multiple outcomes, and multiple pathways to learning and achievement in multiple contexts"*[2].

Why you should read this article

People who seem to be doing the same thing are often doing it based on different reasons. Take practising on a squash court. While some people might go to the squash court or sign up for lessons because they want to master the strategies, tactics, and techniques of playing the game well (i.e., they want to master the game), others might seemingly do the same thing because they want to win (i.e. they want to be better than others in the game). While some people might spend a lot of time practising alone and with others because they don't want to make silly mistakes when they play (i.e. they're trying to avoid mistakes), others also spend a lot of time practising to ensure that they don't play worse than others (i.e. they're afraid of losing). All four of these squash players have different motivations to take lessons and practice. In research into the people's motivation (and students are people), we try to take this into account. We also try to look at other things that influence what they do and why they do it, such as whether people think that they are capable of achieving

1   **PINTRICH, P. R.** (2000). MULTIPLE GOALS, MULTIPLE PATHWAYS: THE ROLE OF GOAL ORIENTATION IN LEARNING AND ACHIEVEMENT. *JOURNAL OF EDUCATIONAL PSYCHOLOGY, 92*, 544–555.

2   **PINTRICH, P. R.** (2000). A MOTIVATIONAL SCIENCE PERSPECTIVE ON THE ROLE OF STUDENT MOTIVATION IN LEARNING AND TEACHING CONTEXTS. *JOURNAL OF EDUCATIONAL PSYCHOLOGY, 95*, 667–686.

their goals and to what extent they can influence the outcome. We came across some of these things in Chapter 8, Beliefs about intelligence can affect intelligence and Chapter 10, How you think about achievement is more important than the achievement itself. In addition to these two important determinants of what we actually learn, we can also look at the goals that students have when they study. Paul Pintrich shows in his article on goal orientation that students have different reasons for starting on a task that can be divided into two categories: namely learning or performing.

Abstract of the articles

ADAPTIVE
OUTCOMES
Results which
change based on
process

Mastery goals have been linked to adaptive outcomes in normative goal theory and research; performance goals, to less adaptive outcomes. In contrast, approach performance goals may be adaptive for some outcomes under a revised goal theory perspective. The current study addresses the role of multiple goals, both mastery and approach performance goals, and links them to multiple outcomes of motivation, affect, strategy use, and performance. Data were collected over 3 waves from 8th and 9th graders (N = 150) in their math classrooms using both self-report questionnaires and actual math grades. There was a general decline in adaptive outcomes over time, but these trends were moderated by the different patterns of multiple goals. In line with normative goal theory, mastery goals were adaptive; but also in line with the revised goal theory perspective, approach performance goals, when coupled with mastery goals, were just as adaptive.

The article

At the end of the 1980s – thanks to Paul Pintrich – goal theory emerged to explain student motivation in an educational setting. In his view, this motivation had three components, namely: "(a) value (including task value and achievement goal orientation), (b) expectancies (including control beliefs, self-efficacy beliefs, and expectancy for success), and (c) affect (focusing primarily on test anxiety and self-esteem)" (Harackiewicz & Linnenbrink, 2005, p. 76). Combining multiple theoretical perspectives, he noted the importance of integrating the study of task value with achievement goal research, as a learner's achievement goal orientation might help determine her/his achievement behaviour, while value would affect the strength of the learner's behaviour.

THREE
COMPONENTS OF
MOTIVATION:
• Value
• Expectancies
• Affect

Building on Dweck (1986) and Dweck and Leggett's (1988) work on motivation and learning (see Chapter 8, Beliefs about intelligence can affect intelligence) Pintrich's work concerned the motivation that students need to start working on a task at all: the so-called goal orientation. He distinguished between mastery goals (goals aimed at learning and understanding the material) and performance goals (goals focused on performance). Mastery-oriented students start working on a task because they want to learn and understand how to carry out the task and are intrinsically motivated to do so. On the other hand, performance-oriented students are focused on the grade that they can earn by completing a task; they start working on a task to score and, preferably, get a better grade than their classmates. Their motivation is extrinsic. In Pintrich's (2000) words:

Mastery versus performance goals

> mastery goals orient students to a focus on learning and mastery of the content or task ... In contrast, performance goals orient students to a concern for their ability and performance relative to others and seem to focus the students on goals of doing better than others or of avoiding looking incompetent or less able in comparison to others

(p. 544).

Goal orientation is domain specific

It's important to note here that a person's goal orientation isn't general, but depends on the subject area or even the specific task because goal orientation is affected by a student's feelings of efficacy, task value, interest, positive affect, etc. A high school student learning words in a foreign language might focus on getting good grades on the weekly exams so as to score better than classmates, but be intrinsically motivated in mathematics and simply want to master the material, regardless of how others perform.

In addition to the distinction between mastery and performance orientation, Pintrich brings in a second important difference in goal orientation, namely approach and avoidance. While important for both mastery and performance orientations, this difference is especially important for the latter. If your performance goals are approach oriented, then you want to do better than others and demonstrate your ability and competence (i.e. you want to outperform others). In contrast, if your performance goals are avoidance oriented, then you want to avoid looking stupid or incompetent (i.e. you want to avoid looking bad). This difference also exists with regard to mastery orientation. If your mastery goals are approach oriented, then you'll work on a task because you want to really learn how to do something well. In contrast, if your mastery goals are avoidance oriented, then you'll work on a task because you're afraid that if you don't, you won't master the material or learn everything that can be learnt (see Tables 11.1 and 11.2).

APPROACH Demonstrate ability

AVOIDANCE Avoid looking bad

	Mastery goals	Performance goals
Approach orientation	Focus on mastering the task Own subjective or personal standards for success, progress, understanding	Focus on performing/ looking better than others Normative standards such as grades, class ranking
Avoidance orientation	Focus on avoiding misunderstanding Own subjective or personal standards for what isn't good	Focus on avoiding appearing to be stupid and/ or worse than others Normative standards such as grades, class ranking

TABLE 11.1
FOUR DIFFERENT GOAL ORIENTATIONS WHEN TACKLING A TASK

	Mastery goals	Performance goals
Approach orientation	I want to be able to read and write well in Spanish so I practice this a lot, both at school and at home.	I practice the Spanish words in the workbook every day because I want to get the best grade in Spanish.
Avoidance orientation	I do all of the Spanish exercises in the workbook because I'm afraid that if I don't, then I won't learn to read and write Spanish well.	I practice the Spanish words in the workbook every day because otherwise I'll get the lowest grade in my class.

TABLE 11.2
FOUR DIFFERENT GOAL ORIENTATIONS WHEN TACKLING A TASK WITH RESPECT TO A SUBJECT

Research carried out by Pintrich and his colleagues has revealed that these four different goal orientations are related to different outcomes in the class such as grades, motivation, choice of strategy, and so forth.

What does this all mean? Let's first take a look at those learners with a performance approach goal orientation. Research (e.g. Senko, Hulleman, & Harackiewicz, 2011) has revealed that these learners are motivated to be the best (not the best that they can be but the best within their class), to appear to be the smartest and most competent in the class. As a result, they work hard, put in a lot of effort in exceeding their peers, and generally score well on exams. Learning is not their goal per se; they work to learn but for what we might call "the wrong reason". These learners work hard, but aren't very engaged in their learning and often resort to superficial learning strategies aimed at showing proficiency like memorising.

A bigger problem are those learners with a performance avoidance goal orientation. These learners try, at all costs, to avoid making mistakes so as not to appear to be incompetent. They are generally very anxious, study in a disorganised way, avoid help offered (accepting help is seen as an admission of incompetence), often get low marks, and have little interest in their work. In their studies, they'll avoid taking risks so as to

PERFORMANCE ORIENTATION
Concerned with exam results

lessen their chances of failing, leading them to take well-trodden paths and choose tasks that are simple and don't challenge them. If they fail, then they often become frustrated and give up.

Mastery learners, on the other hand, are less of a problem, regardless of whether they have an approach or an avoidance orientation. In their research, Senko, Hulleman, and Harackiewicz (2011) showed that students who are focused on mastering a task, that is, have a mastery orientation, are very positive about their learning process. They often enjoy their lessons, continue when tasks become difficult, find help easily, can manage themselves well, use in-depth learning strategies, experience positive emotions in the classroom, and see the assignments they have to make as valuable. According to Lisa Bloom (2009), "mastery goals may be optimal for academic engagement" (p. 179). Learners with a mastery goal orientation tend to have higher feelings of self-efficacy, become – via their success – more self-motivated, try harder and work longer, and seek challenges. Mastery avoiders are generally very concerned, disorganised in their study habits, avoid help offered, often get low marks and have little interest in their work. When they "fail", they don't give up, but rather try harder.

CAN STUDENTS PURSUE MULTIPLE GOALS AT THE SAME TIME?

PINTRICH (2000) asked students to fill in a questionnaire about their goal orientation. It showed that students can pursue multiple goals at the same time. They can work for a subject because they want to master the subject, but also because they want to get a good grade. These two orientations are, thus, not mutually exclusive. In fact, pursuing both goals at the same time should yield a theoretical advantage; these learners are not only intrinsically motivated, but also want to get good grades. The question is to what extent it's possible for students to pursue both goals, because the different goals also require a different focus during learning. This can be solved if learners, for example, focus on learning during the semester, but shift their focus to getting a good grade when studying for a test (Senko, Hulleman, & Harackiewicz, 2011).

Conclusions/implications of the work for educational practice

Goal theory gives teachers insight into how students can think and how they can perform tasks. It helps to understand why students do or do not do certain things. The results show that certain orientations in learning are indeed better than others. An orientation to mastery itself will help students develop an intrinsic motivation for a certain subject or task. By learning for mastery they will learn for the long-term and not just for a test. A focus on performance can help students perform better and help them get the best out of themselves, but is often short-term learning. The student learns for the exam, gets a good grade, and then often forgets what has been learnt. Nicholas Soderstrom and Robert Bjork (2015) discuss this in their article "learning versus performance: An integrative review". They write:

The primary goal of instruction should be to facilitate long-term learning – that is, to create relatively permanent changes in comprehension, understanding, and skills of the types that will support long-term retention and transfer. During the instruction or training process, however, what we can observe and measure is performance, which is often an unreliable index of whether the relatively long-term changes that constitute learning have taken place.

(p. 176).

Both orientations can occur at the same time and both can help students with their learning process. The combination is the most beneficial as the student gets a good grade while learning for the long-term. Only the avoiding orientations have the opposite and deleterious effect.

How to use the work in your teaching

Learning is a risky business because, by definition, learning means doing something you don't know how to do. It is, thus, important to make it less risky by reducing the cost of failure. There are a number of ways that you can do this. You can, for example, make sure that your reaction to a mistake is one of interest and support rather than of criticism. It's also a good idea to give your students the chance to view their "failures" (i.e. mistakes) constructively. Give them additional opportunities to learn what they can't do without harsh consequences, giving them the opportunity and even the drive to identify their mistakes and correct them.

Of course, as a teacher, you also have to grade your students, so make sure that your students maintain a positive outlook and don't act based on fear or other negative emotions. Grades can stimulate learners if they feel that a good grade is within their reach if they do their best, but grades are counterproductive if they make students anxious or insecure, especially if they have an avoidance orientation. In that case focus on

RETENTION AND TRANSFER
Not just remembering information but being able to use it

Failure can be a powerful learning tool when viewed constructively

increasing their intrinsic motivation by using formative assessment (see Chapter 19, Assessment *for*, not *of* learning), giving good feedback (Chapter 20, Feed up, feedback, feed forward), and giving them tasks at their own level (Chapter 12, Why scaffolding is not as easy as it looks). To improve intrinsic motivation, emphasise that learning is not about grades; that you're more interested in whether they understand how to solve a task and how to apply the right strategy than whether the answer is correct (see Figure 11.1). In other words, move the focus more to the learning process and less on the result. If you do this, then mistakes may no longer be seen as something to be anxious about and to avoid, but rather as interesting because you can learn from them.

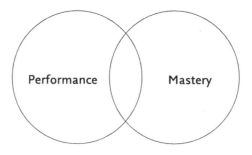

FIGURE 11.1
THE SWEET
SPOT WHERE
PERFORMANCE
MEETS MASTERY

Takeaways

- There are two different goals that play a role in how the learner studies: they can want to master a subject or they can want to perform well.
- Both goals can have positive consequences: the mastery goal learners are often intrinsically motivated, the performance goal-oriented learners often achieve higher marks.
- Learning because you are trying to avoid failure (or even not mastering the subject) has negative effects on the learning processes of students.
- Students can pursue both orientations (i.e. mastery and performance) at the same time.
- Teach students that making mistakes is neither scary nor bad because you can learn from those mistakes.
- This means that you need to make the classroom a safe place so that students will take the risks involved in learning.
- When you give your students a learning task, design them just beyond their current ability level but within their reach.
- Try to encourage performance goal approach learners to learn in a deeper way (i.e. not just memorise, but understand) and to discourage "avoiders" from choosing the easiest way for the easiest tasks.

References

BLOOM, L. A. (2009). *CLASSROOM MANAGEMENT: CREATING POSITIVE OUTCOMES FOR ALL STUDENTS.* UPPER SADDLE RIVER, NJ: PEARSON EDUCATION.

DWECK, C., & LEGGETT, E. (1988). A SOCIAL-COGNITIVE APPROACH TO MOTIVATION AND PERSONALITY. *PSYCHOLOGICAL REVIEW, 95,* 256–273. AVAILABLE FROM HTTP://CITESEERX.IST.PSU.EDU/VIEWDOC/DOWNLOAD?DOI=10.1.1.583.9142&REP=REP1&TYPE=PDF.

DWECK, C. S. (1986). MOTIVATIONAL PROCESSES AFFECTING LEARNING. *AMERICAN PSYCHOLOGIST, 41,* 1040–1048.

HARACKIEWICZ, J. M., & LINNENBRINK, E. A. (2005). MULTIPLE ACHIEVEMENT GOALS AND MULTIPLE PATHWAYS FOR LEARNING: THE AGENDA AND IMPACT OF PAUL R. PINTRICH. *EDUCATIONAL PSYCHOLOGIST,* 40(2), 75–84. AVAILABLE FROM WWW.RESEARCHGATE.NET/PUBLICATION/247522707_MULTIPLE_ACHIEVEMENT_GOALS_AND_MULTIPLE_PATHWAYS_FOR_LEARNING_THE_AGENDA_AND_IMPACT_OF_PAUL_R_PINTRICH.

MISCHEL, W., EBBESEN, E. B., & RASKOFF ZEISS, A. (1972). COGNITIVE AND ATTENTIONAL MECHANISMS IN DELAY OF GRATIFICATION. *JOURNAL OF PERSONALITY AND SOCIAL PSYCHOLOGY, 21,* 204–218. AVAILABLE FROM HTTPS://PAGES.UCSD.EDU/~NCHRISTENFELD/DOG_READINGS_FILES/CLASS%203%20-%20MISCHEL%201972.PDF.

PINTRICH, P. R. (2000). MULTIPLE GOALS, MULTIPLE PATHWAYS: THE ROLE OF GOAL ORIENTATION IN LEARNING AND ACHIEVEMENT. *JOURNAL OF EDUCATIONAL PSYCHOLOGY, 92,* 544–555.

SENKO, C., HULLEMAN, C. S., & HARACKIEWICZ, J. M. (2011). ACHIEVEMENT GOAL THEORY AT THE CROSSROADS: OLD CONTROVERSIES, CURRENT CHALLENGES, AND NEW DIRECTIONS. *EDUCATIONAL PSYCHOLOGIST,* 46(1), 26–47.

SODERSTROM, N. C., & BJORK, R. A. (2015). LEARNING VERSUS PERFORMANCE: AN INTEGRATIVE REVIEW. *PERSPECTIVES ON PSYCHOLOGICAL SCIENCE, 10,* 176–199. AVAILABLE FROM WWW.RESEARCHGATE.NET/PUBLICATION/275355435_LEARNING_VERSUS_PERFORMANCE_AN_INTEGRATIVE_REVIEW.

Suggested readings and links

SVINICKI, M. D. (2005). STUDENT GOAL ORIENTATION, MOTIVATION, AND LEARNING. *IDEA PAPER #41.* **MANHATTAN, KA: THE IDEA CENTER.**

AVAILABLE FROM WWW.DOE.IN.GOV/SITES/DEFAULT/FILES/CTE/NCTEB-STUDMOTIV.PDF.

GOAL ORIENTATION THEORIES. **IN THIS VIDEO PROFESSOR BRETT JONES SHOWS WHAT GOAL THEORY IS AND ITS IMPLICATIONS FOR EDUCATION.**

AVAILABLE FROM WWW.YOUTUBE.COM/WATCH?V=IONAS7_9Q34.

THE MARSHMALLOW TEST – THIS "TEST" (MISCHEL, EBBESEN, & RASKOFF ZEISS, 1972) WAS MEANT TO DETERMINE HOW YOUNG CHILDREN DEAL WITH FRUSTRATION AND DELAYING GRATIFICATION.

AVAILABLE FROM WWW.YOUTUBE.COM/WATCH?V=QX_OY9614HQ.

PART III

WHICH LEARNING ACTIVITIES SUPPORT LEARNING

Back in the dark ages of teaching, we thought of students as either blank slates or sponges. They know nothing when they begin and we offer them information that they can suck up like a sponge sucks up water. Languid and completely dependent on others, they merely respond to external stimuli without thinking.

Admittedly, sometimes this behaviourist approach works pretty well. Think of practising addition and multiplication tables by repeating them together with the rest of the class in first or second grade or repeatedly making maths sums through a computer program (i.e. drill-and-practice). This way you learn to automatise math skills without having to think about it too deeply, which makes more complex math tasks a lot easier.

But since the 1960s we know that in most cases students are neither blank slates nor sponges and that learning really requires thinking and focused learning activities. In this section we cover some of the ways that teachers can support learning activities that students must undertake to effectively, efficiently, and enjoyably learn. Topics covered include the role of scaffolding for learning, tutoring and other instructional techniques, effective problem-solving, and mathemagenic activities (those activities that give birth to learning).

12 WHY SCAFFOLDING IS NOT AS EASY AS IT LOOKS

SCAFFOLDING

12 WHY SCAFFOLDING IS NOT AS EASY AS IT LOOKS

PAPER "The role of tutoring in problem solving"[1]

QUOTE *"Well executed scaffolding begins by luring the child into actions that produce recognizable-for-him solutions. Once that is achieved, the tutor can interpret discrepancies to the child. Finally the tutor stands in a confirmatory role until the tutee is checked out to fly on his own".*

Why you should read this article

How do young meerkats learn to hunt and eat scorpions without being killed? More importantly, how do adult meerkats "teach" them? Well first the adults provide them with a dead scorpion with the stinger removed to allow them to begin the process. Next they bring them a dead scorpion with the stinger attached to take things up a notch and finally they bring them a live scorpion with all guns blazing to complete their training. This would seem that meerkats are expert teachers who can differentiate learning to suit the learner but actually it is thought that they are responding to pup calls and carrying out this task on instinct instead of complex thought.[2] What makes teaching a distinctly human affair is characterised by what Gergely and Csibra (2011, p. 1149) describe as "the cognitive mechanisms that enable the transmission of cultural knowledge *by communication* between individuals".

Intentional teaching versus instinctive teaching

At the time this paper was written, there was a belief that humans were really the only species who truly teach in an "intentional" way (Bruner, 1972; Hinde, 1971). The young meerkat may well be learning how to hunt scorpions but to what extent are they being purposefully *instructed* through communication? The authors of this paper, David Wood,

---

1 **WOOD, D., BRUNER, J., & ROSS, G.** (1976). THE ROLE OF TUTORING IN PROBLEM SOLVING. *JOURNAL OF CHILD PSYCHOLOGY AND CHILD PSYCHIATRY, 17,* 89–100.

2 WWW.YOUTUBE.COM/WATCH?TIME_CONTINUE=60&V=48RHTGTNXRI.

Jerome Bruner, and Gail Ross sought to explore how purposeful and communicative instruction happens between humans, specifically an adult and a group of 3, 4, and 5-year-olds as they try and solve a problem using wooden blocks.

Prior to the publishing of this article, problem-solving or skill acquisition activities were traditionally seen as lone activities, and social interaction was usually framed as modelling and imitation. However situations where there is a tutor or teacher involved (i.e. someone who is an expert and knows how to resolve a particular problem) involve a much more nuanced dynamic. The term given to this process by the authors was "scaffolding", and in doing so they created one of the most influential and commonly used terms in teacher training today. However as we shall see, the term covers a highly complex process requiring great skill and deftness from the teacher and, like the meerkat learning to hunt scorpions, it can very easily go wrong if not done properly.

SCAFFOLDING
Guided support given to learners which is systematically removed as they learn

Abstract of the article

The study examines the process of tutoring where an adult or expert assists someone who is not an adult or an expert. This is explored through a task where an adult tutor teaches children aged between 3 and 5 to build a model of something which is, at first, outside their range of ability. This tutorial process is somewhat different to a traditional one where the expert knows the answer and the tutor does not. We examine a 'natural' tutorial to further understanding regarding natural and automated teaching approaches. This study is not the testing of an hypothesis but rather a systematic description of how the children react to these different forms of assistance. The focus here is on problem-finding activities as opposed to problem-solving activities (Mackworth, 1965).

The article

This article focuses on a study in which the authors examined how 30 children aged 3, 4, and 5 responded to an adult teacher giving them assistance in a task where they had to fit together 21 blocks into a pyramid. The tasks were designed to be entertaining in order to engage the children but also challenging and within their capabilities. A central aim of the teacher was to allow the children to figure things out for themselves as much as possible, and to provide only verbal support initially and intervene only if necessary. The relative success or failure of the child would determine the actions of the teacher.

Provide support and intervene when necessary

As the children attempted to solve the problem, the teacher responded to three types of behaviour. First, if the child ignored the task and simply played with the blocks she would present constructed pairs of blocks to get them started. If the child had begun to construct but had overlooked a feature, the teacher would gently use a verbal cue to get them back on task. Lastly, if the child began to construct in the way modelled to them, the teacher would allow them to correct any errors that they encountered.

THE EXPERIMENTAL TASK

THE TASK was to build a pyramid of blocks that would fit together (see Figure 12.1). After 5 minutes of playfully experimenting with the blocks, the actual task began. Usually the teacher then showed the child how to connect two blocks, but, if they had already connected two blocks together, she picked them up as an example and asked the student to make more. If the student simply ignored the question, the teacher showed the connected blocks to them again. If the child had started with the blocks but forgotten something, the teacher drew attention to it verbally. Where possible, she let the student go ahead.

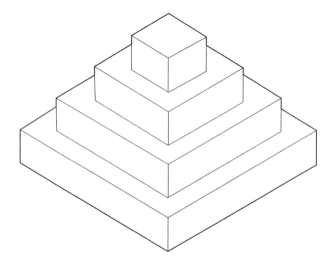

FIGURE 12.1
A REPRESENTATION OF THE BLOCK TASK OF WOOD ET AL.

As you might expect, the behaviour varied between the 3-, 4-, and 5-year-olds and each group had different needs. Interestingly, there was a difference in how effective the help offered was. For example, when teachers attempted to explain the solution to the 3-year-olds, it was only effective one out of every five times; however this method worked more than 50% of the time with 5-year-olds. Clearly, different age groups required different levels of assistance. For the 3-year-olds, the proportion of completely unassisted constructions was 64–65%, for the 4-year-olds it was 79.3%, and for the 5-year-olds it was 87.5%.

The researchers concluded that the role of the teacher with the 3-year-olds was mainly to keep them on task. It will come as no surprise to any parent that these children completely ignored the teacher's suggestions, despite the fact that they could recognise the beginning of an effective solution such as fitting two blocks together. With the 4-year-olds, there was more listening to the teacher, who was able to provide encouragement and correction as the task proceeded. The 5-year-olds were able to ask the teacher for support and check their solutions. Crucially, the authors claim that scaffolding "withers away" for the 5-year-old children and they speculate that for a 6-year-old, that support would be unnecessary.

From these observations, the authors define scaffolding as helping the child into actions that have a *recognisable-for-him* [sic] solution. In other words, the teacher is able to assist the child in recognising the journey they are about to take. As the authors state, *"comprehension of the solution must precede production*. That is to say, the learner must be able to recognise a solution to a particular class of problems before he is himself able to produce the steps leading to it without assistance" (p. 90). The important point here is that the child must understand the relationship between means and ends before they begin the task or as the authors neatly put it, "comprehension precedes production" (p. 94).

Another important element of this process is the way in which the teacher needs to keep two opposing things in mind at once. Not an easy task, but then teaching is a complex business. Problem-solving has a deep structure that is not always apparent until nearing the end of production and in providing effective scaffolding, the teacher needs to not only bear in mind the deep structure and correct solution but also the tutee's current conception of that deep structure and possible solution. Only then will a teacher be able to offer the right form of assistance. As the authors state, this means that, in effect, the teacher needs two theories to bear in mind during instruction.

UNDERSTANDING THE DESIRED OUTCOME IS KEY
Comprehension precedes production

TWO THEORIES
Instructor must keep in mind the deep structure and the current state

THE TWO THEORIES

Without both of these, he [sic] can neither generate feedback nor devise situations in which his feedback will be more appropriate for *this* tutee in *this* task at *this* point in task mastery. The actual pattern of effective instruction, then, will be both *task* and *tutee* dependent, the requirements of the tutorial being *generated* by the interaction of the tutor's two theories.

(p. 94)

Conclusions/implications of the work for educational practice

The key element of this article is the close definition of scaffolding, which the authors then systematically describe more precisely as having six different "functions":

1. *Recruitment*: The teacher must somehow elicit the problem solver's interest in the task and the kinds of skills needed to complete it.
2. *Reduction in degrees of freedom*: This essentially refers to the teacher simplifying the task to a much smaller number of possibilities so that the tutee is not overwhelmed. For the confused novice, the choice between a right step and an obviously wrong one is much easier than a wide array of different steps which they can't tell apart.
3. *Direction maintenance*: Keeping the tutee interested and focused on the task in hand is a vital part of scaffolding, especially when (s)he would experience success on a simpler part of the overall task such as pairing two blocks and want to keep doing that repeatedly as opposed to taking the next step.
4. *Marking critical features*: The teacher should mark out or emphasise key milestones in the development of the task. The key thing here is to make visible discrepancies between where the child is at the moment and where they need to go next.
5. *Frustration control*: Having empathy concerning the possible frustration of the child is a vital aspect of scaffolding and requires deft skill as there is a danger that if the teacher makes it too easy, then the child can develop too much dependency on the teacher.
6. *Demonstrating*: It is not enough to simply model solutions to a task, the effective teacher will perform an "idealization" of the task to be performed. This can be an execution of the problem to be solved by the child, who may have already partially executed the problem. By elaborately performing the task, the teacher allows the child to more easily imitate the steps required to solve the problem.

COMBINING SKILLS

WHEN SOLVING A PROBLEM, there is a hierarchical skills structure. Before you can take on a higher level of skills, you must first master the underlying skill. If we translate this into the block problem that Wood and his colleagues used, you could say that pupils first have to learn how to recognise blocks and learn how to connect them. Once they have mastered these two skills, they can combine them into the skill where they immediately take two matching blocks and connect them. It is therefore important that the lower order skills are achieved first.

How to use the work in your teaching

Scaffolding is a highly complex process requiring a wide range of skills from the instructor or teacher. To properly scaffold, the teacher needs to possess and show a range of emotional skills such as empathy and patience. (S)he also needs to know when and how to provide close support and also when and how to take it away. Finally, they need to be able to hold two mental models at once; their own mental model of the overall problem to be solved and crucially, the child's mental model to be solved. Leading the child to being able to see the discrepancies between where they are at in their own journey and the problem to be solved is the key skill required and not an easy thing to do. Rather like the delicate task of building a pyramid of blocks used in this study, if any part of the scaffolding is shaky, then the whole thing can come crashing down. Possibly the first thing to think about when introducing novel things to your students, of course after determining what the learning goal is, is to not make the lesson too long. Model and/or demonstrate what the student needs to do. We know that modelling, especially when you also verbalise what you're doing, including your thought processes (primarily for older students), is a very effective way of teaching something new. This is closely related to what is known as the *zone of proximal development* (Vygotsky, 1978). You then need to give your student sufficient time to practice constantly checking for understanding or skill, but – and here's the complication – don't let them flounder too long. At this point you need to give just-in-time and "level appropriate" assistance. Finally, remove the scaffolding when the learner is capable of doing it alone!

ZONE OF PROXIMAL DEVELOPMENT
Difference between what the learner can do without guidance and what they can do with it

Takeaways

- Pupils from different levels need different ways of guidance while solving a problem.
- Scaffolding is actually a form of differentiation.
- Students must first master a low-level skill before they can handle a skill of the next level.
- With scaffolding you offer the right support (i.e. support that is just above the level of the student; this helps you to reach a higher level for the student).
- The scaffolding must be reduced as the pupil can do it alone.
- It's crucial to not only understand the problem to be solved but also to be able to see the learners' conceptions of the problem to be solved and help them see the difference.

References

BRUNER, J. S. (1972). NATURE AND USES OF IMMATURITY. *AMERICAN PSYCHOLOGIST*, 27, 1–22.

CSIBRA, G., & GERGELY, G. (2011). NATURAL PEDAGOGY AS EVOLUTIONARY ADAPTATION. *PHILOSOPHICAL TRANSACTIONS OF THE ROYAL SOCIETY OF LONDON. SERIES B, BIOLOGICAL SCIENCES*, 366(1567), 1149–1157. AVAILABLE FROM WWW.RESEARCHGATE.NET/ PUBLICATION/50226360_NATURAL_PEDAGOGY_AS_EVOLUTIONARY_ADAPTATION.

HINDE, R. A. (1971). DEVELOPMENT OF SOCIAL BEHAVIOUR. IN A. M. SCHRIER AND F. STOLLNITZ (EDS.) *BEHAVIOR OF NON-HUMAN PRIMATES*, (VOL. 3, PP. 1–60). NEW YORK, NY: ACADEMIC PRESS.

MACKWORTH, N. H. (1965). ORIGINALITY. *AMERICAN PSYCHOLOGIST*, 20(1), 51–66.

VYGOTSKY, L. S. (1978). *MIND IN SOCIETY: THE DEVELOPMENT OF HIGHER PSYCHOLOGICAL PROCESSES*. CAMBRIDGE, MA: HARVARD UNIVERSITY PRESS.

WOOD, D., BRUNER, J., & ROSS, G. (1976). THE ROLE OF TUTORING IN PROBLEM SOLVING. *JOURNAL OF CHILD PSYCHOLOGY AND CHILD PSYCHIATRY*, 17, 89–100. AVAILABLE FROM WWW.RESEARCHGATE.NET/PUBLICATION/228039919_THE_ROLE_OF_TUTORING_IN_PROBLEM_SOLVING.

Suggested readings and links

SAUGSTAD, P., & RAAHEIM, K. (1960). PROBLEM-SOLVING, PAST EXPERIENCE AND

AVAILABILITY OF FUNCTIONS. *BRITISH JOURNAL OF PSYCHOLOGY*, 51, 97–104.

FISHER, D., & FREY, N. (2010). SCAFFOLDS FOR LEARNING: THE KEY TO GUIDED INSTRUCTION. IN *GUIDED INSTRUCTION: HOW TO DEVELOP CONFIDENT AND SUCCESSFUL LEARNERS, CHAPTER 1.* **ALEXANDRIA, VA: ASCD.**

AVAILABLE FROM HTTP://WWW.ASCD.ORG/PUBLICATIONS/ BOOKS/111,017/CHAPTERS/SCAFFOLDS-FOR-LEARNING@-THE-KEY-TO-GUIDED-INSTRUCTION.ASPX

MULVAHILL, E. (AUGUST 31, 2018). 10 WAYS TO SCAFFOLD LEARNING RUNG BY RUNG (BLOG).

AVAILABLE FROM
WWW.WEARETEACHERS.COM/WAYS-TO-SCAFFOLD-LEARNING/.

THE ROOM 241 TEAM (OCTOBER 2, 2012). FOR TEACHERS: SIMPLE TIPS TO UTILIZE SCAFFOLDING IN EDUCATION.

AVAILABLE FROM HTTPS://EDUCATION. CU-PORTLAND.EDU/BLOG/CLASSROOM-RESOURCES/ SCAFFOLDING-IN-EDUCATION-AND-HOW-YOU-CAN-UTILIZE-IT/.

A VIDEO ABOUT SCAFFOLDING CHILDREN'S LEARNING IS

AVAILABLE FROM WWW.YOUTUBE.COM/WATCH?V=5HWDBSX_KDO.

JEROME BRUNER – HOW DOES TEACHING INFLUENCE LEARNING?

JEROME S. BRUNER, HAD JUST TURNED 99 LESS THAN A WEEK BEFORE THIS VIDEO WAS FILMED.

AVAILABLE FROM WWW.YOUTUBE.COM/WATCH?V=ALJVAUXQHDS.

13 THE HOLY GRAIL

ONE-TO-ONE TUTORING

13 THE HOLY GRAIL
Whole class teaching and one-to-one tutoring

PAPER   "The 2 sigma problem: The search for methods of group instruction as effective as one-to-one tutoring"[1]

QUOTE   *"The tutoring process demonstrates that most of the students do have the potential to reach this high level of learning. I believe an important task of research and instruction is to seek ways of accomplishing this under more practical and realistic conditions than the one-to-one tutoring, which is too costly for most societies to bear on a large scale. This is the '2 sigma' problem" (p. 4).*

Why you should read this article

What is the optimum strategy for batting in baseball? If a home run gives the greatest reward, why wouldn't a player try to hit a home run every time? Well the conditions which allow for a player to hit a home run are relatively rare and run a high risk of punishment if not executed exactly right. Attempting to swing for the fences every time can mean a player is struck out more often than not, and so the regular strategy is to vary one's game, incorporating a range of techniques that when performed alone might not deliver major results, but when used in combination, can add up to something far greater than the individual sum of its parts.

One-to-one (1:1) tutoring is the teaching equivalent of a home run. As this article shows, it delivers far superior results than conventional teaching (the average tutored student's performance is above 98% of pupils in a conventional class), however it's a costly enterprise and so it's rare that the average student gets to be tutored individually. For the most part, students are taught in classes averaging 25–30, and so the puzzle that Benjamin Bloom poses is: given that we cannot teach every pupil individually, which teaching methods will work *in combination* to provide

1   **BLOOM, B.** (1984). THE 2 SIGMA PROBLEM: THE SEARCH FOR METHODS OF GROUP INSTRUCTION AS EFFECTIVE AS ONE-TO-ONE TUTORING. *EDUCATIONAL RESEARCHER, 13*(6), 4–16.

2 SIGMA
Two standard
deviations

the same results of individual tutoring? Bloom refers to this conundrum as the "2 sigma problem" and as we shall see, it's a problem with no clear solution.

Abstract of the article (abridged from introduction)

Two University of Chicago doctoral students in education, Anania (1982, 1983) and Burke (1984), completed dissertations in which they compared student learning under the following three conditions of instruction: 1. conventional. 2. mastery learning. 3. tutoring. [.] the most striking of the findings is that under the best learning conditions we can devise (tutoring), the average student is 2 sigma above the average control student taught under conventional group methods of instruction. The tutoring process demonstrates that most of the students do have the potential to reach this high level of learning. I believe an important task of research and instruction is to seek ways of accomplishing this under more practical and realistic conditions than the one-to-one tutoring, which is too costly for most societies to bear on a large scale. This is the "2 sigma" problem. Can researchers and teachers devise teaching–learning conditions that will enable the majority of students under group instruction to attain levels of achievement that can at present be reached only under good tutoring conditions?

The article

This article focuses on a study done by two doctoral students in which they compared student learning under three conditions:

1. *Conventional*. Students learn from a teacher in a regular class dynamic of around 30 students where tests are given periodically.

MASTERY
LEARNING
Pupils achieve
prerequisite level
before moving onto
new content

2. *Mastery learning*. Students in the same class size are given the same instruction and the same formative tests but are also given corrective procedures and parallel tests to indicate how well the students have mastered the subject matter.

3. *Tutoring*. Students learn from a teacher alone or in maximum groups of two or three. They are given the same formative tests but with the mastery format outlined above.

Students were randomly assigned to one of the three conditions and the same amount of instruction was given to all three groups apart from the corrective work in the latter two groups. The study occurred over 11 periods of instruction over a three-week period.

As one might expect, there were notable differences in final achievement between the groups. The average student in the tutored group performed a lot better – about two standard deviations (2 sigma) above the control (conventional) group. The average student in the mastery learning group was about one standard deviation above the average of the control class.

WHAT ARE STANDARD DEVIATION AND EFFECT SIZE?

STANDARD
DEVIATION
How measurements
are spread out

STANDARD DEVIATION (*sd* or σ – the Greek letter sigma) is a number used to represent how measurements are spread out in relation to an average of a group or population. This can be heights, weights, achievement in school, etc. For IQ, for example, the population average is 100 and the standard deviation is 15. This means that an IQ of 85 or 115 differs 1 σ from the population and an IQ of 70 or 130 differs 2 σ. Also, 68.2% of the population falls within 1 σ of the average (thus between an IQ of 85 and 115) and 95.6% of the population within 2 σ (between 70 and 130; see Figure 13.1).

EFFECT SIZE
Size of the difference
between two
teaching approaches

Effect size (d) is a measurement used to express the size of a particular effect, for example to quantify the size of the difference between two different teaching approaches. In general we speak of a small (*d* = 0.2), medium (*d* = 0.4), or large (*d* = 0.6) effect size. John Hattie defined d = 0.4 as the hinge point because in his studies he found that this effect size is approximately what one will see if we do nothing special but just measure achievement gains after one year of school (i.e. pure maturation[2]). That means if an intervention doesn't exceed this 0.4 you could have just as well done nothing and let the child age, and if it's less than 0.4, then it actually hindered learning.

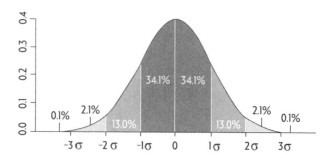

FIGURE 13.1
STANDARD
DEVIATION

---

2   THIS IS ESPECIALLY THE CASE IN CHILDREN.

What is particularly striking is that the average tutored student score was above 98% of the students in the control class, meaning that the vast majority of students in this study have the capability to achieve a high level of learning under the right conditions (see Figure 13.3). The question then posted by the Bloom is: Can we develop a way of achieving the same kind of results from the tutoring conditions under *group* teaching conditions? Bloom refers to this dilemma as the "2 sigma problem".

FIGURE 13.2
ACHIEVEMENT DISTRIBUTION FOR STUDENTS UNDER CONVENTIONAL, MASTERY LEARNING, AND TUTORIAL INSTRUCTION (FROM BLOOM, 1984)

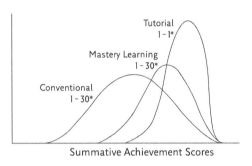

The elephant in the room here of course is the fact that modern societies can't afford to have 1:1 tutors for every single student. However, Bloom sensationally claims that if research on the 2 sigma problem can yield practical methods that the average teacher can learn in a short period of time with little more spending than there is on conventional approaches, then it would be "an educational contribution of the greatest magnitude". In a very real sense, Bloom is searching for the holy grail of education, so what does he suggest might be these practical methods?

ALTERABLE AND STATIC VARIABLES
Things you can change and things you can't

Well Bloom makes a distinction between things you *can* change, which he calls "alterable variables", and things you probably *can't* change, which he terms "stable" or "static variables". Alterable variables are things like the quality of teaching, use of time, formative testing, rate of learning, and home environment (see Table 13.1). Stable variables are elements such as the personality of the teachers, measures of intelligence (though this is highly debatable!), the formal tests to be sat, and the socioeconomic status of families. However not all of these variables are equal. With the help of various meta-analyses, Bloom created a table of alterable variables, with 1:1 tutoring at the top with an effect size of 2 and things like cooperative learning lower down with an effect size of 0.8.

SYNERGISTIC EFFECT
Cumulative interaction of two or more elements

His central claim is that there is a synergistic effect in the combination of these alterable variables put together. In other words, the right mix of things that you *can* do something about could have a dramatic impact on student learning. Put even more simply, though 1 + 1 usually equals 2, in this case it 1 + 1 might equal more than 2. The combination of two or more elements produces an effect greater than their individual components.

		Effect size	Percentile equivalent
	D Tutorial instruction	2.00	98
	D Reinforcement	1.20	
	A Feedback-corrective (ML)	1.00	84
	D Cues and explanations	1.00	
(A)	D Student classroom participation	1.00	
	A Student time on task	1.00[b]	
	A Improved reading/study skill	1.00	
	C Cooperative learning	.80	79
	H Homework (graded)	.80	
	D Classroom morale	.60	73
	A Initial cognitive prerequisites	.60	
	H Home environment intervention	.50[b]	69
	D Peer & cross-age remedial tutoring	.40	66
	D Homework (assigned)	.30	62
	D Higher order questions	.30	
(D)	B New science & math curricula	.30[b]	
	D Teacher expectancy	.3	
	C Peer group influence	.20	58
	B Advance organisers	.20	
	Socio-economic status (for contrast)	.25	60

TABLE 13.1
THE EFFECTS OF SELECTED ALTERABLE VARIABLES ON STUDENT ACHIEVEMENT FROM BLOOM (1984) ADAPTED FROM WALBERG (1984)

NOTE

This table was adapted from Walberg (1984) by Bloom.
[a]Object of change process:
A: Learner | B: Instructional material/ C: Home environment or peer group | D: Teacher
[b]Averaged or estimated from correlational data or from several effect sizes

So what is it about whole class instruction that makes it so inferior to 1:1 tutoring? Well for a start, Bloom suggests that many teachers are only getting feedback on what students are learning from a small sample of high achievers in the class, usually the ones who raise their hands. This can be contrasted with 1:1 tutoring where at every point, the learning is checked and more explanation and clarification given if needed. To address this, he advises strategies that are fairly commonplace today such as getting feedback from a random sample of students in the lesson (often referred to as a "hands down policy" or "cold calling") but at the time these ideas would have been novel to many teachers. His main idea here was not to change the methods of teachers but rather to encourage them to teach to a cross-section of the class as opposed to the ones who are naturally more involved.

So what is the magic recipe? What things should be combined to achieve an effect as powerful as 1:1 tutoring? One thing Bloom is certain about is that one of them should be mastery learning, or what he terms the "feedback-corrective" process. Mastery learning is an instructional approach where students are tested on material learned and if they get less than 90% in a test then they are given additional instruction on that material until they get over 90% or until they have "mastered" the content. In Figure 13.3, the variables are classified as A (the learner), B (the instructional material), C (the home environment), and D (the teacher and teaching process). Interestingly, Bloom speculates that two variables from different categories used together may be additive whereas two variables from the same categories might not be as effective. Variety is the spice of learning it seems.

"FEEDBACK-CORRECTIVE" PROCESS
Tutor identifies errors and provides explanation and clarification

Conclusions/implications of the work for educational practice

Essentially, Bloom is asking how we can teach whole groups of children in a way that essentially might be as effective as 1:1 tutoring. His solution to this is, first, that you need to combine a variety of different approaches, but not all approaches are equal. Although he advocates a variety of different techniques (some of which are vague discussions around critical thinking and student engagement), one firm suggestion is mastery learning as one of the methods to definitely be included. He then later suggests a method called cue-participation-reinforcement (Nordin, 1979, 1980); an approach which seeks to provide better guidance to teachers on more effective cues (explanations) and to generate greater student engagement. The combination of these two approaches, Bloom suggests, might lead to an effect size of 1.7 on the higher mental processes (Tenenbaum, 1982). Although this is still short of solving the 2 sigma problem, it does at least come close.

CUE-PARTICIPATION-REINFORCEMENT
Behaviourist model of teaching to which Bloom added corrective feedback

The key idea in this article is that there are things that we can do something about in instruction and things we can do nothing about and that we should not only focus on the things we can do something about, but also focus on the two or three most effective things and do them together. Broadly speaking, Bloom is advocating for a more personalised form of learning where individualised instruction is tailored to the needs of individual students based on performance (which is the dynamic which makes 1:1 tutoring so effective) however the problem of opportunity cost still remains. Although mastery learning is possible with whole class conventional teaching, it's still time-intensive to have to go over material at different rates for different pupils. This is why Bloom's 2 sigma problem is cited as a guiding principle for the use of technology in personalised instruction. Despite the promises of Silicon Valley however, it's a riddle that hasn't been solved yet and so the search for the holy grail continues.

How to use the work in your teaching

As well as a discussion on instructional methods, this article also discusses the nature of instructional materials used, for example the use of more sophisticated textbooks that take into account the sequential nature of topics and how they allow for schemata to be built. Also discussed are pre-organisers or advance organisers (see Chapter 6, What you know determines what you learn). The use of these materials has an effect size of 0.2, which is not likely to add much to solving the 2 sigma problem, however Bloom claims that it is likely that

> a combination of advance organizers at the beginning of a new topic, further organizational aids during the chapter or unit, as well as appropriate questions, summaries, or other organizational aids at the end of the unit may have a substantial effect on the student's learning of that chapter (p. 9)

Put simply, introducing knowledge organisers at the *beginning* of a topic of study is likely to be very beneficial for learning, not just as a revision resource at the end.

Another alternative variable discussed is the home environment. Attention is paid to a number of studies which look at ways of fostering greater parental engagement. One study found that groups of parents meeting a parent educator for two hours, twice a month over a period of six months had a strong impact on student learning and effected significant changes in the home environment, although it is conceded that this approach is probably not very cost-effective. Bloom speculates that because mastery learning takes place in the school and parent support occurs in the home environment, that these two approaches work in a sort of "pincer movement" and represent a strong solution to the 2 sigma problem, particularly if started early.

Parental engagement can greatly enhance attainment

Interestingly, when the student learning in a regular class setting is compared to tutoring it is noted that approximately 20% of the students do equally as well as the tutored students. That is to say that these students would not do any better than if they had been individually tutored. However, another way of looking at that is that 80% of students in a regular classroom don't do as well as students who have been tutored 1:1. Bloom accounts for this by claiming that teachers treat students unequally in most classroom settings, with some students

Teachers can tend to focus on a limited number of students

getting encouragement and praise while others are largely ignored. The results in the teacher getting feedback from a relatively small number of students and so is missing out on the kind of specific and actionable feedback and direction that one would get in an individual situation. The key thing here is to get feedback on the whole class learning from a random sample of students in the lesson rather than from confident individuals who give the impression everyone understands the material.

Ultimately, to solve the 2 sigma problem and deliver results that are as close to possible to 1:1 tutoring, teachers should use mastery learning approaches in combination with more active student participation so that teaching can be more responsive to all students, not just a minority. For Bloom, there is clearly a law of diminishing returns in whole class instruction and he offers no hard and fast rules for solving the problem but invites educators to pick up the challenge, a challenge still being wrestled with today.

Takeaways

- Most students can achieve high results given the right instructional approach.
- By combining different instructional techniques in different ways we might be able to enormously increase learning.
- When using knowledge organisers, *when* you use them is as important as *how* you use them.
- Parental involvement such as meeting the teacher or instructor twice a month could have a big impact.
- Instead of taking feedback from the same students, ask a random sample.
- Mastery learning is one part of the solution to the 2 sigma riddle and can achieve significant results.

References

ANANIA, J. (1982). THE EFFECTS OF QUALITY OF INSTRUCTION ON THE COGNITIVE AND AFFECTIVE LEARNING OF STUDENTS. (DOCTORAL DISSERTATION, UNIVERSITY OF CHICAGO, 1981). *DISSERTATION ABSTRACTS INTERNATIONAL, 42,* 4269A.

ANANIA, J. (1983). THE INFLUENCE OF IN-STRUCTIONAL CONDITIONS ON STUDENT LEARNING AND ACHIEVEMENT. *EVALUATION IN EDUCATION: AN INTERNATIONAL REVIEW SERIES, 7*(1), 1–92.

BLOOM, B. (1984). THE 2 SIGMA PROBLEM: THE SEARCH FOR METHODS OF GROUP INSTRUCTION AS EFFECTIVE AS ONE-TO-ONE TUTORING. *EDUCATIONAL RESEARCHER, 13*(6), 4–16. AVAILABLE FROM WEB.MIT.EDU/5.95/WWW/READINGS/BLOOM-TWO-SIGMA.PDF.

BURKE, A.J. (1984). STUDENTS' POTENTIAL FOR LEARNING CONTRASTED UNDER TUTORIAL AND GROUP APPROACHES TO INSTRUCTION. (DOCTORAL DISSERTATION, UNIVERSITY OF CHICAGO, 1983). *DISSERTATION ABSTRACTS INTERNATIONAL, 44,* 2025A.

NORDIN, A. B. (1979). *THE EFFECTS OF DIFFERENT QUALITIES OF INSTRUCTION ON SELECTED COGNITIVE, AFFECTIVE, AND TIME VARIABLES.* UNPUBLISHED DOCTORAL DISSERTATION, UNIVERSITY OF CHICAGO.

NORDIN, A. B. (1980). IMPROVING LEARNING: AN EXPERIMENT IN RURAL PRIMARY SCHOOLS IN MALAYSIA. *EVALUATION IN EDUCATION: AN INTERNATIONAL REVIEW SERIES, 4,* 143–263.

TENENBAUM, G. (1982). *A METHOD OF GROUP INSTRUCTION WHICH IS AS EFFECTIVE AS ONE-TO-ONE TUTORIAL INSTRUCTION.* UNPUBLISHED DOCTORAL DISSERTATION, UNIVERSITY OF CHICAGO.

WALBERG, H. J. (1984). IMPROVING THE PRODUCTIVITY OF AMERICA'S SCHOOLS. *EDUCATIONAL LEADERSHIP,* 41(8), 19–27.

Suggested readings and links

ANDERSON, S. A. (1994). *SYNTHESIS OF RESEARCH ON MASTERY LEARNING.* **US DEPARTMENT OF EDUCATION, OFFICE OF EDUCATION, RESEARCH AND IMPROVEMENT, EDUCATIONAL RESOURCES INFORMATION CENTER (ERIC).**

AVAILABLE FROM HTTPS://FILES.ERIC.ED.GOV/FULLTEXT/ED382567.PDF.

AUSUBEL, D. (1960). THE USE OF ADVANCE ORGANIZERS IN THE LEARNING AND RETENTION OF MEANINGFUL VERBAL MATERIAL. *JOURNAL OF EDUCATIONAL PSYCHOLOGY,* 51, 267–272.

BLOOM, B. S. (MARCH 1968). LEARNING FOR MASTERY. *UCLA – CSEIP – EVALUATION COMMENT,* 1(2), 1–11.

AVAILABLE FROM HTTP://PROGRAMS.HONOLULU.HAWAII.EDU/INTRANET/ SITES/PROGRAMS.HONOLULU.HAWAII.EDU.INTRANET/FILES/UPSTF-STUDENT-SUCCESS-BLOOM-1968.PDF

VYGOTSKY, L. S. (1978). INTERACTION BETWEEN LEARNING AND DEVELOPMENT. IN M. COLE, V. JOHN-STEINER, S. SCRIBNER, & E. SOUBERMAN (EDS.), *MIND IN SOCIETY: THE DEVELOPMENT OF HIGHER PSYCHOLOGICAL PROCESSES* **(PP. 79–91). CAMBRIDGE, MA: HARVARD UNIVERSITY PRESS.**

AVAILABLE FROM WWW.FACULTY.MUN.CA/CMATTATALL/VYGOTSKY_1978. PDF.

SPOTLIGHTING THE BENJAMIN BLOOM TWO-SIGMA "PROBLEM", AS A STEP TOWARDS EDUCATIONAL REFORMATION TOWARDS WIDESPREAD MASTERY-BASED LEARNING.

AVAILABLE FROM HTTP://KAIROSFOCUS.BLOGSPOT.COM/2012/08/ CAPACITY-FOCUS-55A-SPOTLIGHTING.HTML.

ADDRESSING THE "2 SIGMA PROBLEM": A REVIEW OF BILL FERSTER'S TEACHING MACHINES.

AVAILABLE FROM HTTPS://JITP.COMMONS.GC.CUNY.EDU/ADDRESSING-THE-2-SIGMA-PROBLEM-A-REVIEW-OF-BILL-FERSTERS-TEACHING-MACHINES/.

STANDARD DEVIATION – EXPLAINED AND VISUALIZED.

AVAILABLE FROM WWW.YOUTUBE.COM/WATCH?V=MRQTXL2WX2M.

MASTERY LEARNING.

AVAILABLE FROM WWW.YOUTUBE.COM/WATCH?V=GWA48XRNLH0.

14 PROBLEM-SOLVING

PROBLEM-SOLVING

14 PROBLEM-SOLVING
How to find a needle in a haystack

PAPER   "Human problem solving"[1]

QUOTE   *"Problem solving was regarded by many, at that time, as a mystical, almost magical, human activity — as though the preservation of human dignity depended on man's remaining inscrutable to himself, on the magic-making processes remaining unexplained".*

Why you should read this article

Back in the 1980s, every kid in my neighbourhood had a Rubik's cube. I can remember often picking one up and having several attempts at various solutions but I don't remember ever solving it. The challenge was both simple and complex: twist the cube until every face had nine panels of the same colour. Sounds straightforward until you learn that the cube had 3 billion combinations but only one solution as a 1980s TV commercial claimed.[2] How then could a child (or adult for that matter) solve such a problem with seemingly impossible odds?

As popular as the cube itself were the guides on how to solve it. In 1981, three of the top ten best-selling books in the US were books on how to solve the Rubik's cube (Singmaster, 1994). The solution cannot be found randomly and requires two key elements: first knowing *where* to start and second knowing *what* to do. A decade before, Newell and Simon came up with their theory of how people solve problems, using computer simulated problems which began to lift the lid on the mystical nature of problems like the Rubik's cube. They posited that people have "problem spaces", an internalised representation of the problem that looks very different than the external representation of the problem. What is so important about their work is that they managed to shine a light on those inner processes and demystify a lot of the "magic" of problem-solving.

PROBLEM SPACE
Internal
conceptualisation of
a problem

1   **NEWELL, A., & SIMON, H. A.** (1972). *HUMAN PROBLEM SOLVING.* ENGLEWOOD CLIFFS. NJ: PRENTICE-HALL.
2   TELEVISIONARCHIVES (OCTOBER 23, 2008). *RUBIK'S CUBE COMMERCIAL 1981.* RETRIEVED APRIL 10, 2019 – VIA YOUTUBE.

Abstract of the article (abridged)

Instead of tracing history here, we should like to give a brief account of the product of the history, of the theory of human problem-solving that has emerged from the research. The theory makes reference to an information-processing system, the problem solver, confronted by a task. The task is defined objectively (or from the viewpoint of an experimenter, if you prefer) in terms of a task environment. It is defined by the problem solver, for purposes of attacking it, in terms of a problem space. The shape of the theory can be captured by four propositions (Newell & Simon, 1972):

1. A few, and only a few, gross characteristics of the human information-processing system are invariant over task and problem solver.
2. These characteristics are sufficient to determine that a task environment is represented (in the information-processing system) as a problem space, and that problem-solving takes place in a problem space.
3. The structure of the task environment determines the possible structures of the problem space.
4. The structure of the problem space determines the possible programs that can be used for problem-solving.

These are the bones of the theory.

Problem solver is an information processing system

The article

Until relatively recently, the process of human problem-solving was largely a mystery. Behaviourists contended that problem-solving was reproductive in nature; in other words, people will *reproduce* something which worked before to solve a problem. Gestalt psychologists saw problem-solving in a very different way. For them the process is characterised by individuals reconstituting or shifting around elements of the problem mentally until they have a "Eureka!" moment where they suddenly "get it". However, in the early 1970s, Allen Newell and Herbert Simon explored the nature of problem-solving using computer programmes (simulations) and found that humans solve problems in somewhat surprising ways.

GESTALT PSYCHOLOGY Holistic view of behaviour and the mind

A central idea in their work is the idea of "problem spaces". When encountering a problem to be solved, humans will represent this as a range of different solutions to be searched in internal memory (i.e. their long-term memory). This is distinct from the task environment, which is the way the problem looks externally. Essentially, when encountering a problem, we will represent the present state, the goal state, and a range of possibilities in between. However, problem spaces can be very large and searching through an index of possible problem solutions can be near impossible.

Consider the Hanoi Tower problem (Figure 14.1) where there are a number of circular blocks and three pegs and the aim is to move all the blocks to the right peg in their current order but only moving one block at a time, and the final kick in the teeth; you cannot put a bigger block on top of a smaller one. If there are four blocks, most humans can eventually solve this problem through trial and error. However if there are five or more blocks, the problem space contains a range of variables that are simply too large to search through, unless you have the right heuristic or "key" to use.

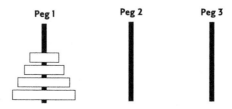

FIGURE 14.1
THE TOWER OF
HANOI PROBLEM[3]

However, a key element of success in solving this problem is not searching the entire problem space, but rather searching within a smaller, pre-defined area that is much more manageable and likely to produce a solution. In other words, knowing *where* to look is as important as *what* to look for. As Newell and Simon put it, "We need not be concerned with how large the haystack is, if we can identify a small part of it in which we are quite sure to find a needle" (p. 151).

Within these so-called knowledge spaces there are differing sources of information and structure. "Structure" as defined by Newell and Simon is the opposite of randomness. The presence or absence of random structures determine whether an individual will blindly search for an answer, trying every possible eventuality, or whether they search for a solution in a systematic way. The key difference here in terms of success is the ability to predict which areas to look at so you can search selectively rather than randomly.

Structure is the opposite of randomness

Each knowledge state or "step" is defined as a node; for example having three blocks on the left peg is the starting node for the Hanoi Tower problem. The action one can take to reach the next node is defined as the "operator". So essentially there are two options available to the problem solver: *where* to begin solving the problem (node) and *how* to solve it (operator). A common method of achieving this is through means–end analysis.

An important point made by the authors is to do with representation and language. If we accept that a problem has both an internal representation and an external one, and that the human problem

---

3   WWW.MATHCS.EMORY.EDU/~CHEUNG/COURSES/170/SYLLABUS/13/HANOI.HTML (ACCESSED APRIL 11, 2019).

A problem solver
must encode and
decode a problem

solver needs information in the form of text or images to encode and decode the problem, then a problem arises when trying to evaluate that translation process. In other words, it's very difficult to know the exact internal process of problem-solving, or as the authors put it: "It is a little like building a program to translate from English to Language X, where no one will tell us anything about Language X" (p. 157). The authors contend that this translation process or "Language X" will eventually be researched and explained.

Conclusions/implications of the work for educational practice

A key ability to solve problems is a heightened search ability that is largely determined by the presence or absence of knowledge – if you don't know what you're looking for, then how do you know what to look for and how do you know when you find it? As the authors point out, A. D. de Groot (1965) made an interesting observation of choice in chess players where the tree of move sequences did not look like a "bushy growth" but rather a "bundle of spindly explorations". After exploring each possibility, expert players would return to the base position to evaluate further possibilities for exploration, a process de Groot referred to as "progressive deepening". This method is intrinsically human in nature and accounted for by the limitations of working memory. This is an important difference between human problem-solving and computer programmes which have a near infinite search functionality of different permutations. Taking into account the limitations of working memory (see Chapter 2, Take a load off me) it's clear that having a strong mental representation of a problem to be solved is useful for students and rather like the best-selling guides on how to solve the Rubik's cube, this means an expert giving explicit guidance to a novice. Encouraging students to "discover" a solution to the Rubik's cube might be fun for 10 minutes but will not allow them to solve it (unless they have 30,000 hours to randomly stumble across it). Similarly, having students work in groups to find a solution will be just as useless unless one of them has an internalised "problem space" with the solution.

PROGRESSIVE
DEEPENING
When chess masters
work out a series
of moves and
possibilities internally

How to use the work in your teaching

When showing students how to solve a particular problem, it's vital that they have the opportunity to independently solve that problem to put into practice what they have learned. This approach is often criticised as a "drill and kill" approach which can demotivate students but as Simon would later point out, this view is not supported by evidence:

The importance of
practice

"DRILL AND KILL"?

[THE] CRITICISM OF PRACTICE (called "drill and kill", as if this phrase constituted empirical evaluation) is prominent in constructivist writings. Nothing flies more in the face of the last 20 years of research than the assertion that practice is bad. All evidence, from the laboratory and from extensive case studies of professionals, indicates that real competence only comes with extensive practice (e.g. Hayes, 1985; Ericsson, Krampe, & Tesche-Romer, 1993). In denying the critical role of practice one is denying children the very thing they need to achieve real competence. The instructional task is not to "kill" motivation by demanding drill, but to find tasks that provide practice while at the same time sustaining interest.

(Anderson, Reder, & Simon, 1999, p. 21)

A good example of this is the multiplication times tables. By committing these to memory from a young age, students can free up their cognitive bandwidth to creatively attack problems and find solutions. Furthermore, by using worked examples (see Chapter 17, Why discovery learning is a bad way to discover things) of how to solve particular problems and giving them plenty of time to practice them, instructors can endow students with internalised problem spaces that are invaluable when encountering new problems with similar underlying structures.

In addition, it is hugely important that students are searching for solutions selectively rather than randomly. In this sense, the teacher needs to monitor whether or not students have the right amount of knowledge to begin creatively exploring a problem. If their internal problem space is not sufficient, then they will be merely guessing; in other words, making sure that learners have the prerequisite prior knowledge (see Chapter 6, What you know determines what you see). This might work for a simple problem with limited combinations but is useless for more complex problems. Modelling to students (see Chapter 24, Making things visible) where to start working on a problem is hugely important – asking students to find the proverbial needle in a haystack would be cruel, but narrowing *where* to begin and then a range of possible actions allows them a way to be successful and become more motivated in the future. An expert can see where they have taken a wrong turn, a novice can't; so when teaching someone such experiments in chemistry or physics, it's helpful to signpost the path for students so if they become lost, they can return to a particular node and start again from there.

Takeaways

- Problems to be solved are represented differently in our internal world than they look in the external world.
- Knowing *where* to start with a problem can be as important as knowing *how* to solve it.
- Having mental models of similar problems can help problem-solving. The teacher is the person best suited to model it.
- You can help novices by breaking down larger problems into smaller steps.
- Students are successful when they can search problem spaces *selectively* rather than *randomly*.

References

ANDERSON, J. R., REDER, L. M., & SIMON, H. A. (1999). APPLICATIONS AND MISAPPLICATIONS OF COGNITIVE PSYCHOLOGY TO MATHEMATICS EDUCATION. *TEXAS EDUCATION REVIEW, 1*, 29–49.

DE GROOT, A. D. (1965). *THOUGHT AND CHOICE IN CHESS* (2ND ED.). THE HAGUE AND THE NETHERLANDS: MOUTON PUBLISHERS.

ERICCSON, K. A., KRAMPE, R. T., & TESCHE-ROMER, C. (1993). THE ROLE OF DELIBERATE PRACTICE IN THE ACQUISITION OF EXPERT PERFORMANCE. *PSYCHOLOGICAL REVIEW, 100*, 363–406.

HAYES, J. R. (1985). THE PROBLEMS IN TEACHING GENERAL SKILLS. IN J. SEGAL, S. CHIPMAN, & R. GLASER (EDS.), *THINKING AND LEARNING, VOL. 2*. HILLSDALE, NJ: ERLBAUM.

NEWELL, A., & SIMON, H. A. (1972). *HUMAN PROBLEM SOLVING*. ENGLEWOOD CLIFFS, NJ: PRENTICE-HALL.

SINGMASTER, D. (1994). THE UTILITY OF RECREATIONAL MATHEMATICS. IN R. K. GUY AND R. E. WOODROW (EDS.), *THE LIGHTER SIDE OF MATHEMATICS: PROCEEDINGS OF THE EUGÈNE STRENS MEMORIAL CONFERENCE ON RECREATIONAL MATHEMATICS AND ITS HISTORY*. CAMBRIDGE, MA: CAMBRIDGE UNIVERSITY PRESS.

TELEVISION ARCHIVES. (OCTOBER 23, 2008). *RUBIK'S CUBE COMMERCIAL 1981*. RETRIEVED APRIL 10, 2019 – VIA YOUTUBE.

Suggested readings and links

ANDERSON, J. R. (1993). PROBLEM SOLVING AND LEARNING. *AMERICAN PSYCHOLOGIST, 48*(1), 35–44.

A GOOD INTRODUCTION TO PROBLEM-SOLVING WITH USEFUL EXAMPLES IS

AVAILABLE FROM HTTP://PSYCHOLOGICALRESOURCES.BLOGSPOT.COM/2011/01/PROBLEM-SOLVING.HTML.

A BRIEF OVERVIEW OF NEWELL AND SIMON'S GPS (GENERAL PROBLEM-SOLVER) PROGRAMME IS

AVAILABLE FROM WWW.INSTRUCTIONALDESIGN.ORG/THEORIES/GENERAL-PROBLEM-SOLVER/.

AN INTERACTIVE VERSION OF THE HANOI TOWER PROBLEM IS

AVAILABLE FROM WWW.MATHSISFUN.COM/GAMES/TOWEROFHANOI.HTML.

15 ACTIVITIES THAT GIVE BIRTH TO LEARNING

MATHEMAGENIC ACTIVITIES

15 ACTIVITIES THAT GIVE BIRTH TO LEARNING

PAPER   "The concept of mathemagenic activities"[1]

QUOTE   *"You can lead a horse to water but the only water that gets into his stomach is what he drinks".*

Why you should read this article

Ernst Rothkopf begins his 1970 article on how people learn with this metaphor: "You can lead a horse to the water, but the only water that gets into his stomach is what he drinks". For Rothkopf, while learning depends on what is offered (i.e. the water) it depends more on what the learner does with what is offered (i.e. what (s)he drinks). To learn, we must cognitively process what is offered. Whether and how we process the incoming information determines what we learn and remember. Rothkopf calls activities that promote learning *mathemagenic activities* (Greek: *manthanein* = that which is learnt + *gignesthai* = to be born). His theory of mathemagenic activities was one of the first theories that saw the learner as central to the learning process as opposed to the curriculum or the teacher.

MATHEMAGENIC
That which gives
birth to learning

You could say that students have veto power over their learning. If they read a text or listen to a lesson and are focused on the facts, then they'll learn and probably remember the facts. In contrast, if while reading or listening they think about how to use the information, then they'll – hopefully – learn how to apply it. And of course, if they don't do anything with the information, then they'll learn nothing. In other words, you as the teacher can offer everything, but in the end it's the learner who has the last word. The learner has to process the material that you offer and this process of processing is what ultimately determines what's learnt. That doesn't mean that you have nothing to add to the equation. You can be the driving force to stimulate students to carry out those activities that promote learning.

1   **ROTHKOPF, E. Z.** (1970). THE CONCEPT OF MATHEMAGENIC ACTIVITIES. *REVIEW OF EDUCATIONAL RESEARCH, 40*, 325–336. DOI: 10.3102/00346543040003325.

There are many activities that a student can carry out to process the material. Some have a positive effect on learning (are mathemagenic), some are neutral (they neither help nor hinder learning), and some even work counterproductively (they are called mathemathantic; *thanatos* = death; see Chapter 27, When teaching kills learning). For example, research shows that presenting learners with questions before or after the to-be-learnt materials or giving a quiz (see Chapter 21, Learning techniques that really work) induce specific *mathemagenic positive* activities. Other activities such as highlighting, underlining, or re-reading texts are, in principle, *mathemagenic neutral* activities.[2] Then there are activities such as attuning tasks to so-called learning styles or summarising something without having learnt to make a good summary. These activities are actually *mathemagenic negative*; that is, they interfere with learning. Rothkopf adds a fourth category, namely *mathemagenic unknown*.

MATHEMATHANTIC
That which kills learning

Abstract of the article

Psychologists write from time to time in human language. Some years ago, I submitted the report of an experiment about mathemagenic behaviour to a journal. The article started with the sentence, "You can lead a horse to water but the only water that gets into his stomach is what he drinks". The editor, probably judging this alimentary (i.e., relating to nourishment or nutrition), deleted the sentence. I regretted this not only because the little phrase pleased me but also because the problem of the not-drinking horse was and is a useful metaphor for explaining why the study of mathemagenic activities is a challenging enterprise for the educational psychologist.

The proposition is simple. In most instructional situations, what is learned depends largely on the activities of the student. It therefore behoves those interested in the scientific study of instruction to examine these learning activities, i.e., the "drinking habits" of students.

The singular importance of certain learner activities first impressed me in connection with a theoretical analysis of frame formats programmed instruction. Student responses and the immediate feedback of knowledge of results had been interpreted in that context as having a direct effect on the acquisition of subject matter knowledge. Analysis led to the rejection of this interpretation and to the belief that these operations affect the inspection activities of the students instead. The inspection activities then determine what is learned.

A similar conclusion was reached in attempts to understand attention-like phenomena in earlier experiments on learning from written

---

2   A NOTE NEEDS TO BE MADE HERE. THE ACTIVITIES THEMSELVES DON'T HELP OR HINDER. HOWEVER, IF THEY ARE CARRIED OUT INSTEAD OF MATHEMAGENIC POSITIVE ACTIVITIES, LEARNING WHAT COULD BE LEARNED ISN'T.

sentences. This prompted me to coin the word mathemagenic to refer to attending phenomena derived from the Greek root *mathemain* – that which is learned and *gignesthai* – to be born. Mathemagenic behaviors are behaviors that give birth to learning. More specifically, the study of mathemagenic activities is the study of the student's actions that are relevant to the achievement of specified instructional objectives.

The concept of mathemagenic activity implies that the learners play an important role in determining what is learned.

The article

In order to get a grip on which activities are mathemagenic and which are not, Rothkopf posits that we first need to describe the activities precisely and then link them to a particular learning objective in a given situation. These last two aspects are extremely important because learning is a complex process. For him,

> any definition of mathemagenic activity that is broad enough to encompass all activities that produce any learning (or performance changes) in any situation is too broad to be useful ... Performance changes in different situations may depend on different actions by the student ... [distinguishing] ... (a) instructional settings and (b) specific characterizations of instructional materials."
>
> (p. 327)

Rothkopf himself primarily studied written materials and distinguished three categories of mathemagenic activities:

THE THREE
CATEGORIES OF
MATHEMAGENIC
ACTIVITIES:
Orientation,
Acquisition,
Translation and
processing

(1) *Orientation*: Moving students towards what they have to learn. This includes attracting and retaining attention as well as controlling activities that distract or disturb others.
(2) *Object acquisition*: Focusing the attention and studying of the student on certain things and in a certain way.
(3) *Translation and processing*: This involves influencing what and how the student looks at the material, how it is translated into internal speech or representations, and the mental accompaniments of reading such as discrimination, segmentation, and the processing of the information offered in the brain.

We can observe the first two activities fairly directly. However whether the learner actually processes the information, and thus learns, can only be indirectly derived from other behaviours such as whether they can apply a concept after having been given application questions in the text. This third category includes three closely intertwined actions:

(3a) *Translation*: Visually focusing on parts of the text and vocalisations of what is being read (which can sometimes be sub-audible).

(3b) *Segmentation*: Syntactically analysing what has been read such that it is broken down into smaller units which are then related to each other. A typical way to "observe" this was to follow the intonation of the student when reading.

(3c) *Processing*: Assimilating new information from the text into existing schemata and actions. This is difficult to "see", except by testing or questioning by the teacher or fellow students.

The sequence of mathemagenic activities carried out by the learner goes from less to more abstract; that is from certain physically observable behaviours (e.g. eye and muscle movement) to non-observable deeper processing. By examining mathemagenic activities and describing them as precisely as possible in behaviours, we can get a grip on what students have to do to achieve a certain learning goal in a particular situation. While Rothkopf only had rudimentary tools to follow these activities such as respiration (breathing patterns) and intonation (segmentation and intonation when reading), nowadays researchers have more precise ways to map out learning activities and thus see which activities are mathemagenic and which are not (see the box "The eye as portal to the brain").

THE VALUE OF
EYE-TRACKING
Where one looks,
for how long and in
what sequence

THE EYE AS PORTAL TO THE BRAIN

RESEARCHERS can now precisely map our eye movements when they look at a text, picture, combination of the two, or situation with so-called eye- or gaze-trackers. These trackers allow us to see and follow exactly what someone is looking at, for how long, the pattern of fixations, where the eyes jump to, and so on. These eye-tracking measurements give us an impression of the thinking processes that take place in the learner's mind.

Kim, Aleven, and Dey (2014), for example, compared how novices and experts look at and solve geometry problems (see Figure 15.1). It's clear that completely different strategies are used.

Also, because tracking devices are becoming smaller, more mobile, and cheaper, we can conduct research into what students see in certain situations. For example, research on eye movements of teachers-in-training (novices) and expert teachers when managing a classroom can yield insight into the strategies they use. In Figure 15.1 below we can see that expert teachers look at (and

(Continued)

(Continued)

process) what's going on in a classroom differently than teachers-in-training (Van Den Bogert, 2016).

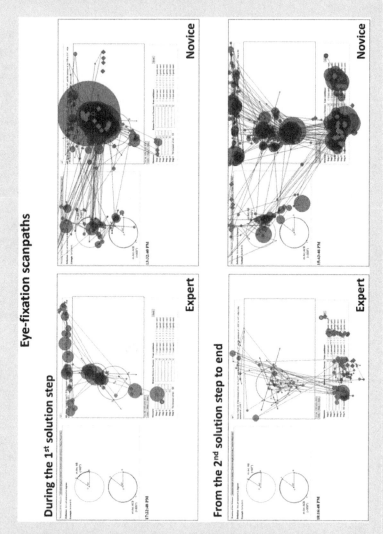

FIGURE 15.1
THE EYE-MOVEMENTS OF EXPERTS AND NOVICES SOLVING A GEOMETRY PROBLEM
(FROM KIM, ALEVEN, & DEY, 2014)

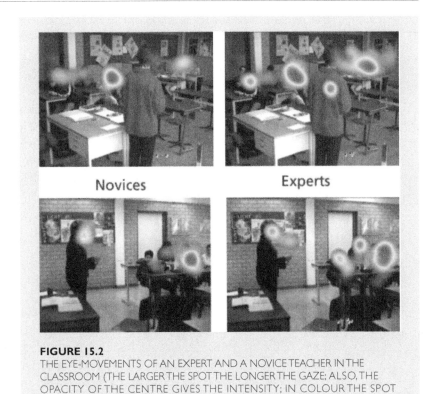

FIGURE 15.2
THE EYE-MOVEMENTS OF AN EXPERT AND A NOVICE TEACHER IN THE
CLASSROOM (THE LARGER THE SPOT THE LONGER THE GAZE; ALSO, THE
OPACITY OF THE CENTRE GIVES THE INTENSITY; IN COLOUR THE SPOT
GOES FROM GREEN TO AMBER TO RED LIKE A TRAFFIC LIGHT)

Conclusions/implications of the work for educational practice

Attending to mathemagenic activities has two concrete consequences
for educational practice. The first is an emphasis on "investment in
the instructional environment" (p. 334). Since 1970 we've seen radical
changes in learning materials which are now seen as normal, but weren't
then. Most textbooks were minimal. Attention guidance techniques such
as interspersing questions in texts, presenting learning objectives prior to
a chapter, and using prompting and focusing devices in multimedia are
examples of this.

The second consequence is that we now pay more attention to what
students actually do. Rothkopf wrote: "Emphasis in instruction is on
promoting those activities in the student that will allow him [*sic*] to
achieve instructional goals with available materials. This is truly a
student-centered approach" (p. 334). As a side note here, we see that
Rothkopf called this promoting of mathemagenic activities in learners
as student-centred! The view of learners as sponges that absorb
information has shifted to learners as active participants in their own

The paradox of
Rothkopf's "student-
centred" approach

learning process. As a teacher you can be very focused on the curriculum, pondering questions such as: Which method should I use? What are the objectives of my lesson? In which order do I teach? Though all are important questions, to promote actual student learning you must also take into account the learning process. If you don't, your clever lessons fall on deaf ears. Rothkopf focuses this learning process in his theory by looking at which learning and thinking activities the learner must undertake to learn from the offered subject matter. By paying attention to this when (shaping) your lessons, you support your students' learning. We'll give you some tips for this in the next section. While many of them will be pretty straightforward for many teachers, it still makes sense to be aware of the necessary processing activities for achieving specific learning objectives in specific situations. In doing so, it can offer a new perspective on how to teach.

How to use the work in your teaching

As a teacher, you can stimulate mathemagenic activities in different ways. Orientation and object acquisition (selection), for example, benefit from a quiet and orderly classroom. It's important that students are seated properly and that they can listen or read without disruption. Tom Bennett refers to this as creating a positive classroom climate. This also means that different distractors are not available such as mobile phones, tablets, or laptop screens when they are not necessary for the lesson. You can also encourage and help your students to focus on what they're doing. Think of making the objective crystal clear before starting on a lesson, implementing reward systems, or building quiet moments into your lessons. Though translation and processing is carried out in the students' minds, you can shape this. For example, making use of adjunct questions (Hamaker, 1986; Rothkopf, 1966, 1972) or other prompting techniques prior to, during, or after reading a text, listening to a presentation or a podcast (Popova, Kirschner, & Joiner, 2014), watching a video (Kirschner, 1978), and even working on a learning task or using a simulation can shape the way students think about the content or carry out their work. Adjunct questions and other similar prompts not only ensure proper orientation and object acquisition, but also have a major impact on processing. Questions can concern specific facts or concepts ("Where is X?" or "What is the definition of X?"), application of knowledge or thinking ("What is meant by X?" or "Where can you put X more to use?") or even stimulate thought ("Why does X work here and not here?" or "Why doesn't/won't X work in this situation?"). The last category of questions is known as epistemic questions or tasks (Ohlsson, 1995). By consistently asking a certain type of question or giving a

A positive classroom climate supports orientation and object acquisition

ADJUNCT QUESTIONS Questions inserted into a text to draw attention and steer how one reads and learns

specific type of assignment, you influence how students read/listen, translate, and process the information (i.e. learning behaviour). They then have this question in mind when reading/listening, even when no question is asked.

Takeaways

- Learning is a combination of object orientation, selection, translation, and processing that takes place in the learner. A teacher can try to make the learning objects available, but what is learnt depends on what the learner does with them.
- The lessons that you prepare can be very sophisticated, but if your students don't do anything with them or do the "wrong" thing with them (e.g. memorise instead of apply), then they won't learn properly.
- With good use of questions, learning objectives, and assignments you can steer your students' learning in the direction that you want (e.g. to learn facts or to apply knowledge).
- Certain ambient factors such as appropriate student behaviour, classroom climate, and the appropriate use of technology are critical to stimulating mathemagenic activities. Get these right first.
- For those training teachers or line-managing teachers, it's helpful to focus less on "teaching" and more on the overall conditions that the teacher has set that engender student learning.

References

HAMAKER, C. (1986). THE EFFECTS OF ADJUNCT QUESTIONS ON PROSE LEARNING. *REVIEW OF EDUCATIONAL RESEARCH, 56,* 212–242.

KIM, S., ALEVEN, V., & DEY, A. (2014). UNDERSTANDING EXPERT-NOVICE DIFFERENCES IN GEOMETRY PROBLEM-SOLVING TASKS: A SENSOR-BASED APPROACH. PAPER PRESENTED AT THE CHI'14 EXTENDED ABSTRACTS ON HUMAN FACTORS IN COMPUTING SYSTEMS (PP. 1867–1872). NEW YORK, NY: ACM. AVAILABLE FROM WWW.CS.CMU.EDU/~SJUNIKIM/PUBLICATIONS/CHI2014_WIP_GEOMETRY_LEARNING.PDF.

KIRSCHNER, P. A. (1978). THE EFFECT OF ADJUNCT QUESTION POSITION, TYPE, AND THE PRESENCE OR ABSENCE OF FEEDBACK ON LEARNING FROM A VIDEOTAPED LESSON. D. BROOK AND P. RICE (EDS.), *ASPECTS OF EDUCATIONAL TECHNOLOGY XII.* LONDON, UK: KOGAN PAGE.

OHLSSON, S. (1995) LEARNING TO DO AND LEARNING TO UNDERSTAND: A LESSON AND A CHALLENGE FOR COGNITIVE MODELLING. IN P. REIMANN AND H. SPADA (EDS.), *LEARNING IN HUMANS AND MACHINES: TOWARDS AN INTERDISCIPLINARY LEARNING SCIENCE* (PP. 37–62). LONDON, UK: PERGAMON.

POPOVA, A., KIRSCHNER, P. A., & JOINER, R. (2014). ENHANCING LEARNING FROM LECTURES WITH EPISTEMIC PRIMER PODCASTS ACTIVITY – A PILOT STUDY. *INTERNATIONAL JOURNAL OF LEARNING TECHNOLOGY, 9,* 323–337.

ROTHKOPF, E. Z. (1966). LEARNING FROM WRITTEN INSTRUCTIVE MATERIALS: AN EXPLORATION OF THE CONTROL OF INSPECTION BEHAVIOR BY TEST-LIKE EVENTS. *AMERICAN EDUCATIONAL RESEARCH JOURNAL, 3,* 241–249.

ROTHKOPF, E. Z. (1970). THE CONCEPT OF MATHEMAGENIC ACTIVITIES. *REVIEW OF EDUCATIONAL RESEARCH, 40,* 325–336.

ROTHKOPF, E. Z. (1972). VARIABLE ADJUNCT QUESTION SCHEDULES, INTERPERSONAL INTERACTION, AND INCIDENTAL LEARNING FROM WRITTEN MATERIAL. *JOURNAL OF EDUCATIONAL PSYCHOLOGY, 63,* 87–92.

ROTHKOPF, E. Z. (1996) CONTROL OF MATHEMAGENIC ACTIVITIES. IN D. H. JONASSEN, (ED.), *HANDBOOK OF RESEARCH ON EDUCATIONAL COMMUNICATIONS AND TECHNOLOGY* (PP. 879–896). NEW YORK, NY: MCMILLAN.

VAN DEN BOGERT, N. J. (2016). *ON TEACHERS' VISUAL PERCEPTION AND INTERPRETATION OF CLASSROOM EVENTS USING EYE TRACKING AND COLLABORATIVE TAGGING METHODOLOGIES.* UNPUBLISHED DOCTORAL DISSERTATION. EINDHOVEN SCHOOL OF EDUCATION, EINDHOVEN, THE NETHERLANDS. AVAILABLE FROM HTTPS://PURE.TUE.NL/WS/FILES/12966900/20160116_BOGERT.PDF.

Suggested readings and links

IN A 2005 INTERVIEW ERNST ROTHKOPF DISCUSSES HIS VIEW ON MATHEMAGENIC ACTIVITIES AND HIS MANY RESEARCH STUDIES ON THIS TOPIC: ROTHKOPF, E., & SHAUGHNESSY, M. F. (2005). AN INTERVIEW WITH ERNST ROTHKOPF: REFLECTIONS ON EDUCATIONAL PSYCHOLOGY. *NORTH AMERICAN JOURNAL OF PSYCHOLOGY,* 7(1), 51–58.

PART IV

THE TEACHER

John Hattie assesses and discusses no fewer than 138 different influences on learning in his book *Visible Learning*.[1] And what, or rather who, emerges as the most important for the learning process of students? Indeed, the teacher.

Noblesse oblige, and how! If teachers want to live up to their positive influence, they must be directive, authoritative, caring, active, and passionately involved in teaching and learning. On top of this, the teacher needs deep conceptual domain knowledge and skills necessary to be able to teach a subject and give meaningful feedback to each student. Finally, top all of this off with the ability to precisely determine whether their lessons really work and the picture is complete. But then, in Hattie's words, it is also irrefutable that it is "what teachers know, do, and care about which is very powerful in this learning equation".[2]

In this part we give you some useful tips to help you achieve this ideal. For example, we discuss how you can give effective feedback, how you can best support learning, how direct instruction works and why, but also why discovery learning doesn't work.

1   **HATTIE, J.** (2009). *VISIBLE LEARNING: A SYNTHESIS OF OVER 800 META-ANALYSES RELATING TO ACHIEVEMENT.* LONDON: ROUTLEDGE.
2   **HATTIE, J.** (2003). TEACHERS MAKE A DIFFERENCE: WHAT IS THE RESEARCH EVIDENCE? *AUSTRALIAN COUNCIL FOR EDUCATIONAL RESEARCH: ANNUAL CONFERENCE ON BUILDING TEACHER QUALITY.* MELBOURNE, AUSTRALIA. AVAILABLE FROM HTTPS://RESEARCH.ACER.EDU.AU/CGI/VIEWCONTENT. CGI?ARTICLE=1003&CONTEXT=RESEARCH_CONFERENCE_2003.

16 ZOOMING OUT TO ZOOM IN

ELABORATION THEORY OF INSTRUCTION

16 ZOOMING OUT TO ZOOM IN

PAPER   "The elaboration theory of instruction"[3]

QUOTE   *"The simple-to-complex sequence prescribed by the Elaboration Theory helps to ensure that the learner is always aware of the context and importance of the different ideas that are being taught. It allows the learner to learn at the level of complexity that is most appropriate and meaningful to him or her at any given state in the development of one's knowledge"*

Why you should read this article

As a young musician, Claude Debussy was greatly influenced by the German composer Richard Wagner and once considered his music to represent the birth of modern music, but in later years he began to feel that his work was not as significant as he previously thought and later referred to him as "a beautiful sunset that was mistaken for a dawn".[4]

The use of analogy is really a form of heuristic which aims to illuminate meaning by introducing a new concept and relating it to a concept already known to the learner. To someone who was not knowledgeable of the music of either composer, or indeed the genre as a whole, it would be impossible to discern whether Wagner was as ground-breaking as many thought he was but by using the comparison of a sunset and a dawn as an analogy, Debussy is able to illuminate the novice as to how that might make sense and orient them towards a deeper appreciation, or at least initiate them into a first stage of understanding of the debate.

ELABORATION
THEORY
Content should be
ordered from simple
to complex

The use of analogy is just one component of elaboration theory, a model for the sequencing and organising instruction on a course

---

3   **REIGELUTH, C., & STEIN, F.** (1983). THE ELABORATION THEORY OF INSTRUCTION. IN C. REIGELUTH (ED.), *INSTRUCTIONAL DESIGN THEORIES AND MODELS*, HILLSDALE, NJ: ERLBAUM ASSOCIATES.
4   **DEBUSSY, C.** (1971). L'INFLUENCE ALLEMANDE SUR LA MUSIQUE FRANCAISE. IN *MONSIEUR CROCHE* (P. 67). PARIS: EDITIONS GAILLIMARD.

of content developed by Charles Reigeluth in the 1970s and 1980s. The organising structure for a particular course may be conceptual, procedural, or theoretical and requires various strategy components such as "epitomising" or giving the ultimate concrete examples of a particular concept and providing analogy to initiate the learner into a particular domain of knowledge. In the intervening years, elaboration theory has been well received by the community and has been highly influential in course design and the sequencing of instruction.

Summary of the article (adapted from the chapter)

The elaboration theory's prescriptions are based both on an analysis of the structure of knowledge and on an understanding of cognitive processes and learning theories. As with other theories, goals form the basis for prescribing models. The most important aspect of all three models is a specific kind of simple-to-complex sequence, which is an extension of Ausubel's *subsumptive sequencing*, Bruner's *spiral curriculum*, and Norman's *web learning*. This sequencing pattern helps to build stable cognitive structures, provides a meaningful context for all instructional content, and allows for a meaningful context for all instructional content and meaningful application-level learning from the very first "lesson". Gagné's learning-prerequisite sequences are then introduced only as they become necessary within each lesson, and systematic integration and review are provided at the end of each lesson and unit. Also, each lesson is adjusted in certain ways to make it appropriate for the ability level of the students in relation to the complexity or difficulty of the content.

SUBSUMPTIVE
SEQUENCING
General to complex

SPIRAL
CURRICULUM
Revisiting content
with increasing
complexity each
time

The article

Using an analogy, the authors liken the initial stage of elaboration theory to looking at a picture with a zoom lens. You begin with an overview or wide-angle view of things which allows you to see the component parts and how they relate to one another, however with no detail. From there you can zoom into the component parts and look more closely at its individual elements and their subtleties (in contrast to "cutting" to a detail). Then you zoom back out again and consider how those individual elements relate to the whole picture again. These smaller constituent parts are what Robert Gagné (1968, 1977) referred to as *learning prerequisites* which represent the fact that in order to acquire new knowledge, certain previous knowledge is needed to fully understand it (see also Chapter 6, What you know determines what you learn).

LEARNING
PREREQUISITES
Foundational
knowledge needed
to build new
knowledge

For example, when looking at Picasso's "Guernica" as a whole, it seems to be an abstract collection of unrelated images. However, when the viewer zooms in, they can see a bull, a horse and numerous faces contorted with pain. When they learn that the bull and horse are significant images in Spanish culture and that Guernica was the site of a bombing during the Spanish Civil war where many civilians were killed, they can begin to attribute meaning where previously there was none. These elements of knowledge coalesce to form a deeper understanding and appreciation of the work through a process of zooming in and out and connecting various elements, previously unconnected.

Reigeluth (1979, pp. 8–9) summed this up as follows:

> A person starts with a wide angle view, which allows one to see the major part of the picture and the major relationships among those parts (e.g. the composition or balance of the picture), but without any detail.
>
> Zooming in at one level on a given part of the picture allows the person to see the major subparts.
>
> After having studied those subparts and their interrelationships, the person could then zoom back out to the wide-angle view to review the other parts of the whole picture and to review the context of this part within the whole picture.
>
> The person continues this pattern of zooming in at one level to see the major subparts of a part and zooming back out for context and review, until the whole picture has been seen at the first level of detail.
>
> The person follows the same zoom-in/zoom-out pattern for the second level of detail, the third level, and so on, until the desired level of detail is reached.

The seven components of elaboration theory

The authors' outline of elaboration theory features seven major strategy components: (1) an elaborative sequence, (2) learning-prerequisite sequences, (3) summary, (4) synthesis, (5) analogies, (6) cognitive strategies, and (7) learner control. The most important of these is the initial stage where the emphasis should be on introducing the overall topic or course with the aim of moving from simple-to-complex components in the instructional design. At this stage a key concept, procedure, or principle should be *epitomised* with additional layers of complexity being added appropriately later on. According to Reigeluth (1979), such an epitome is a "perfect example" of the to-be-learned material plus it also has what he calls "a single orientation" in that it emphasises only one kind of content. Simply stated, an epitome is the simplest and most fundamental example of an idea; the exemplary example. Epitomising is differentiated from summarising a topic by introducing a small element of the concept at a concrete level with applicable examples, which then allows the learner to build on those and relate them to subsequent concepts, procedures, or principles.

EPITOME
The exemplary example

A *summariser* is a strategy component which gives a concise statement of what has been learned with typical easy-to-remember examples and a diagnostic test to be taken by the learner. A *synthesiser* will integrate what has already been learned with the bigger picture and aims to increase student motivation and agency by creating more continuity between new knowledge and the learner's prior knowledge. The use of analogy is recommended to relate new or difficult knowledge to familiar knowledge. For example, when teaching iambic pentameter in poetry, the teacher might use the analogy of rhythm in a contemporary song which may be familiar to the learners. *Cognitive strategies* are strategy components which explicitly harness the cognitive architecture of the brain by using less domain-specific elements such as diagrams, mnemonics, or paraphrases. However this component veers somewhat dangerously close to the idea of generic skills which is less supported by more recent evidence (Tricot & Sweller, 2014). The *learner control* component refers to the process where the learner has more agency over the entire domain of knowledge due to the knowledge they have acquired and are then best placed to use metacognitive strategies to decide where to focus their attention on what they wish to review or attend to more closely to plug any gaps they might have. A key element of this last component is that material will have been presented in a simple-to-complex sequence with various concepts clearly labelled so that the learner can choose where to select and review the relevant content.

They also note that there are two fundamental types of sequencing strategies, namely a topical sequencing where a topic or task is taught to that level of understanding or competence which is necessary to go to the next level, and spiral sequencing where learners study the material in a number of rounds, going deeper or broader in each round. Within each of these two sequencing strategies, one can choose to go from simple to complex, general to detailed, or concrete to abstract.

Designing instruction according to the elaboration model has two major phases. The first phase is structuring the subject matter. This is done in the following six steps (see Figure 16.1):

1. Select how you want to organise the content based on what your instruction hopes to achieve. Should it be conceptual, procedural, or theoretical?
2. Develop an organising structure in the most detailed/complex version that the student needs to learn (i.e. detailed content analysis or task description).
3. Analyse the organising structure to determine which aspect(s) of content should be presented in the epitome and which in each level of elaboration. This is the "skeleton".

SYNTHESISER
Presentation device to help learners integrate new content

Learner control supports agency of the learner

PHASE 1 Structure the subject matter

4. Put some meat on the skeleton by adding the other two types of content plus facts at the lowest appropriate levels of detail. For example, if you chose in the first step for a conceptual organisation, then add the necessary procedural and theoretical content.

5. Establish the scope and depth of each lesson that will comprise each level. How broad and deep do your students need to learn?

6. Plan the internal structure of each lesson. Determine what is prerequisite to what, what is needed to understand the whole, and what analogies, synthesisers, and summarisers you'll use. Finally, specify the content of each expanded epitome.

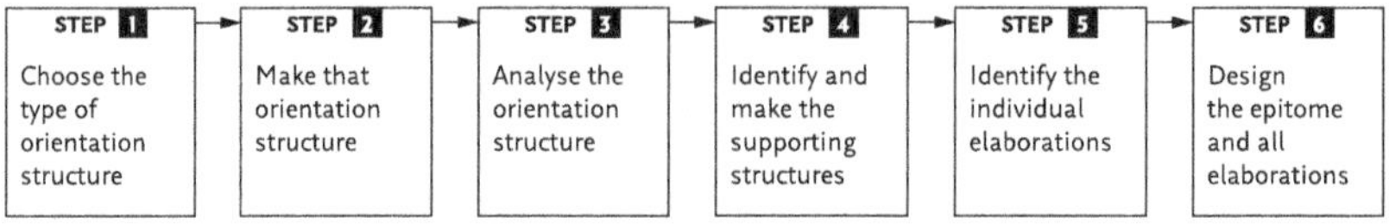

FIGURE 16.1
THE SIX-STEP DESIGN PROCEDURE FOR STRUCTURING THE INSTRUCTION IN ANY COURSE ENTAILING COGNITIVE SUBJECT MATTER (REIGELUTH & STEIN, 1983, P. 371)

STEP 1	STEP 2	STEP 3	STEP 4	STEP 5	STEP 6
Choose the type of orientation structure	Make that orientation structure	Analyse the orientation structure	Identify and make the supporting structures	Identify the individual elaborations	Design the epitome and all elaborations

PHASE 2
Design the instruction

Having done this we can begin with phase 2, namely designing the actual instruction (Reigeluth, 1979; Reigeluth & Stein, 1983). First, we present the epitome. Having done this we present what is known as a level-1 elaboration, which provides detail of the aspect of the epitome that is most important or contributes most to an understanding of the whole structure. We follow this by a summariser with an expanded epitome, which is followed by another level-1 elaboration with a summariser and an expanded epitome until all aspects of the content in the epitome have been elaborated at that level. Then a deeper – level-2 – elaboration is presented and so forth until the level of detail/complexity specified by the objectives is attained in all aspects of the content. See Figure 16.2.

Reigeluth and Stein define a summariser as an additional instructional strategy component of elaboration theory which provides 1) a concise statement of each concept, idea or fact that has been taught; 2) a reference example or a relatively easy to remember example of that reference; and 3) some kind of self-test for each of the ideas. Furthermore, there are two types of summariser: an internal summariser which appears at the end of each lesson and reviews only the content covered in that lesson, and a within-set summariser which covers all the material that has been taught up until this point in the "set of lessons" which refers to any single lesson and the lesson on which it elaborates in addition to the coordinate lessons that also elaborate on that lesson. For example, when studying a novel such as "The Great Gatsby" the teacher might use some form of advance organiser (see Chapter 6, What you know determines what you learn) featuring a definition of the American dream and an easy to understand example and then set a quiz on the

EXAMPLE
Internal and within-set summarisers

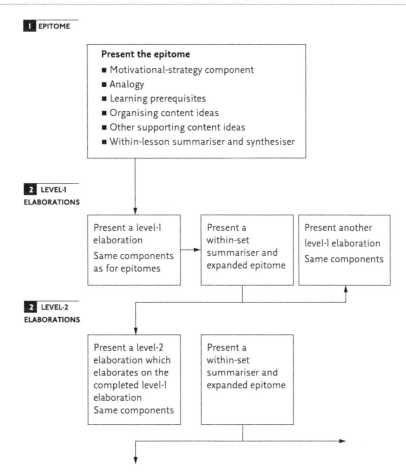

FIGURE 16.2
A DIAGRAMMATIC
REPRESENTATION
OF THE
ELABORATION
MODEL OF
INSTRUCTION
(REIGELUTH &
STEIN, 1983, P. 367)

sequence of events and that relates to the American dream in Chapter 4 covered in that lesson. For homework, the teacher might set a quiz on all new vocab encountered in Chapters 1–4.

Space doesn't allow us to discuss all of the different aspects of this theory. We, however, strongly recommend going to the original sources (links are given in the references; Reigeluth, 1979; Reigeluth & Stein, 1983) as they present many examples of epitomes, sequences, and structures for using elaboration theory in many different fields (government, STEM, language, etc.).

Conclusions/implications of the work for educational practice

Reigeluth and Stein stress that elaboration theory is mainly to be used at a macro level and is most helpful when looking at the "big picture". Essentially it's a series of strategic components to be considered when planning the sequencing and organising of a course which borrowed from emerging cognitive psychology at the time.

The core idea in elaboration theory is a deceptively simple one: when designing a sequence of lessons units, content should be presented in a simple way at first and then with increasingly complexity, but crucially the student must have a sound contextual understanding of the broad domain within which to process and assimilate new knowledge, skills, and concepts. This has many implications, particularly in terms of curriculum design; indeed Reigeluth notes that his work draws heavily on the concept of the spiral curriculum (Bruner, 1960) which asserts that no content is too "difficult" for students if it is presented in the right way. Bruner wrote: "We begin with the hypothesis that any subject can be taught effectively in some intellectually honest form to any child at any stage of development" (p. 33).

How to use the work in your teaching

As stated, the most important element of elaborative teaching is not just the sequencing of content from simple to increasingly complex, but the introduction of new content in relation to previously understood knowledge, skills and concepts. Reigeluth and Stein provide a number of examples of how to provide epitomes at the outset of a course. For example, when introducing a course on economics one might begin instruction by selecting or "epitomising" the concept of supply and demand and then zooming in and out as necessary.

THEORETICAL EPITOME FOR AN INTRODUCTORY COURSE IN ECONOMICS:

Organising content (principles) – the law of supply and demand

(a) An increase in price causes an increase in the quantity supplied and a decrease in the quantity demanded.
(b) A decrease in price causes a decrease in the quantity supplied and an increase in the quantity demanded.

Supporting content – concepts of price, supply, demand, increase, decrease

There has been a recent shift towards carefully considering curriculum design, particularly in the UK where the government inspection body will now examine the ways in which schools are choosing, sequencing, and designing course content. One positive aspect of this is that it moves us away from the idea of learning as a single unit (a lesson) where teachers must demonstrate student progress within that unit. By considering how a particular "set" of lessons might link with and "elaborate" on previous lessons, we can begin to see how student learning takes place over many different phases and is cumulative in nature. 3 gives a good model of what you can do to implement the elaboration theory in your teaching, particularly when considering the sequencing of content and the use of summarisers.

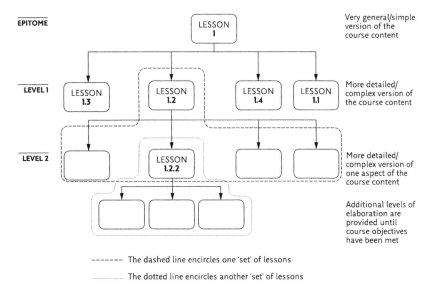

FIGURE 16.3
A DIAGRAMMATIC
REPRESENTATION
OF A SET OF
LESSONS
(REIGELUTH &
STEIN, 1983, P. 359)

------- The dashed line encircles one 'set' of lessons

·············· The dotted line encircles another 'set' of lessons

Takeaways

- Begin a course by "epitomising" a key concept or idea and then zooming in or out using it to build connections in the learner's knowledge base.
- Use summarisers at the end of a lesson to consolidate knowledge and relate to the "bigger picture" through quizzes.
- Use analogies to relate new knowledge to familiar concepts and ideas.
- Sequence your lessons/curricula either from simple to complex, general to detailed, or concrete to abstract.
- Once the learner has a sound understanding of a domain of knowledge, then allow them more control over which areas they need to zoom in on to consolidate knowledge.

References

BRUNER, J. S. (1960). *THE PROCESS OF EDUCATION.* CAMBRIDGE, MA: HARVARD UNIVERSITY PRESS.

DEBUSSY, C. (1971) L'INFLUENCE ALLEMANDE SUR LA MUSIQUE FRANCAISE, IN F. LESEUR (ED.), *MONSIEUR CROCHE* (PP. 67). PARIS: EDITIONS GAILLIMARD.

GAGNÉ, R. M. (1968). LEARNING HIERARCHIES. *EDUCATIONAL PSYCHOLOGIST,* 6(L), L–6.

GAGNÉ, R. M. (1977). *THE CONDITIONS OF LEARNING* (3RD ED.). NEW YORK, NY: HOLT, RINEHART & WINSTON.

REIGELUTH, C. M. (1979). IN SEARCH OF A BETTER WAY TO ORGANIZE INSTRUCTION: THE ELABORATION THEORY. *JOURNAL OF INSTRUCTIONAL DEVELOPMENT, 2*(3), 8–15. AVAILABLE FROM WWW.RESEARCHGATE.NET/PUBLICATION/226063833_THE_ELABORATION_THEORY_OF_ INSTRUCTION_A_MODEL_FOR_SEQUENCING_AND_SYNTHESIZING_INSTRUCTION_11.

REIGELUTH, C. M., & STEIN, F. (1983). THE ELABORATION THEORY OF INSTRUCTION. IN C. REIGELUTH (EDS.), *INSTRUCTIONAL DESIGN THEORIES AND MODELS: AN OVERVIEW OF THEIR CURRENT STATUS* (PP. 335–381). HILLSDALE, NJ: ERLBAUM ASSOCIATES. AVAILABLE FROM WWW.RESEARCHGATE.NET/ PUBLICATION/243768474_THE_ELABORATION_THEORY_OF_INSTRUCTION_19.

TRICOT, A., & SWELLER, J. (2014). DOMAIN-SPECIFIC KNOWLEDGE AND WHY TEACHING GENERIC SKILLS DOES NOT WORK. *EDUCATIONAL PSYCHOLOGY REVIEW, 26,* 265–283.

Suggested readings and links

THE WEBSITE INSTRUCTIONALDESIGN.ORG GIVES A GOOD OVERVIEW OF ELABORATION THEORY.

AVAILABLE FROM HTTPS://WWW.INSTRUCTIONALDESIGN.ORG/THEORIES/ ELABORATION-THEORY/.

THE DESIGN THEORY DATA BASE PRESENTS THIS OVERVIEW OF ELABORATION THEORY.

AVAILABLE FROM HTTP://JCSITES.JUNIATA.EDU/STAFF/PHEASAJ/INSYS525/ ELABORATION.HTML.

IF YOU WANT TO KNOW MORE ABOUT HOW TO SEQUENCE ACCORDING TO ELABORATION THEORY, HERE'S A GOOD ARTICLE: REIGELUTH, C. M., MERRILL, M. D., WILSON, B. G., & SPILLER, R. T. (1980). THE ELABORATION THEORY OF INSTRUCTION: A MODEL FOR SEQUENCING AND SYNTHESIZING INSTRUCTION. *INSTRUCTIONAL SCIENCE, 9,* 195–219.

AVAILABLE FROM WWW.RESEARCHGATE.NET/PUBLICATION/226063833_ THE_ELABORATION_THEORY_OF_INSTRUCTION_A_MODEL_FOR_ SEQUENCING_AND_SYNTHESIZING_INSTRUCTION_11.

IMPORTANT CRITIQUE OF ELABORATION THEORY WITH SOME FURTHER RECOMMENDATIONS: WILSON, B. & COLE, P. A. CRITICAL REVIEW OF ELABORATION THEORY *ETR&D* (1992). *40,* 63. DOI: 10.1007/ BF02296843.

A VIDEO WHICH GIVES AN OVERVIEW OF THE MAIN TENETS OF THE ELABORATION THEORY OF INSTRUCTION.

AVAILABLE FROM HTTPS://WWW.YOUTUBE.COM/WATCH?V= 8RPBANBKPAS.

17 WHY DISCOVERY LEARNING IS A BAD WAY TO DISCOVER THINGS/WHY INQUIRY LEARNING ISN'T

DISCOVERY LEARNING

17 WHY DISCOVERY LEARNING IS A BAD WAY TO DISCOVER THINGS/WHY INQUIRY LEARNING ISN'T

PAPER "Why minimal guidance during instruction does not work: an analysis of the failure of constructivist, discovery, problem-based, experiential, and inquiry-based teaching"[1]

QUOTE *"Learning, simply stated, means that there has been a change made in one's long-term memory".*

Why you should read this article

LEARNING
A change in long-term memory

This paper poses a fundamental question, namely what do we mean by learning? Decades of evidence on how the brain actually works suggests that the answer is a relatively simple one: Learning, simply stated, means that there has been a change made in one's long-term memory. Arising from this then is the question of how best to affect those changes through teaching. This seminal article makes the claim that if you use approaches where there is minimal guidance from the teacher and where students are encouraged to discover things for themselves, then you are ignoring the basic processes of human cognitive architecture. This article is important as it is one of the first to use developments in cognitive psychology to challenge a dominant orthodoxy in teaching, namely that direct instruction or teacher-led learning is a less effective approach than allowing learners to discover knowledge for themselves. This view has its roots in Rousseau's model of learning where the child should discover things for themselves and when you try to teach them, their "shining,

---

[1] **KIRSCHNER, P. A., SWELLER, J., & CLARK, R. E.** (2006). WHY MINIMAL GUIDANCE DURING INSTRUCTION DOES NOT WORK: AN ANALYSIS OF THE FAILURE OF CONSTRUCTIVIST, DISCOVERY, PROBLEM-BASED, EXPERIENTIAL, AND INQUIRY-BASED TEACHING. *EDUCATIONAL PSYCHOLOGIST*, 46(2), 75–86.

polished brain reflects, as in a mirror, the things you show them, but nothing sinks in".[2] By looking closely at recent research from cognitive psychology, specifically the claims of cognitive load theory and the limitations of working memory, this article has proven to be a *cri de coeur* for teachers who simply want to teach and students who want to learn.

Abstract of the article

Evidence for the superiority of guided instruction is explained in the context of our knowledge of human cognitive architecture, expert–novice differences, and cognitive load. Although unguided or minimally guided instructional approaches are very popular and intuitively appealing, the point is made that these approaches ignore both the structures that constitute human cognitive architecture and evidence from empirical studies over the past half-century, which consistently indicate that minimally guided instruction is less effective and less efficient than instructional approaches that place a strong emphasis on guidance of the student learning process. The advantage of guidance begins to recede only when learners have sufficiently high prior knowledge to provide "internal" guidance. Recent developments in instructional research and instructional design models that support guidance during instruction are briefly described.

The article

MINIMALLY GUIDED INSTRUCTION
The learner discovers what should be learnt

In this conceptual article, Paul A. Kirschner, John Sweller, and Richard E. Clark confront the concept of *minimally guided instruction* (i.e. constructivist, discovery, problem-based, experiential, and inquiry-based teaching) head on. They dispute the two main assumptions underlying teaching using minimal guidance, namely that (1) having learners construct their own solutions to "authentic" problems or acquire complex knowledge in information-rich settings leads to the most effective learning experience and (2) knowledge can best be acquired through experience based on the procedures of the discipline (i.e. seeing the pedagogic content of the learning experience as identical to the methods and processes or the way experts gain knowledge within the discipline being studied; Kirschner, 1992). In such programmes, minimal guidance is offered in the form of process- or task-relevant information that is available if learners choose to use it. Advocates of this approach imply that instructional guidance that provides or embeds learning strategies in instruction interferes with the natural processes by which learners draw on their unique, prior experience and

---

2   **ROUSSEAU, J.-J.** (1979). *EMILE, OR ON EDUCATION.* TRANS. ALLAN BLOOM. NEW YORK, NY: BASIC BOOKS.

Explicit or direct instruction

preferred learning approach to construct new, situated knowledge that will achieve their goals. They contrast the minimally guided approach with what they call *explicit instructional guidance* (also known as direct instructional guidance); an approach which provides information that fully explains the concepts and procedures that students are required to learn as well as learning strategy support that is compatible with human cognitive architecture.

Different types of instruction

MINIMALLY GUIDED INSTRUCTION is when teachers offer partial or minimal guidance so that learners are expected to discover some or all of the concepts and skills they are supposed to learn on their own. This approach has been given various names, including discovery learning, problem-based learning, inquiry learning, experiential learning, and constructivist learning.

EXPLICIT INSTRUCTIONAL GUIDANCE is when teachers *fully explain* the concepts and skills that students are required to learn. The provided guidance can be achieved through a variety of media, such as lectures, modelling, videos, computer-based presentations, and realistic demonstrations. It can also include class discussions and activities – if the teacher ensures that through the discussion or activity, the relevant information is explicitly provided and practised.

Their arguments are based on the premise that instructional procedures that ignore the structures that constitute human cognitive architecture are not likely to be effective or efficient. Human cognitive architecture is concerned with the manner in which our cognitive structures are organised, using Atkinson and Shiffrin's (1968) sensory, working, and long-term memory model as its base. As sensory memory is not relevant here, they only consider the relations between working and long-term memory, in conjunction with the cognitive processes that support learning. Long-term memory is viewed as the central, dominant structure of our human cognitive architecture, whereby learning is defined as "a change in long-term memory".

LONG-TERM MEMORY
Where information is held indefinitely in schemata

Working memory – where conscious processing occurs – has two well-known characteristics: when processing novel information, it's very limited in duration and in capacity. Almost all information stored in working memory and not rehearsed is lost within 30 seconds (Peterson & Peterson, 1959) and the capacity of working memory is limited to only a very small number of elements ranging from 7 according to Miller (1956) to 4±1 (Cowan, 2001).

WORKING MEMORY
Where new information is processed

These memory structures and their relations have direct implications for instructional design (e.g. Sweller, 1999; Sweller, van Merriënboer, & Paas, 1998). Inquiry- and problem-based instruction requires learners to search a problem space for problem-relevant information making heavy demands on working memory. This working memory load doesn't contribute to the accumulation of knowledge in long-term memory because while working memory is being used to search for problem solutions, it is not available and cannot be used to learn.

The article concludes that after about 50 years (now 60) of advocacy for minimally guided instruction, there is no real body of research supporting the approach. In so far as there is any evidence from controlled studies, it almost uniformly supports direct, strong instructional guidance rather than constructivist-based minimal guidance during the instruction of novice to intermediate learners. Even for students with considerable prior knowledge, strong guidance while learning is most often found to be equally effective as unguided approaches. Not only is unguided instruction normally less effective, there is evidence that it may have negative results when students acquire misconceptions or incomplete and/or disorganised knowledge.

UNGUIDED
INSTRUCTION
Can lead to
misconceptions

Conclusions/implications of the work for educational practice

Based upon this article we can make a number of conclusions along with implications for teaching and learning.

First, when designing lessons we need to be mindful of the possibilities and limitations of our *human cognitive architecture*, and specifically working memory, long-term memory, and the interactions between them. Working memory (short term memory) is extremely limited in both capacity and duration. Long-term memory stores a virtually unlimited amount of knowledge and skills on a more-or-less permanent basis, containing cognitive schemata that incorporate multiple elements of information into a single element.

COGNITIVE LOAD
THEORY
The amount of
mental effort
required to perform
a task

Intrinsic load versus
extraneous load

Related to this is *cognitive load theory* which holds that optimal learning can only occur when instruction is aligned with human cognitive architecture. It concerns itself with techniques to reduce the load on working memory so as to facilitate the changes in long-term memory associated with schema acquisition. Instrumental here is the reduction of a learning task's extraneous load (i.e. the way the material is presented or the activities required of the learner) to allow optimal processing of a learning task's intrinsic load (i.e. the complexity of the task as determined by the number of novel learning elements and the interaction between those elements, and the expertise of the learner).

It's also important to note that instructional methods should decrease extraneous cognitive load – that is, choosing an instructional approach that optimally supports and guides learning – so that the limited cognitive resources available can be devoted to effective and efficient learning. The support and guidance given minimises extrinsic load so that learners can focus their resources on the intrinsic demands of the learning.

Constructivist, discovery, problem-based, experiential, and inquiry-based teaching, due to their inherent nature, tax working memory in such a way that it impedes effective and efficient learning. Such approaches require learners to search a problem space for problem-relevant information which makes heavy demands on working memory. Also, that working memory load doesn't contribute to the accumulation of knowledge in long-term memory because while it's being used to search for problem solutions, it's not available and cannot be used to learn.

The goal of instruction is not to have learners search for and discover information, but rather to give them specific support for guidance about how to cognitively manipulate information in ways that are consistent with a learning goal, and store the result in long-term memory. Approaches which achieve this are: modelling with and without explanations, worked/worked-out examples which are faded into partially worked examples and finally are faded into conventional tasks without support (see Van Merriënboer & Kirschner, 2018), process worksheets, and so forth.

Finally, for students with considerable prior knowledge, strong support and guidance while learning is most often found to be equally effective to unguided and minimally guided approaches. And it's not only the case that unguided instruction is less effective and/or efficient, but there is evidence that this way of teaching may have negative results when students acquire misconceptions or incomplete and/or disorganised knowledge.

Minimally guided instruction increases extraneous load

WORKED EXAMPLES Solutions to problems explicitly shown in solution steps

How to use the work in your teaching

Start with worked-out examples of a task where a full solution is shown and which students then have to apply to a new task. In other words, they follow the sequence of steps. Then move to completion assignments – also known as partially worked-out examples – where a partial solution is given and students must carry out the "empty" steps themselves to complete it. Subsequently remove – one by one – the presented steps until the learner is, eventually, left with a problem that (s)he has to solve without any support. In other words, begin with a model (a complete example), gradually remove completed steps which the learner has to complete independently, and finally leave just the to-be-solved problem or task. This approach acts as a form of *scaffolding*. Below (Figure 17.1) is an example of a simple visual worked-out example.

Determining the Measure of an Angle in a Triangle

Ex 1: Point O is the centre of a circle and AB is a tangent to the circle.
In △ OAB, ∠AOB =58°. Determine the measure of ∠ OBA

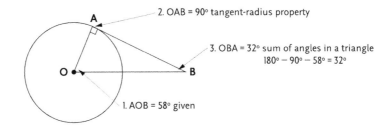

2. OAB = 90° tangent-radius property

3. OBA = 32° sum of angles in a triangle
180° − 90° − 58° = 32°

1. AOB = 58° given

FIGURE 17.1
A GEOMETRY
WORKED-
EXAMPLE
DEMONSTRATING
THE TANGENT-
RADIUS PROPERTY

Maximum guidance is provided by modelling examples or process-oriented worked examples because they confront learners with how to carry out a task, simultaneously explaining why the task is being carried out the way it is. A modelling example is, thus, similar to a worked-out example studied and evaluated by the learner, but it also pays explicit attention to the processes needed to reach an acceptable solution.

Breaking down the subject content, sequencing delivery so that sub-tasks are taught individually before being explained together as a whole. The idea is to not overwhelm a student too early on in the introduction of new work. An example is that if you want to teach someone to play squash, don't instruct them to think about her/his footing, the way (s) he holds the racquet, the stroke of the racquet etc. all at once. Let her/him play first only concentrating on the footing. Once this has been mastered, shift the concentration to holding the racquet, and so forth. This is known as *emphasis manipulation*; learners carry out the whole task from beginning to the end, but different parts are emphasised as the learning progresses.

EXAMPLE
Emphasis
manipulation

PROCESS
WORKSHEET
Heuristic guidance
through a task
solution

A *process worksheet* provides learners with the phases to go through to carry out a learning task, heuristically guiding them through the process. The learner uses the process worksheet as a guide for carrying out the task. For each phase, rules-of-thumb are provided as to how to successfully complete the phase. These rules-of-thumb may be in the form of statements (e.g. when doing A, consider X, Y, and/or Z) or guiding questions (e.g. what aspect(s) of X, Y, and/or Z should you take into account doing A and why?). The latter form (also known as epistemic questions) had the advantage of triggering learners to think about what they need to do rather than just mechanically trying to carry out the instructions. An example of a process worksheet is the presentation of the series of steps (i.e. phases and sub-phases) that a student-chef needs to go through when planning a meal, along with rules-of-thumb such as: the amount of time needed to marinate and cook the meat is based on the surface area and not the weight.

Simple ≠ Easy
Complex ≠ Difficult

SIMPLE IS NOT THE SAME AS EASY, AND COMPLEX IS NOT THE SAME AS DIFFICULT.

Well-designed guided instruction ensures that learners are not overwhelmed by the complexity of a task. This means that the tasks are ordered from simple to complex with the necessary support and guidance given when needed. Important to note here is that simple is not the same as easy, and complex is not the same as difficult. The simplicity/complexity of a task is related to its intrinsic load; that is the number of new information elements contained in the task and the interactions between those elements. For example, a simple task in learning about electricity has few elements (one or two bulbs with a singular source of current either in series or parallel) whereas a complex task can have multiple elements combined in multiple ways.

Takeaways

- Learning is a change in long-term memory.
- Working memory is where conscious processing occurs. It is severely limited in duration and capacity.
- Long-term memory is virtually unlimited. It contains huge amounts of information concerning the area organised in schemata.
- Any instructional procedure that ignores the structures that constitute human cognitive architecture is not likely to be effective.
- Minimally guided instruction challenges working memory and, thus, inhibits/hampers effective and efficient learning.
- Explicitly (guided) instruction takes human cognitive architecture into account and, thus, supports/facilitates effective and efficient learning.
- While there is a substantial body or research supporting explicitly guided instruction, more than a half-century of promotion of minimally guided learning has not produced a body of research supporting its use.

References

ATKINSON, R., & SHIFFRIN, R. (1968). HUMAN MEMORY: A PROPOSED SYSTEM AND ITS CONTROL PROCESSES. IN K. SPENCE AND J. SPENCE (EDS.), *THE PSYCHOLOGY OF LEARNING AND MOTIVATION* (VOL. 2, PP. 89–195). NEW YORK, NY: ACADEMIC PRESS. AVAILABLE FROM WWW.RCA. UCSD.EDU/SELECTED_PAPERS/2_HUMAN%20MEMORY_A%20PROPOSED%20SYSTEM%20AND%20 ITS%20CONTROL%20PROCESSES.PDF.

COWAN, N. (2001). THE MAGICAL NUMBER 4 IN SHORT-TERM MEMORY: A RECONSIDERATION OF MENTAL STORAGE CAPACITY. *BEHAVIORAL AND BRAIN SCIENCES, 24,* 87–114.

KIRSCHNER, P. A. (1992). EPISTEMOLOGY, PRACTICAL WORK AND ACADEMIC SKILLS IN SCIENCE EDUCATION. *SCIENCE AND EDUCATION,* 1(3), 273–299. AVAILABLE FROM HTTPS://DSPACE.LIBRARY. UU.NL/BITSTREAM/HANDLE/1874/12698/KIRSCHNER_92_EPISTEMOLOGY_PRACTICAL_WORK_ ACADEMIC_SKILLS_SCIENCE_EDUCATION.PDF.

MILLER, G. A. (1956). THE MAGICAL NUMBER SEVEN, PLUS OR MINUS TWO: SOME LIMITS ON OUR CAPACITY FOR PROCESSING INFORMATION. *PSYCHOLOGICAL REVIEW, 63,* 81–97.

PETERSON, L., & PETERSON, M. (1959). SHORT-TERM RETENTION OF INDIVIDUAL VERBAL ITEMS. *JOURNAL OF EXPERIMENTAL PSYCHOLOGY, 58,* 193–198.

SWELLER, J. (1999). *INSTRUCTIONAL DESIGN IN TECHNICAL AREAS.* CAMBERWELL, AUSTRALIA: ACER PRESS.

SWELLER, J., VAN MERRIËNBOER, J. J. G., & PAAS, F. (1998). COGNITIVE ARCHITECTURE AND INSTRUCTIONAL DESIGN. *EDUCATIONAL PSYCHOLOGY REVIEW, 10,* 251–296. AVAILABLE FROM WWW. CSUCHICO.EDU/~NSCHWARTZ/SWELLER%20VAN%20MERRIENBOER%20AND%20PASS%201998.PDF.

VAN MERRIËNBOER, J. J. G., & KIRSCHNER, P. A. (2018). *TEN STEPS TO COMPLEX LEARNING* (3RD ED.). NEW YORK, NY: ROUTLEDGE.

Suggested readings and links

MAYER, R. (2004). SHOULD THERE BE A THREE-STRIKES RULE AGAINST PURE DISCOVERY LEARNING? THE CASE FOR GUIDED METHODS OF INSTRUCTION. *AMERICAN PSYCHOLOGIST, 59*(1), 14–19.

Richard Mayer posits that there is sufficient research evidence to make any reasonable person sceptical about the benefits of discovery learning – practiced under the guise of cognitive constructivism or social constructivism – as a preferred instructional method. He reviews research on discovery of problem-solving rules culminating in the 1960s, discovery of conservation strategies culminating in the 1970s, and discovery of LOGO programming strategies culminating in the 1980s. He concludes that, overall, learning is best supported by instructional methods involving cognitive activity instead of behavioural activity, instructional guidance instead of pure discovery, and curricular focus instead of unstructured exploration.

AVAILABLE FROM HTTP://TICTRABALHODEPROJECTO.PBWORKS.COM/F/ SHOULD%20THERE%20BE%20A%20THREE-STRIKES%20RULE%20AGAINST%20 PURE.PDF.

SWELLER, J. (2016). WORKING MEMORY, LONG-TERM-MEMORY, AND INSTRUCTIONAL DESIGN. *JOURNAL OF APPLIED RESEARCH IN MEMORY AND COGNITION*, 5, 360–367.

John Sweller discusses the use of cognitive load theory to design instruction, making use of David Geary's theory of evolutionary educational psychology. The premises underlying the use of cognitive load theory assume that: (1) we have not specifically evolved to learn the topics taught in educational and training institutions; (2) these topics require learners to acquire domain-specific rather than generic–cognitive knowledge; and (3) we have not evolved to acquire domain-specific concepts and skills which require explicit instruction. For these reasons, cognitive load theory has been developed to provide techniques that reduce unnecessary working memory load when dealing with explicitly taught, biologically secondary, domain-specific knowledge.

AVAILABLE FROM HTTPS://READER.ELSEVIER.COM/READER/SD/PII/
S2211368115000935?TOKEN=D022673CEFD05BC9CDDEBFF63 E6B6BD8
B24906BC1D993 C9253559A12CD14D537FF19CA47669D2464F1
F897F1E50CF327.

A VIDEO EXPLAINING COGNITIVE LOAD THEORY.

AVAILABLE FROM WWW.YOUTUBE.COM/WATCH?V=STJ-MKTGRFS.

18 DIRECT INSTRUCTION

DIRECT INSTRUCTION

18 DIRECT INSTRUCTION

PAPER "Principles of instruction. Research-based strategies that all teachers should know"[1]

QUOTE *"The most successful teachers spent more time in guided practice, more time asking questions, more time checking for understanding, and more time correcting errors".*

Why you should read this article

Robert Pondiscio, Senior Fellow and Vice President for External Affairs at the Thomas B. Fordham Institute in the US, published a blog in which he called direct instruction the Rodney Dangerfield of curricula. Rodney Dangerfield was an American comedian who constantly complained that he didn't get any respect, no matter what he did. Poor Rodney.[2]

Engelmann's model of Direct Instruction (DI)

The same seems to be true for direct instruction. But before discussing the article by Barak Rosenshine, we need to say that there is Direct Instruction and direct instruction. Yes, there is not one, but rather two types! The first is Direct Instruction (with capital DI). This is a model for instruction that emphasises well-developed, carefully planned lessons, focusing on small learning steps with clearly defined and prescribed learning tasks. This model was developed by the American Siegfried Engelmann (Oregon University). His theory is that clear instruction should eliminate misconceptions and will/could lead to more effective and efficient learning. Educational/instructional techniques that are used with DI are, for example, working groups, participation labs, discussions, lectures, seminars, workshops, observation, active learning, practical assignments, and internships.

1   **ROSENSHINE, B.** (2010) *PRINCIPLES OF INSTRUCTION*. INTERNATIONAL ACADEMY OF EDUCATION, UNESCO. GENEVA, SWITZERLAND: INTERNATIONAL BUREAU OF EDUCATION.ROSENSHINE, B. V. (2012, SPRING). PRINCIPLES OF INSTRUCTION. RESEARCH-BASED STRATEGIES THAT ALL TEACHERS SHOULD KNOW. *AMERICAN EDUCATOR, 36*(1), 12–19.

2   PARTS OF THIS CHAPTER LEAN STRONGLY ON TWO BLOGS WRITTEN BY THE FIRST AUTHOR AND MIRJAM NEELEN ON THEIR WEBSITE *3-STAR LEARNING EXPERIENCES* (HTTPS://3STARLEARNINGEXPERIENCES. WORDPRESS.COM/).

The second type of direct instruction (with lowercase di) was introduced by Barak Rosenshine in 1976/1979. He used the term direct instruction for a collection of variables that are significantly related to optimal learning.

Abstract of the articles

This article presents 10 research-based principles of instruction, along with suggestions for classroom practice. These principles come from three sources: (a) research in cognitive science, (b) research on master teachers, and (c) research on cognitive supports. Each is briefly explained in this article. Even though these are three very different bodies of research, there is "no conflict at all" between the instructional suggestions that come from each of these three sources. In other words, these three sources supplement and complement each other. The fact that the instructional ideas from three different sources supplement and complement each other gives teachers faith in the validity of these findings.

The article

Brophy (1979) summarised Rosenshine's "small di" as follows: Instructors 1) emphasise academic goals, 2) ensure that learners are involved in learning, 3) select the learning objectives and monitor learner progress, 4) structure the learning activities and give immediate academically focused feedback, and 5) create a task-oriented yet "relaxed" learning environment. In essence, direct instruction:

Rosenshine's model of direct instruction (di)

- sets the stage for learning via introductions and review of what has been learnt
- presents clear explanation of what to do
- models the process/shows how to do something
- guides practice in which the process is monitored
- encourages independent practice, but only after the teacher is confident that the students will be successful
- provides assessment of student progress and closure of the learning experience (i.e. reviews what the lesson was about)

In 2012, Barak Rosenshine, emeritus professor of educational psychology at the University of Illinois, published an article in *American Educator* magazine about instructional principles that have proven their value time and again. The article was an adapted version of a report that he wrote in 2010 for UNESCO. In that article he extracted principles from research in cognitive science, research on master teachers, and research on cognitive supports for learning. The major strength of

Direct Instruction IS	Direct Instruction ISN'T
Skill based with active student participation	Drill and practice
Holistic where the whole task is modelled	Limited to learning isolated facts and procedures
Integrates smaller learning units into meaningful wholes	Teaching basic skills in isolation from meaningful contexts
Developmentally appropriate; tailored to students' learning and attentional needs	A one size fits all approach
Geared towards understanding where student progress is constantly monitored	Geared towards rote learning of facts and procedures
Usable in all different contexts and areas	Usable only for basic skills All teacher directed

FIGURE 18.1
ROSENSHINE'S
TEN GOLDEN
PRINCIPLES

this synthesis is, even though these are three very different bodies of research, there is no conflict whatsoever between the instructional suggestions that they provide. Here are his ten golden instruction principles (see Figure 18.1).

Principle 1: Begin a learning experience with a short review of previous learning

PRIOR
KNOWLEDGE
Establish connections

Reviewing what you've learnt reinforces learning and retention by establishing connections between what we already know and the new information that is coming. By beginning each session with a short review, we refresh our memory and activate our prior knowledge (see Chapter 6, What we know determines what we learn). Daily review is especially important for things that need to be used often as repetition helps automate the retrieval of that information. It allows for the effortless retrieval of words, concepts, procedures, etc. from our memory which we need to solve problems, carry out tasks and understand new subject matter.

Principle 2: Present new learning material in small steps and help students practice with it

SMALL STEPS
Offer new
information
incrementally

Our working memory is very small: it can hold between four and seven pieces of new information at any one time. Those chunks are processed and stored in our long-term memory as schemata. Too much information overwhelms our working memory and the working memory will simply no longer process it. Always offer small amounts of information, then help students practice it and only go to the next step if the previous one is mastered.

Principle 3: Ask a large number of questions to support connections between new materials and prior learning

RETRIEVAL
PRACTICE
Ask lots of questions

Answering questions helps students to practice what has just been presented (i.e. new information) and to then to make connections between that new information and with what they have already learnt. This is especially the case for "how and why" questions, so-called epistemic questions. The most successful teachers appear to spend more than half of their lessons teaching, demonstrating and asking questions. Also, asking a teacher can also determine how well the students have learnt, whether they themselves taught properly, and whether further or different instruction is needed. To this end, it's also useful to ask students to explain how they came to the answer.

Principle 4: Provide models and worked examples; this supports learners to solve problems faster or better

COGNITIVE
SUPPORTS
Worked examples
and models

Or even better, be a model. Students need what Rosenshine calls "cognitive" support to learn how to carry out tasks and solve problems. By acting as a model and also telling them about what you're thinking, what you're doing, what working steps you're taking, and why you're doing what you're doing you can show them how to do it properly.

Principle 5: Guide your students in practising with new learning material

Simply offering new material isn't enough. In addition to review and repetition (Principle 1), sufficient and varied practice and testing are required. Pupils must spend time reformulating, expanding on, and summarising new material if you want them to store it properly in their long-term memory. This increases the retrieval strength of the information. Look at it this way: It's easy to store something in a drawer, but it can be very difficult to remember exactly where you left it. Practice helps us remember where it is! You as a teacher can help this rehearsal process by asking students questions, because good questions require them to process and review what they have learnt.

QUESTIONING
Helps students
understand and
remember content

Principle 6: Check whether students have really understood what you've taught

UNDERSTANDING
Check for
understanding often

Effective teachers very often check whether students are actually learning the new subject matter. They not only check the product, but also the process of learning. In this way, they not only promote the processing of the material, they can also check whether students actually learn well and also whether they have actually understood the material. By the way, this also helps you to see whether the students have acquired misconceptions.

Principle 7: Obtain a high success rate

It's important that students achieve success (small steps; Principle 2 helps this) as success breed self-efficacy, a feeling of achievement, and ultimately the motivation to continue. Also, it's important that learners have mastered prerequisite knowledge for further learning. Effective teachers check whether their students are successful often. This isn't for grading (assessment of learning), but rather as a learning strategy (assessment for learning). This was discussed in Chapter 19, Assessment *for*, not *of* learning and Chapter 21, Learning techniques that really work. This last is what is known as retrieval practice. And although practice makes perfect, this is only if students or learners don't practice mistakes. If the practice doesn't lead to success, chances are that the student is practising the wrong thing. And ingrained errors – as well as misconceptions – are very difficult to eradicate.

Principle 8: Provide scaffolds for difficult tasks

In addition to explaining things yourself (see Principle 4), you can also give your students temporary support that is used to assist them. These so-called scaffolds are gradually withdrawn as they become more competent. There are many types of scaffolds. Best known are worked (out) examples where the solution steps are gradually removed until the learner solves a problem or carries out a task without support or process worksheets where the process is laid out step for step and also is gradually diminished. In this way you offer students temporary cognitive support. Eliminating more and more steps, you break down the scaffold piece by piece, gradually guiding your students towards independent implementation.

Principle 9: Require and monitor independent practice

You can't endlessly take your students by the hand; in the end they have to be able to do it themselves. Let them practice independently and check whether they can really do it or whether more and/or different (guided or unguided) practice is needed. Rosenshine (2010, p. 24) writes: "When material is overlearned it can be recalled automatically, and doesn't take up any space in our working memory. When students become automatic in an area, they can then devote more of their attention to comprehension and application".

Principle 10: Engage students in weekly and monthly review

Students need to have extensive practice in order to develop well-connected and automatic knowledge. In other words, you need to activate what they have learnt regularly. It's important here to note

REVIEW OFTEN
Interleave and space
student practice

that this review should be varied (i.e. interleaved) and spread over time (i.e. distributed) so as to help them develop strong and rich schemata. By returning to something that has already been learned often – but with the necessary time in between so that they can gain new knowledge in new and different situations – the connections in the schemata are strengthened and they become richer and more extensive.

Now the question is, does direct instruction (both the uppercase and lowercase version) work? The first real evidence of the efficacy of direct instruction was a very large scale study known as *Project Follow Through*. This project was a US government funded project meant to determine the best way to teach "at-risk children" from kindergarten through third grade. From 1968–1977, more than 200,000 children took part in this project which compared 22 different models of instruction ranging from open education through constructivism/discovery learning to DI. The results were crystal clear. Siegfried Engelmann's DI method had the highest gains. Cathy Watkins (1997) writes:

PROJECT FOLLOW
THROUGH
Largest experimental
project in education
ever

> The Follow Through experiment was intended to answer the question "what works" in educating disadvantaged children. If education is defined as the acquisition of academic skills, the results of the Follow Through experiment provide an unequivocal answer to the question. The evidence provided by the Follow Through experiment clearly indicates that the instructional methods employed in the Direct Instruction and Behavior Analysis models are most effective in teaching the skills necessary for basic literacy and mathematical competence.
>
> (p. 42)

Not only did students who received DI have significantly higher academic achievement, but they also had higher self-esteem and self-confidence than students whose instruction followed any other programme. It is interesting that subsequent research found that the DI children continued to outperform their peers, were more likely to finish high school, and more likely to go on to higher education.

Stockard and colleagues (2018) conducted a meta-analysis of studies on direct instruction. They included more than 400 studies that were carried out between 1966 and 2016. The research papers included subjects such as language, reading, maths, and spelling, as well as subjects that also focused on learning outcomes, affective outcomes (e.g. learner attitudes, confidence, self-esteem, and behaviour), perceptions from the instructor about the effectiveness of the process, and parent opinions. All effects of direct instruction were positive and significant, except for the affective outcomes, which were positive but not significant. In other words, direct instruction (1) has a positive effect on learning, (2) instructors and parents are positive about it, and (3) it doesn't hurt learner attitudes, confidence, self-esteem, and behaviour. That sounds hopeful to say the least, we'd say.

Furtak and colleagues (2012) also carried out a meta-analysis, including experimental and quasi-experimental studies on discovery learning. They investigated 37 studies, completed between 1996 and 2006. The authors characterise this period as the decade in which curriculum innovation (especially in physics) clearly focused on discovery learning. They found an overall positive effect; however, the effect of the instructor-driven activities were much larger (effect size 0.40) than learner-driven activities. This might very well be the case, because discovery learning over time has started to show many similarities to high quality direct instruction. In other words, discovery learning works *if* (and only *if*) the instructor provides clear guidance during the discovery process!

Last but not least, Andersen and Andersen (2017) investigated the possible (side-) effects of learner-centred education on inequality. In this case, learner-centred education means an educational approach in which 1) learners set their own goals, 2) activities are tailored to the individual learner, 3) learners are responsible for (self-)directing their learning and seek help from the instructor at their own initiative, 4) learners are actively seeking knowledge, 5) educational methods are focused on individual learning and collaboration (often with ICT support), and 6) the instructors' role is to coach and facilitate. In a study with over 56,000 learners in 825 Danish schools, the effects of learner-centred education on academic achievement from learners with various socio-economic backgrounds were analysed (its measurement was based on the highest educational degree from the parents, which is an often-used measure of socio-economic status). The researchers found that overall learner-centred education had a negative impact on the academic achievement of the learners; however (and this is worrisome), that effect was larger for learners whose parents had a lower socio-economic status. Therefore, the unfortunate conclusion is that learner-centred education appears to increase inequality in education.

Conclusions/implications of the work for educational practice

There are a lot of things that people think direct instruction is and isn't. Here is a handy table (see Table 18.1) to help understand this.

Direct Instruction *is*	Direct Instruction *isn't*
• skill based with active student participation	• drill and practice
• holistic where the whole task is modelled	• limited to learning isolated facts and procedures
• integrates smaller learning units into meaningful wholes	• teaching basic skills in isolation from meaningful contexts
• developmentally appropriate; tailored to students' learning and attentional needs	• a one size fits all approach
• geared towards understanding where student progress is constantly monitored	• geared towards rote learning of facts and procedures
• usable in all different contexts and areas	• usable only for basic skills
• allows students the opportunity to monitor and direct their own learning	• all teacher directed

TABLE 18.1
WHAT DIRECT INSTRUCTION IS AND ISN'T (ADAPTED FROM GOEKE, 2018)

How to use the work in your teaching

The article has possibly the most directly implementable guidance for the classroom. The simplest way to explain how to use Barak Rosenshine's principles is to follow them.

Takeaways

We cannot say it better than Rosenshine (2010, p. 7) himself, so:

- Begin a lesson with a short review of previous learning.
- Present new material in small steps with student practice after each step.
- Limit the amount of material students receive at one time.
- Give clear and detailed instructions and explanations.
- Ask a large number of questions and check for understanding.
- Provide a high level of active practice for all students.
- Guide students as they begin to practice.
- Think aloud and model steps.
- Provide models of worked-out problems.
- Ask students to explain what they have learnt.
- Check the responses of all students.
- Provide systematic feedback and corrections.
- Use more time to provide explanations.
- Provide many examples.

- Re-teach material when necessary.
- Prepare students for independent practice.
- Monitor students when they begin independent practice.

References

ANDERSEN, I. G., & ANDERSEN, S. C. (2017). STUDENT-CENTERED INSTRUCTION AND ACADEMIC ACHIEVEMENT: LINKING MECHANISMS OF EDUCATIONAL INEQUALITY TO SCHOOLS' INSTRUCTIONAL STRATEGY. *BRITISH JOURNAL OF SOCIOLOGY OF EDUCATION, 38*, 533–550.

BROPHY, J. (1979). ADVANCES IN TEACHER RESEARCH. *JOURNAL OF CLASSROOM INSTRUCTION*, 15, 1–7.

FURTAK, E. M., SEIDEL, T., IVERSON, H., & BRIGGS, D. C. (2012). EXPERIMENTAL AND QUASI-EXPERIMENTAL STUDIES OF INQUIRY-BASED SCIENCE TEACHING: A META-ANALYSIS. *REVIEW OF EDUCATIONAL RESEARCH, 82*, 300–329. AVAILABLE FROM WWW.RESEARCHGATE.NET/ PUBLICATION/256648693_EXPERIMENTAL_AND_QUASI-EXPERIMENTAL_STUDIES_OF_INQUIRY- BASED_SCIENCE_TEACHING_A_META-ANALYSIS.

GOEKE, J. L. (2018). *EXPLICIT INSTRUCTION: A FRAMEWORK FOR MEANINGFUL DIRECT TEACHING.* UPPER SADDLE RIVER, NJ: MERRILL.

ROSENSHINE, B. (2010). *PRINCIPLES OF INSTRUCTION.* INTERNATIONAL ACADEMY OF EDUCATION, UNESCO. GENEVA, SWITZERLAND: INTERNATIONAL BUREAU OF EDUCATION. AVAILABLE FROM WWW.IBE.UNESCO.ORG/FILEADMIN/USER_UPLOAD/PUBLICATIONS/ EDUCATIONAL_PRACTICES/EDPRACTICES_21.PDF.

ROSENSHINE, B. V. (1976). CLASSROOM INSTRUCTION. IN N. GAGE (ED.), *THE PSYCHOLOGY OF TEACHING METHODS, 75TH YEARBOOK OF THE NATIONAL SOCIETY FOR THE STUDY OF EDUCATION.* CHICAGO, IL: UNIVERSITY OF CHICAGO PRESS.

ROSENSHINE, B. V. (1979). CONTENT, TIME, AND DIRECT INSTRUCTION. IN P. L. PETERSON AND H. J. WALBERG (EDS.), *RESEARCH ON TEACHING: CONCEPTS. FINDINGS AND IMPLICATIONS* (PP. 28–56). BERKLEY, CA: MCCUTCHAN PUBLISHING.

ROSENSHINE, B. V. (2012, SPRING). PRINCIPLES OF INSTRUCTION. RESEARCH-BASED STRATEGIES THAT ALL TEACHERS SHOULD KNOW. *AMERICAN EDUCATOR, 36* (1), 12–19. AVAILABLE FROM WWW. AFT.ORG/SITES/DEFAULT/FILES/PERIODICALS/ROSENSHINE.PDF.

STOCKARD, J., WOOD, T. W., COUGHLIN, C., & KHOURY, C. R. (2018. ONLINE FIRST). THE EFFECTIVENESS OF DIRECT INSTRUCTION CURRICULA: A META-ANALYSIS OF A HALF CENTURY OF RESEARCH. *REVIEW OF EDUCATIONAL RESEARCH.* AVAILABLE FROM HTTP://ARTHURREADINGWORKSHOP.COM/WP-CONTENT/UPLOADS/2018/05/ STOCKARDDIMETAANALYSIS2018.PDF.

WATKINS, C. L. (1997). *PROJECT FOLLOW THROUGH: A CASE STUDY OF CONTINGENCIES INFLUENCING INSTRUCTIONAL PRACTICES OF THE EDUCATIONAL ESTABLISHMENT.* CAMBRIDGE, MA: CAMBRIDGE CENTER FOR BEHAVIORAL STUDIES. AVAILABLE FROM WWW.BEHAVIOR.ORG/RESOURCES/901.PDF.

Suggested readings and links

WHAT IS EXPLICIT INSTRUCTION?

AVAILABLE FROM HTTPS://GRANITESCHOOLS.INSTRUCTURE.COM/ FILES/64552171/DOWNLOAD?DOWNLOAD_FRD=1.

EXPLORING THE FOUNDATIONS OF EXPLICIT INSTRUCTION.

AVAILABLE FROM HTTPS://EXPLICITINSTRUCTION.ORG/DOWNLOAD/ SAMPLE-CHAPTER.PDF.

THE NATIONAL INSTITUTE FOR DIRECT INSTRUCTION (NIFDI) IS THE WORLD'S FOREMOST DIRECT INSTRUCTION (DI) SUPPORT PROVIDER. THIS WEBSITE PROVIDES INFORMATION AND RESOURCES FOR ADMINISTRATORS, TEACHERS AND PARENTS TO HELP THEM MAXIMISE STUDENT ACHIEVEMENT THROUGH DI.

AVAILABLE FROM WWW.NIFDI.ORG/.

CARNINE, D., (2000). WHY EDUCATION EXPERTS RESIST EFFECTIVE PRACTICES (AND WHAT IT WOULD TAKE TO MAKE EDUCATION MORE LIKE MEDICINE).

AVAILABLE FROM WWW.WRIGHTSLAW.COM/INFO/TEACH.PROFESSION. CARNINE.PDF.

TOM SHERRINGTON – BARAK ROSENSHINE'S PRINCIPLES OF INSTRUCTION PAPER – RESEARCHED 2019.

AVAILABLE FROM WWW.YOUTUBE.COM/WATCH?V=YR1DFO5XOPO.

EXPLORING BARAK ROSENSHINE'S SEMINAL PRINCIPLES OF INSTRUCTION: WHY IT IS THE MUST-READ FOR ALL TEACHERS.

AVAILABLE FROM HTTPS://TEACHERHEAD.COM/2018/06/10/EXPLORING-BARAK-ROSENSHINES-SEMINAL-PRINCIPLES-OF-INSTRUCTION-WHY-IT-IS-THE-MUST-READ-FOR-ALL-TEACHERS/.

DIRECT INSTRUCTION GETS NO RESPECT (BUT IT WORKS).

AVAILABLE FROM HTTPS://3STARLEARNINGEXPERIENCES.WORDPRESS. COM/2018/05/01/DIRECT-INSTRUCTION-GETS-NO-RESPECT-BUT-IT-WORKS/.

WILL THE EDUCATIONAL SCIENCES EVER GROW UP?

AVAILABLE FROM HTTPS://3STARLEARNINGEXPERIENCES.WORDPRESS. COM/2017/01/10/WILL-THE-EDUCATIONAL-SCIENCES-EVER-GROW-UP/.

19 ASSESSMENT *FOR*, NOT *OF* LEARNING

ASSESSMENT FOR LEARNING

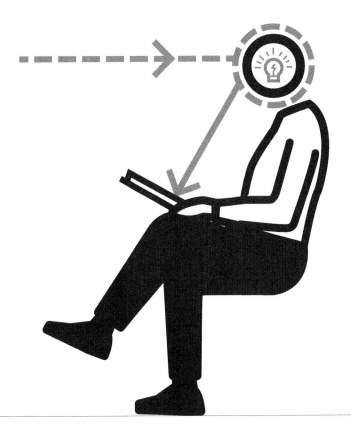

19 ASSESSMENT *FOR*, NOT *OF* LEARNING

PAPER   "Assessment and classroom learning"[1]

QUOTE   *"Feedback should be more work for the recipient than the donor".*[2]

Why you should read this article

In thinking about education research and its relevance to the classroom, one helpful term to consider is that of "best bets". It seems self-evident that because teacher and pupil time is so precious and because of the elusive way in which learning happens, we should focus on what is more likely to yield the best learning gains based on the best available evidence. Possibly the strongest "bet" we know of is high quality feedback and over the last 20 years the practice of formative assessment or "assessment for learning" as it would be later known, became one of the most influential approaches to classroom practice we know of.

FORMATIVE ASSESSMENT
Allows teachers to respond to learner's needs

In this seminal article, Paul Black and Dylan Wiliam present a strong case for the use of formative assessment as a means of not just reducing the gap between pupil achievement and underachievement but for raising pupil achievement overall. Feedback is often cited as the most effective intervention there is, giving the most "bang for your buck", but surprisingly not all feedback is good. A review by Avraham Kluger and Angelo DeNisi (1996) found that while the overall effect size of feedback was powerful (0.4), there were huge discrepancies between the effects with around two out of every five showing a negative effect. In other words, some pupils would have been more successful if they had had no feedback at all. It's not the giving of feedback per se but rather the type of feedback

FEEDBACK
Not always a positive impact

1   **BLACK, P., & WILIAM, D.** (1998). ASSESSMENT AND CLASSROOM LEARNING. *ASSESSMENT IN EDUCATION: PRINCIPLES, POLICY & PRACTICE*, 5(1), 7–74.

2   **WILIAM, D.** (2011). *EMBEDDED FORMATIVE ASSESSMENT.* BLOOMINGTON, IN: SOLUTION TREE PRESS.

given, possibly combined with the way it's given. The question is thus: What kinds of feedback are effective, and how can teachers use them?

In the 1990s, Wiliam and Black reviewed a great number of studies on assessment completed between 1988 and 1998 (comprised of a total of 681 publications) and what they found was that assessment *for* learning as opposed to assessment *of* learning produced substantial improvement in student outcomes. This distinction (Gipps, 1994) claimed that approaches to assessment that were formative in nature, that is to say they were more focused on responding to a piece of work in a way that informed what the student and teacher needed to do next, and which viewed feedback as an interaction between teacher and pupil (*for* learning) were far more effective than summative feedback in the form of simply giving grades and comments (*of* learning).

Assessment for learning versus asesssment of learning

Abstract of the article

This article is a review of the literature on classroom formative assessment. Several studies show firm evidence that innovations designed to strengthen the frequent feedback that students receive about their learning yield substantial learning gains. The perceptions of students and their role in self-assessment are considered alongside analysis of the strategies used by teachers and the formative strategies incorporated in such systemic approaches as mastery learning. There follows a more detailed and theoretical analysis of the nature of feedback, which provides a basis for a discussion of the development of theoretical models for formative assessment and of the prospects for the improvement of practice.

The article

In this article, the authors review studies published between 1988 and 1998 comprised of a total of 681 publications. The studies ranged from pupils aged 5 right up to undergraduates. The studies suggest that formative assessment practices are very powerful with typical effect sizes of formative assessment interventions recorded between 0.4 and 0.7. These are big gains. To put this in perspective, the authors note that: "An effect size gain of 0.7 in the recent international comparative studies in mathematics would have raised the score of a nation in the middle of the pack of 41 countries (e.g., the U.S.) to one of the top five". (Black & Wiliam, 1998a, p. 141) These findings would have big implications not just for the classroom teacher but for policy makers at a local, national and indeed international level.

EFFECT SIZE Measure of an intervention's impact

HOW LARGE IS THE EFFECT?

THE MOST FREQUENTLY mentioned magnitude of the effect of formative testing on learning is an improvement between 0.4 and 0.7. What these numbers mean exactly becomes clear when you express them in percentages (the so-called superiority percentage). These percentages indicate the likelihood that a random student from the formative assessment group will do better than someone from the control group (without formative assessment). For the effect size 0.4 that percentage is 61% and for 0.7 it is 69%. A meta-analysis by Neal Kingston and Brooke Nash from 2011 shows that this is an overestimation. The true effect size of formative testing is more in the direction of 0.25 or 57% (Kingston & Nash, 2011).

FORMATIVE
ASSESSMENT
Modify teaching and
learning activities

The term formative assessment has a long history in education, with it usually being attributed to Scriven (1967), however as Black and Wiliam state, formative assessment "does not have a tightly defined and widely accepted meaning" (p. 7). This points to a core problem in the implementation of the research, namely that it's often a kind of crystal ball through which anyone can see anything they want. They define formative assessment as "encompassing all those activities undertaken by teachers, and/or by their students, which provide information to be used as feedback to modify the teaching and learning activities in which they are engaged" (p. 7). In their view, formative assessment relates to a sequence of two actions: (1) the learners' perception that there is a gap between their goal and the present state of their knowledge, understanding, and/or a skill, and (2) what learners do to close that gap and attain the desired goal.

In reviewing the literature on teacher assessment practices, the authors found three major themes: first, formative assessment is not well understood by most teachers and is poor in practice. Second, the external pressure of local and national accountability exerts a strong influence on its efficacy. Lastly, to implement it properly requires substantial changes in teachers' perception of their own role and their classroom practice.

Another key point is that what students want and what *we want them to want* are often two completely different things. Many students "do not aspire to learn as much as possible, but are content to 'get by', to get through the period, the day or the year without any major disaster, having made time for activities other than school work" (Perrenoud, 1991, p. 92). The authors then lay out the challenge with formative assessment;

not only do we aim for students to learn material and then know it at some time in the future, but we also want them to *know what they don't know* and then be able and motivated to do something about it, to put in place actions which will lead to a closing of the gap between aspired goals and outcomes. As a side note here: This prepares them for their futures without the need of twenty-first century skills hype.

Another issue is that students often don't recognise feedback as a first step for them to take towards success but rather as an overall judgement of ability (Tunstall & Gipps, 1996). The work of Purdie and Hattie (1996) in Japanese and Australian students showed a cultural difference in students' response to feedback; some saw it as a means to succeed and some just didn't want it. A key point here is that it's not just enough to *provide* feedback – students need to *want* the feedback. If the feedback is not desired, then it disappears into the ether (or the bottom of their book bags or backpacks). Furthermore, students with a more mastery orientated approach to learning as opposed to a performance-orientated approach are far more likely to seek out, take on and ultimately act upon feedback (see Chapter 8, Beliefs about intelligence can affect intelligence and Chapter 11, Where are we going and how do we get there?). Thus, the authors are keen to emphasise the importance of self-concept on formative assessment.

One more key point made in this article is that formative assessment practices are particularly effective for low-performing students and so reduces the gap in achievement and raises the level of achievement overall. This has significant implications as such students are often demotivated and can be disruptive for other students and can then go on to be "alienated from society and to become the sources and the victims of serious social problems". (Black & Wiliam, 1998b, p. 142)

In summing up, the authors state that formative assessment practices are hugely powerful and that the associated practices are not marginal changes in teacher practice and require additional support and guidance. Additionally, the kinds of significant gains are dependent on a wide range of factors that are often beyond the control of the classroom teacher such as managerial focus on summative data or the quality of the relationships between teacher and pupil for example.

Conclusions/implications of the work for educational practice

The central takeaway from this article is that assessment of pupil progress needs to have more than a summative function in order for it to affect learning; it must inform both the teacher and student *what to do next*. One of the problems with the word "assessment" however is that it

Unwanted feedback is counter-productive

Formative assessment informs rather than judges

has certain, often pejorative, connotations. Indeed Dylan Wiliam would later say in an interview in the *Times Educational Supplement* that "The big mistake that Paul and I made was calling this stuff 'assessment' … because when you use the word assessment, people think about tests and exams" (Stewart, 2012). In fact, he would later say that he wished he had called it "responsive teaching" as opposed to assessment for learning.[3] Crucially also as stated earlier, there is an important distinction to be made between assessment *of* learning and assessment *for* learning (Gipps, 1994) which are two entirely different things. Black et al (2002, p. i) define assessment *for* learning as:

> any assessment for which the first priority in its design and practice is to serve the purpose of promoting pupils' learning. An assessment activity can help learning if it provides information to be used as feedback, by teachers, and by their pupils, in assessing themselves and each other, to modify the teaching and learning activities in which they are engaged.

The article has considerable implications, not just for the classroom teacher but also for school leaders in terms of the way in which they view the function of assessments. For example, many schools have an "assessment week" where year groups take tests and are given grades which are then recorded centrally and used for reports. But how many schools have a "feedback week"? A time where there is not just a stronger dialogue between teacher and student about the test but also a dedicated time given for the student to refine and improve and for the teacher to review and modify what they will teach next. In this way, assessments are truly responsive.

Feedback week
as opposed to
assessment week

 Essentially this article makes the claim that assessment which seeks to inform next steps is one of the most effective ways we know to improve pupil achievement (indeed the gains in using this approach are among the largest ever reported for educational interventions); however, they are at pains to state that a critical set of conditions need to be met in order to harness that effectiveness, which are a lot harder than one might think. Indeed it is interesting to note that some recent discussion has asked whether the subsequent use of assessment for learning over the last 20 years can be considered a success or failure (Christodoulou, 2017).

---

3   **WILIAM, D.** (2013). EXAMPLE OF A REALLY BIG MISTAKE: CALLING FORMATIVE ASSESSMENT FORMATIVE ASSESSMENT AND NOT SOMETHING LIKE RESPONSIVE TEACHING. TWITTER BLOG AVAILABLE AT: HTTPS://TWITTER.COM/DYLANWILIAM/STATUS/393045049337847808 (ACCESSED JUNE 12, 2019).

How to use the work in your teaching

Following this article, Wiliam and Black worked with a wide range of schools in 1999 on putting the principles of assessment for learning into practice in the classroom. They explained the research and then collaborated with them on how to implement the findings into their own practice. Among the strategies identified (Black et al., 2003) were:

Assessment for learning in practice

- Marking and feedback: handing back work to students with no grade, only comments. The idea here is to focus more on how to improve rather than how well they've done or gotten wrong.
- Questioning: Instead of asking questions that are factual recall or guessing what's in the teacher's head, teachers should allow more thinking time for deeper understanding.
- Testing schedule: having tests two-thirds of the way through a unit as opposed to the end in order to allow students time to attend to miscomprehensions.
- Peer-assessment and self-assessment: allowing students to look at assessment criteria from exam boards and then use that criteria to evaluate their own work and that of their peers.

According to the researchers, the results were dramatic. By the end of that academic year, the performance on external tests by the students taught by the teachers using formative assessment practices was significantly higher than those not using them in the same school (Black et al., 2003).

Gradeless feedback

Possibly the most radical of these methods is giving back assessments or individual pieces of work with no grades on them. This is where there needs to be a serious conversation within a school about the purpose of assessment. A key question to ask is: does the assessment serve the learning or does the learning serve the assessment? If it's the latter then it's unlikely that students will be truly mastering a domain and it's possible that they are being taught to pass the test. It is also more uncomfortable to have to really think hard about work you have done, where you have gone wrong and how to improve it than it is to look at a grade, but it is undoubtedly more effective. As Wiliam notes "feedback should be more work for the recipient than the donor" (Wiliam, 2011, p.162). The key challenge facing educators is in creating a climate where those challenges are embraced and genuine learning is a central aspiration.

Takeaways

- Make a clear distinction between assessment *of* learning and assessment *for* learning.
- Formative assessment is particularly effective with lower performing students.

- Don't always give a grade when handing back work, try comments only.
- Use questions to not only check understanding but to inform what to teach next.
- Give students rubrics, success criteria and exemplar work and get them to peer-assess each other's work.
- The onus should be put on the student to respond to marked work.

References

BLACK, P., HARRISON, C., LEE, C., MARSHALL, B., & WILIAM, D. (2002). *WORKING INSIDE THE BLACK BOX: ASSESSMENT FOR LEARNING IN THE CLASSROOM.* LONDON: KING'S COLLEGE LONDON DEPARTMENT OF EDUCATION AND PROFESSIONAL STUDIES.

BLACK, P.; HARRISON, C., LEE, C., MARSHALL, B., & WILIAM, D. (2003). *ASSESSMENT FOR LEARNING: PUTTING IT INTO PRACTICE.* BUCKINGHAM: OPEN UNIVERSITY PRESS.

BLACK, P., & WILIAM, D. (1998A). ASSESSMENT AND CLASSROOM LEARNING: *ASSESSMENT IN EDUCATION: PRINCIPLES, POLICY & PRACTICE, 5*(1), 7–74. AVAILABLE FROM WWW.GLA.AC.UK/T4/LEARNINGANDTEACHING/FILES/PGCTHE/BLACKANDWILIAM1998.PDF.

BLACK, P., & WILIAM, D. (1998B). INSIDE THE BLACK BOX: RAISING STANDARDS THROUGH CLASSROOM ASSESSMENT. *PHI DELTA KAPPAN, 80*(2), 139–148. AVAILABLE FROM HTTPS://PDFS.SEMANTICSCHOLAR.ORG/15BC/CADD19DBEB64EE5F0EDAC90E5857E6D5AD66.PDF.

CHRISTODOULOU, D. (2017). *MAKING GOOD PROGRESS.* LONDON: OPEN UNIVERSITY PRESS.

GIPPS, C. V. (1994). *BEYOND TESTING: TOWARDS A THEORY OF EDUCATIONAL ASSESSMENT,* WASHINGTON, DC: FALMER PRESS.

KINGSTON, N., & NASH, B. (2011). FORMATIVE ASSESSMENT: A META-ANALYSIS AND A CALL FOR RESEARCH. *EDUCATIONAL MEASUREMENT: ISSUES AND PRACTICE, 30*(4), 28–37. AVAILABLE FROM HTTPS://ONLINELIBRARY.WILEY.COM/DOI/ABS/10.1111/J.1745-3992.2011.00220.X.

KLUGER, A. N., & DENISI, A. (1996). THE EFFECTS OF FEEDBACK INTERVENTIONS ON PERFORMANCE: A HISTORICAL REVIEW, A META-ANALYSIS, AND A PRELIMINARY FEEDBACK INTERVENTION THEORY. *PSYCHOLOGICAL BULLETIN, 119*, 254–284. AVAILABLE FROM WWW.RESEARCHGATE.NET/PUBLICATION/232458848_THE_EFFECTS_OF_FEEDBACK_INTERVENTIONS_ON_PERFORMANCE_A_HISTORICAL_REVIEW_A_META-ANALYSIS_AND_A_PRELIMINARY_FEEDBACK_INTERVENTION_THEORY

PERRENOUD, P. (1991), TOWARDS A PRAGMATIC APPROACH TO FORMATIVE EVALUATION. IN P. WESTON (ED.), ASSESSMENT OF PUPIL ACHIEVEMENT: MOTIVATION AND SCHOOL SUCCESS (PP. 79–101). AMSTERDAM, THE NETHERLANDS: SWETS AND ZEITLINGER.

PURDIE, N., & HATTIE, H. (1996). CULTURAL DIFFERENCES IN THE USE OF SELF REGULATED LEARNING. *AMERICAN EDUCATIONAL RESEARCH JOURNAL, 33*, 845–871.

SCRIVEN, M. (1967). THE METHODOLOGY OF EVALUATION. IN R. E. STAKE (ED.), *PERSPECTIVES OF CURRICULUM EVALUATION* (VOL. 1, PP. 39–55). CHICAGO, IL: RAND MCNALLY.

STEWART, W. (JULY 13, 2012). THINK YOU'VE IMPLEMENTED ASSESSMENT FOR LEARNING? TIMES EDUCATIONAL SUPPLEMENT. AVAILABLE FROM HTTPS://WWW.TES.COM/NEWS/TES-ARCHIVE/TES-PUBLICATION/THINK-YOUVE-IMPLEMENTED-ASSESSMENT-LEARNING.

TUNSTALL, P., & GIPPS, C. (1996). TEACHER FEEDBACK TO YOUNG CHILDREN IN FORMATIVE ASSESSMENT: A TYPOLOGY. *BRITISH EDUCATIONAL RESEARCH JOURNAL, 22*(4), 389–404.

WILIAM, D. (2011). *EMBEDDED FORMATIVE ASSESSMENT.* BLOOMINGTON, IN: SOLUTION TREE PRESS.

WILIAM, D. (2013). EXAMPLE OF A REALLY BIG MISTAKE: CALLING FORMATIVE ASSESSMENT FORMATIVE ASSESSMENT AND NOT SOMETHING LIKE "RESPONSIVE TEACHING". TWITTER BLOG AVAILABLE AT: HTTPS://TWITTER.COM/DYLANWILIAM/STATUS/393045049337847808.

Suggested readings and link

BLACK, P., & WILIAM, D. (1998B). INSIDE THE BLACK BOX: RAISING STANDARDS THROUGH CLASSROOM ASSESSMENT. *PHI DELTA KAPPAN*, 80(2), 139–148. HTTPS://JOURNALS.SAGEPUB.COM/DOI/PDF/10.1177/003172171009200119

CHRISTODOULOU, D. WHY DID ASSESSMENT FOR LEARNING FAIL? FESTIVAL OF EDUCATION, WELLINGTON COLLEGE.

Assessment for learning is one of the most well-evidenced methods of improving education. Yet, after nearly two decades of intensive training and investment in its principles, educational standards in England haven't risen. Why? Daisy Christodoulou considers some possible explanations.

AVAILABLE FROM WWW.YOUTUBE.COM/WATCH?V=QLPAALDAQQY.

BLACK, P. (2006). ASSESSMENT FOR LEARNING: WHERE IS IT NOW? WHERE IS IT GOING? IN C. RUST (ED.). *IMPROVING STUDENT LEARNING THROUGH ASSESSMENT*, OXFORD CENTRE FOR STAFF AND LEARNING DEVELOPMENT. SLIDE PRESENTATION

AVAILABLE FROM HTTPS://SLIDEPLAYER.COM/SLIDE/783910/.

A VIDEO OF DYLAN WILIAM EXPLAINING ASSESSMENT FOR LEARNING.

AVAILABLE FROM WWW.YOUTUBE.COM/WATCH?V=HIU-JY-XAPG.

LEARNING SCIENCES INTERNATIONAL (PUBLISHED ON SEPTEMBER 11, 2018)

Dylan Wiliam reviews the meaning of assessment for learning. He brings forward five helpful studies. Between them, five research reports synthesise the results of about 4000 research projects on feedback on assessment for learning in schools and colleges and in workplaces. Find out what the data has to say and what it reveals about learning assessment.

AVAILABLE FROM WWW.YOUTUBE.COM/WATCH?V=Q-MYBW36_DA.

GETTING STARTED WITH ASSESSMENT FOR LEARNING.

AVAILABLE FROM HTTPS://CAMBRIDGE-COMMUNITY.ORG.UK/PROFESSIONAL-DEVELOPMENT/GSWAFL/INDEX.HTML.

20 FEED UP, FEEDBACK, FEED FORWARD

FEEDBACK

20 FEED UP, FEEDBACK, FEED FORWARD

PAPER "The power of feedback"[1]

QUOTE *"Effective feedback must answer three major questions asked by a teacher and/or by a student: Where am I going? (What are the goals), How am I going? (What progress is being made toward the goal?), and Where to next? (What activities need to be undertaken to make better progress?)"*

Why you should read this article

Do you remember the first time you learned how to ride a bike? For many of us that would have been with a parent and often resulted in many crashes before you finally took flight. Now if your parent said to you when you crashed "Oh you crashed there, okay now try it again but this time try not to crash", this input from the parent is technically a form of feedback in its broadest sense but is almost completely useless and more likely to put more pressure on the child. Instead, the parent might break down the global skill of "riding a bike" into its component parts and give specific instruction on how to push off, pedal at the right time, balance the frame and guide the handlebars. This form of feedback is likely to result in success because it has a clear goal and provides clear steps on how to get there.

FEEDBACK
A definition

Kluger and DeNisi (1996) define feedback as "actions taken by an external agent to provide information regarding some aspect(s) of one's task performance" (p. 235). However a surprising thing about feedback is that it doesn't always lead to positive outcomes, indeed it often gets in the way of learning. The word feedback implies a responsibility on the teacher and certainly this is true, but what this article clearly shows is that students are most successful when they take responsibility for feedback. As Dylan Wiliam observes, "feedback should be more work for the recipient than the donor" (Wiliam, 2011, p. 129).

Shared responsibility
of teacher and
student

[1] **HATTIE, J., & TIMPERLEY, H.** (2007) THE POWER OF FEEDBACK. *REVIEW OF EDUCATIONAL RESEARCH,* 77, 81–112.

In this article, Hattie and Timperley draw on a vast amount of evidence to make several important conclusions about the purpose and type of feedback. They invite us to view the process as a continuum of instruction and feedback and offer three central questions to be asked when providing feedback along with a four-part model with which to conceptualise the power of feedback.

Abstract of the articles

Feedback is one of the most powerful influences on learning and achievement, but this impact can be either positive or negative. Its power is frequently mentioned in articles about learning and teaching, but surprisingly few recent studies have systematically investigated its meaning. This article provides a conceptual analysis of feedback and reviews the evidence related to its impact on learning and achievement. This evidence shows that although feedback is among the major influences, the type of feedback and the way it is given can be differentially effective. A model of feedback is then proposed that identifies the particular properties and circumstances that make it effective, and some typically thorny issues are discussed, including the timing of feedback and the effects of positive and negative feedback. Finally, this analysis is used to suggest ways in which feedback can be used to enhance its effectiveness in classrooms.

The article

The authors begin with a conceptual analysis of the meaning of the term feedback, which is more slippery than one might think. Possibly the best definition they give, which the authors describe as "an excellent summary", is from Winne and Butler (1994) who write that "feedback is information with which a learner can confirm, add to, overwrite, tune, or restructure information in memory, whether that information is domain knowledge, meta-cognitive knowledge, beliefs about self and tasks, or cognitive tactics and strategies" (p. 5740). This notion of a continuum or trajectory of learning, in which feedback and student agency are symbiotically linked, is a strong theme in this article.

META-COGNITION
Awareness and ownership of one's own learning

A key distinction made by the authors is that feedback and instruction are not the same thing. If students' knowledge of a particular domain is low then more instruction will be better than feedback. If you are learning to drive a car, it is no use for the instructor to tell you to "find the bite point" on the accelerator if you don't know how to use a clutch. As Kulhavy (1977, p. 220) points out "if the material studied is unfamiliar or abstruse, providing feedback should have little effect on criterion performance since there is not a way to relate the new information to what is already known".

Feedback and instruction are not the same thing

As discussed in Chapter 19, the surprising thing about feedback is that some of it is not helpful at all. In Hattie's meta-analysis he also discovered a wide variability in the quality and impact of feedback. Simply providing more feedback is not always useful. The authors cite Kluger and DeNisi (1996) and their finding that the average effect size of feedback was 0.38 yet 32% of the effects were negative. The authors conclude from this that feedback is more effective when it builds on changes from previous trials and when goals are specific and challenging and task complexity is low. Significantly they claim that praise for task performance seems to be ineffective "which is hardly surprising because it contains such little learning-related information" (Hattie & Timperley, 2007, p. 86).

PRAISE
Good for lots of things but not for learning

A central theme of this article is that feedback needs to be directed at the appropriate level of student learning. (Considering again their model of feedback as a continuum between instruction and feedback is important to remember). With that in mind, the authors use a three-part strategy based on three central questions:

FEEDBACK
Three questions to ask

1. *Where am I going?* (What is my goal? What am I trying to achieve?)
2. *How am I going?* (What is my current level of performance relative to my goal?)
3. *Where to next?* (What specific actions do I need to take to reduce the gap?)

They also refer to these three steps as *"feed up, feedback and feed forward"*. In answering the first question, the authors state that it is vital to provide clear goals to students that are unambiguous and attainable, which attempt to close the gap between current understanding and goals: "Feedback cannot lead to a reduction in this discrepancy if the goal is poorly defined, because the gap between current learning and intended learning is unlikely to be sufficiently clear for students to see a need to reduce it" (Hattie & Timperley, 2007, p. 89). In terms of "How am I going?", there is not much guidance given apart from asserting that testing is perhaps not an ideal way of assessing current performance. The last question, "Where to next?" is a crucial one and may include "enhanced challenges, more self-regulation over the learning process, greater fluency and automaticity, more strategies and processes to work on the tasks, deeper understanding, and more information about what is and what is not understood". (Hattie & Timperley, 2007, p. 90)

Feed up, feedback, feed forward

Arising from this, the authors present a four-part model (Figure 20.1) which incorporates:

1. Feedback about the task (FT) is likely to be more powerful if it highlights misinterpretations of key concepts or terms instead of merely pointing out a lack of information.

2. Feedback about the process (FP) is aimed at outlining aspects of the process used to create a product or whatever was carried out.

3. Feedback about the level of self-regulation a student is using (FR) is aimed at providing guidance on how students might better assess how they can metacognitively reflect on their own learning, assess what they need to work on and how to progress.

4. Lastly, feedback that is aimed at the self (FS) is aimed at personal aspects of the student such as saying "Good girl, well done you are a top student".

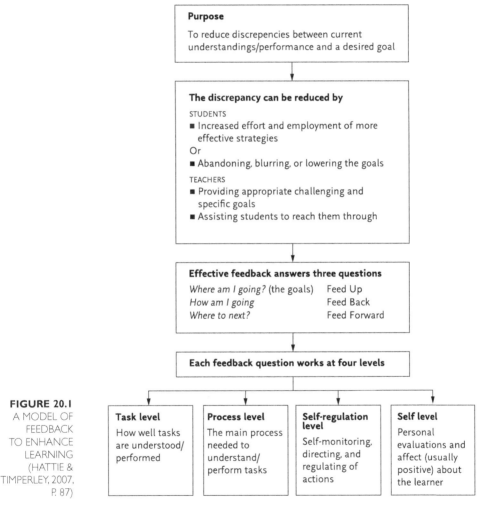

FIGURE 20.1
A MODEL OF FEEDBACK TO ENHANCE LEARNING (HATTIE & TIMPERLEY, 2007, P. 87)

A particularly important part of this model is the self-regulation level. Some students have low self-regulation levels and poor overall self-concept as they are conscious of the fact that "feedback", as they understand it, is a judgement of sorts. In this case, feedback is not always wanted or acted upon. Feedback is particularly powerful when it tells the student what they did well and how to expand on that, but as we saw in Chapter 10 (How you think about achievement is more important than the achievement itself), if overly positive praise or undeserved success is given to the student then the impact of this feedback can be negative as the student will not attribute their performance to effort but rather to external factors. Additionally, feedback can be really powerful when it disconfirms what a student thought they knew: "Feedback has its greatest effect when a learner expects a response to be correct and it turns out to be wrong" (Hattie & Timperley, 2007, p. 95).

An additional problem is that some students view the entire process of feedback as the teacher's responsibility. They expect to be told what they need to achieve, how they are currently doing, and then how to get there. In the initial stages, there is certainly a responsibility on the teacher to provide this information but the students who are really successful will take more ownership of this process.

Disconfirmation is important in learning

Conclusions/implications of the work for educational practice

Essentially, you want the student receiving feedback to act upon information provided to them and to do so they will need a clear picture of where they need to be. Getting students to "take on" this responsibility is key. If the teacher is working twice as hard as the student then something has gone wrong. Providing clear criteria for success, worked examples, and exemplars is particularly helpful. After all, it's impossible to be excellent if you don't know what excellent looks like. From there they need accurate information of their current performance and clear steps on how to reduce the gap between the current state and the aspired outcome.

Feedback works better when the learner has ownership

Additionally, feedback needs to be given in a context. Saying "you need to use more complex vocabulary and terms" is going to be ineffective if the teacher is not specific about what that specific context is. Too much "feedback" is really just information about what is wrong with the student's work. For example, in providing students with feedback on an essay on Shakespeare teachers often use the language of the exam board grade descriptors such as "extensive vocabulary should be used widely"; however, this is not useful information for a student who does not have that wide vocabulary in the first place. Instructing the student to use terms such as "soliloquy" and "iambic pentameter" and pointing them to an area where they might expand on these terms is likely to lead to more learning.

Feedback should clarify and inform

In addition, the goals given to students need to be specific. If the feedback is unrelated to the goal then it is unlikely to reduce the gap between the current level of performance and the intended goal. For example, if the goal of a piece of student writing is to "create a mood in a story" and the student is given feedback on spelling and presentation then they are not likely to improve in their ability to create a mood where the focus might be on the use of tone and imagery which would better address the task.

How to use the work in your teaching

The authors of this article attempt to encourage teachers to view feedback as a continuum in which a productive dialogue occurs. The aim is to get students to think about, and act upon the information they have been given. A helpful model of this is provided by Paul Kirschner, in a presentation in 2017 for the MBO Taalacademie (Vocational High School Language Academy) on "Effective, efficient and enjoyable feedback: Is that possible? And how?" distinguished three forms of feedback (see Figure 20.2). With *corrective feedback* you look at something, say whether it is right or wrong and what it should be. A student does not learn very much from this kind of feedback. This is called *single loop* feedback: It relates to the actions, behaviour and visible effect or result (good/ desirable or wrong/undesirable). A little better is *directive feedback*, in which the teacher tells the student what is wrong and how (s)he can correct it. This is called *double loop* and is about how the task was performed in which the student is told how it can or should be done better. The best type of feedback is knowledge development or *epistemic feedback*. This is called *triple loop* feedback. As a teacher, with this type of feedback you encourage the student to think about the who, what, why, when and how of the task. You ask, for example, "Why did you choose this formula, Aisha? And what would you have done if the task was X? Would you have done it differently?"

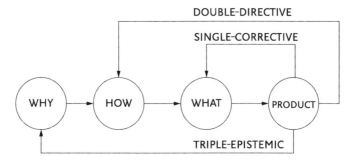

FIGURE 20.2
SINGLE, DOUBLE, AND TRIPLE LOOP FEEDBACK

Feedback is one of the most powerful forms of intervention in education but it is also one of the most misunderstood. Many teachers are now assessed against the progress of their pupils and how much marking is in their students' books, which can result in a situation where feedback is more about showing their own work as opposed to that of their students. To really harness the power of feedback it is vital to cultivate an environment where students have a clear sense of where they are going to, how they are currently doing against that goal, and what to do about it to close that gap.

Takeaways

- If the student doesn't know enough about a topic then they don't need feedback, they need more instruction.
- Feedback needs to be context specific, not general. Saying "use better vocab" is not helpful to students if they don't know what that domain-specific vocab is.
- If the teacher is putting more work into the process than the student, then progress is likely to be impaired.
- Students need to view the process of feedback as one they will ultimately take ownership of.
- Feedback needs to be non-threatening to students in terms of their self-concept.
- Praise that directs the student away from the task and towards the self is unlikely to be beneficial as it contains so little information on how to improve.
- Feedback on the task (FT) is most powerful when it addresses faulty conceptions as opposed to a complete misunderstanding.

References

HATTIE, J., & TIMPERLEY, H. (2007). THE POWER OF FEEDBACK. *REVIEW OF EDUCATIONAL RESEARCH, 77,* 81–112.

KLUGER, A. N., & DENISI, A. (1996). THE EFFECTS OF FEEDBACK INTERVENTIONS ON PERFORMANCE: A HISTORICAL REVIEW, A META-ANALYSIS, AND A PRELIMINARY FEEDBACK INTERVENTION THEORY. *PSYCHOLOGICAL BULLETIN, 119,* 254–284.

KULHAVY, R. W. (1977). FEEDBACK IN WRITTEN INSTRUCTION. *REVIEW OF EDUCATIONAL RESEARCH, 47,* 2, 211–232.

WILIAM, D. (2011). *EMBEDDED FORMATIVE ASSESSMENT.* BLOOMINGTON, MN: SOLUTION TREE PRESS.

WINNE, P. H., & BUTLER, D. L. (1994). STUDENT COGNITION IN LEARNING FROM TEACHING. IN T. HUSEN AND T. POSTLEWAITE (EDS.), *INTERNATIONAL ENCYCLOPEDIA OF EDUCATION* (2ND ED., PP. 5738–5745). OXFORD: PERGAMON.

Suggested readings and links

A VIDEO OF JOHN HATTIE ON VISIBLE LEARNING AND FEEDBACK IS

AVAILABLE FROM WWW.YOUTUBE.COM/WATCH?V=VPQ09EY4PZO.

DYLAN WILIAM'S "FOUR QUARTERS MARKING" – A WORKLOAD SOLUTION?

AVAILABLE FROM HTTPS://CHRONOTOPEBLOG.COM/2017/09/02/
FOUR-QUARTERS-MARKING-A-WORKLOAD-SOLUTION/.

A SUMMARY OF THE ARTICLE WITH SOME USEFUL EXAMPLES OF APPLICATION IN THE CLASSROOM IS

AVAILABLE FROM HTTPS://ROBINBNEAL.COM/2015/04/24/
THE-POWER-OF-FEEDBACK-SUMMARY-PART-ONE/

21 | LEARNING TECHNIQUES THAT REALLY WORK

LEARNING TECHNIQUES

21 | LEARNING TECHNIQUES THAT REALLY WORK

PAPER "Improving students' learning with effective learning techniques: Promising directions from cognitive and educational psychology"[1]

QUOTE *"If simple techniques were available that teachers and students could use to improve student learning and achievement, would you be surprised if teachers were not being told about these techniques and if many students were not using them?"*

Why you should read this article

You have to read and learn from some text. What's the best way to do this? Do you highlight the text with different colour markers? Do you underline in the text? Do you re-read the text? These are all "normal" study approaches, but it does not stop here. Learners often have very astonishing ideas about how they can best learn. Thinking back to our own school careers, we did things like putting a book under our pillow or playing a poem on an endless loop on the tape recorder so that the content could enter our brains during sleep. We've also heard of learners who thought that taking notes with a certain pen would ensure that the content would also appear during the examinations. Think of this as your own magical remember pen. Now these last three are very exceptional ideas and of course we know that they really don't work (especially the first and last ones), but the reason that students do these things is, in essence, good. At the very least they want to get a good grade on an exam and at best they really want to learn and master the substance (see Chapter 8 on how beliefs can influence learning and Chapter 11, Where are we going and how do we get there?).

---

[1] **DUNLOSKY, J., RAWSON, K. A., MARSH, E. J., NATHAN, M. J., & WILLINGHAM, D. T.** (2013). IMPROVING STUDENTS' LEARNING WITH EFFECTIVE LEARNING TECHNIQUES: PROMISING DIRECTIONS FROM COGNITIVE AND EDUCATIONAL PSYCHOLOGY. *PSYCHOLOGICAL SCIENCE IN THE PUBLIC INTEREST, 14*, 4–58.

Students lack knowledge of most effective study methods

As a "calculating student" (nothing pejorative meant here), if there are certain study strategies or approaches that are more effective or efficient than others, then of course it's smart to use the most effective or efficient approach. The only problem here was that most students, and also many or even most teachers, don't have an accurate picture of the effectiveness of their study approach. We'd even venture to state that many don't even know the different effective strategies. After more than a hundred years of research into learning and memory, there are a few things that we know about good and less good approaches. Since the turn of this century, people have been trying to figure out how to remember as much as possible, how to ensure that we forget as little as possible, and how to do this in as little time as possible. The reason that we have our doubts with respect to teachers is because the findings that have emerged from this research aren't yet included in textbooks for teachers (both in research in the US, as well as in the Netherlands and Flanders, Pomerance, Greenberg, & Walsh, 2016; Surma, Vanhoywegen, Camp, & Kirschner, 2018). This is one of the reasons why John Dunlosky and colleagues conducted an overview study of what is known about effective and efficient study approaches. With this knowledge, teachers can better choose between different approaches and apply the best in their education and also teach their pupils to do it themselves.

Abstract of the article

Many students are being left behind by an educational system that some people believe is in crisis. Improving educational outcomes will require efforts on many fronts, but a central premise of this monograph is that one part of a solution involves helping students to better regulate their learning through the use of effective learning techniques. Fortunately, cognitive and educational psychologists have been developing and evaluating easy-to-use learning techniques that could help students achieve their learning goals. In this monograph, we discuss 10 learning techniques in detail and offer recommendations about their relative utility. We selected techniques that were expected to be relatively easy to use and hence could be adopted by many students. Also, some techniques (e.g. highlighting and rereading) were selected because students report relying heavily on them, which makes it especially important to examine how well they work. The techniques include elaborative interrogation, self-explanation, summarization, highlighting (or underlining), the keyword mnemonic, imagery use for text learning, rereading, practice testing, distributed practice, and interleaved practice.

To offer recommendations about the relative utility of these techniques, we evaluated whether their benefits generalize across four

Easy-to-use study techniques

categories of variables: learning conditions, student characteristics, materials, and criterion tasks. Learning conditions include aspects of the learning environment in which the technique is implemented, such as whether a student studies alone or with a group. Student characteristics include variables such as age, ability, and level of prior knowledge. Materials vary from simple concepts to mathematical problems to complicated science texts. Criterion tasks include different outcome measures that are relevant to student achievement, such as those tapping memory, problem solving, and comprehension.

Five techniques received a low utility assessment: summarization, highlighting, the keyword mnemonic, imagery use for text learning, and rereading. These techniques were rated as low utility for numerous reasons. Summarization and imagery use for text learning have been shown to help some students on some criterion tasks, yet the conditions under which these techniques produce benefits are limited, and much research is still needed to fully explore their overall effectiveness. The keyword mnemonic is difficult to implement in some contexts, and it appears to benefit students for a limited number of materials and for short retention intervals. Most students report rereading and highlighting, yet these techniques do not consistently boost students' performance, so other techniques should be used in their place (e.g. practice testing instead of rereading).

The article

John Dunlosky and his colleagues Katherine Rawson, Elizabeth Marsh, Mitch Nathan, and Dan Willingham wrote this article to help students and teachers by looking at what was known from research in cognitive psychology and educational sciences on the effectiveness of different study approaches (they called them learning techniques). They knew from the literature that much was known about effective learning techniques, but that this information often wasn't found in teacher textbooks; both per-service and in-service.

Dunlosky et al. document and discuss ten study techniques, namely: elaborative interrogation, self-explanation, summarisation, highlighting/underlining, keyword mnemonics, imagery for text, rereading, practice testing, distributed practice, and interleaved practice (see Table 21.1). They chose these ten because they're all relatively easy to use independently and would, therefore, be usable by many students.

Highlighting and rereading don't work

They also noted that a number of techniques (e.g. highlighting and rereading) are often used by students and so it was important to know if they actually worked. To this end, they searched the scientific literature for studies on the effectiveness of the different techniques. In addition

TABLE 21.1
THE TEN LEARNING
TECHNIQUES
STUDIED BY
DUNLOSKY ET AL.
(2013)

Technique	Description
1 Elaborative interrogation	Generating an explanation for why an explicitly stated fact or concept is true
2 Self-explanation	Explaining how new information is related to known information, or explaining steps taken during problem solving
3 Summarization	Writing summaries (of various lengths) of to-be-learned texts
4 Highlighting/underlining	Marking potentially important portions of to-be-learned materials while reading
5 Keyword mnemonic	Using keywords and mental imagery to associate verbal materials
6 Imagery for text	Attempting to form mental images of text materials while reading or listening
7 Rereading	Restudying text material again after an initial reading
8 Practice testing	Self-testing or taking practice tests over to-be-learned material
9 Distributed practice	Implementing a schedule of practice that spreads out study activities over time
10 Interleaved practice	Implementing a schedule of practice that mixes different kinds of problems, or a schedule of study that mixes different kinds of material, within a single study session

to looking at whether the learning techniques actually led to better information retention, they also took into account whether the strategies could be used by different students (e.g. different ages, prior knowledge, verbal ability, self-efficacy), with different types of learning material (e.g. vocabulary, lecture content, narrative and expository texts, maps, diagrams), under different learning conditions (e.g. amount of practice, reading vs. listening, intentional vs. incidental learning, individual vs. group learning, listening vs. reading) and for different criterion tasks (e.g. cued recall, free recall, recognition, problem solving, essay writing). The researchers were looking for techniques that could be used by as many students as possible (i.e. that were generalisable). Below are the ten with a short description. In the next part, we look at which ones came out the best.

Dunlosky and his colleagues produced a kind of report card for the different techniques including the generalisability requirements. Table 21.2 lists the assessments. As is apparent, the top two are practice testing and distributed practice. These learning techniques are, therefore, assessed as good (i.e. have high utility). Practice testing and distributed practice work regardless of learner, material, criterion task, learning context, and issues (problems) for implementation.

Technique	Utility	Learner	Material	Criterion tasks	Context	Implement-ation issues
Elaborative interrogation	Moderate	P–I	P	I	I	P
Self-explanation	Moderate	P–I	P	P–I	I	Q
Summarization	Low	Q	P–I	Q	I	Q
Highlighting	Low	Q	Q	N	N	P
Keyword mnemonic	Low	Q	Q	Q-I	Q–I	Q
Imagery use	Low	Q	Q	Q-I	I	P
Rereading	Low	I	P	Q-I	I	P
Practice testing	High	P–I	P	P	P	P
Distributed practice	High	P–I	P	P–I	P–I	P
Interleaved practice	Moderate	I	Q	P–I	P–I	P

Note: A positive (P) rating indicates that available evidence demonstrates efficacy of a learning technique with respect to a given variable or issue. A negative (N) rating indicates that a technique is largely ineffective for a given variable. A qualified (Q) rating indicates that the technique yielded positive effects under some conditions (or in some groups) but not others. An insufficient (I) rating indicates that there is insufficient evidence to support a definitive assessment for one or more factors for a given variable or issue.

Elaborative interrogation, self-explanation, and interleaved practice were judged to be of moderate, but sufficient, utility. There was less good news for summarisation, highlighting/underlining, keyword mnemonics, imagery use, and rereading; techniques which are very often recommended to and used by students. These all had low utility; that is they don't really help students learn. One of these may sound a bit weird, namely summarisation because it's actually a form of self-testing. The reason for this is simple: in order for summarisation to work, you have to be able to make a good summary. However, most students can't! The same might be true for underlining/highlighting.

If you can't separate the wheat from the chaff, you'll highlight/underline too much or the wrong things.

The researchers conclude that, how can it be any different, more research is needed. First, research should fully explore the degree to which the benefits of some techniques generalise to the variables studied (learner, material, etc.) including interactions among the variables that might limit or magnify the benefits of a given technique. Second, research on the benefit of most of the techniques needs to be carried out in representative educational settings.

Conclusions/implications of the work for educational practice

It's probably best to confine ourselves to a discussion of the two best techniques: practice testing and distributed practice.

Distributed practice (spaced practice) is a technique whereby you spread out the study and/or practice time instead of bundling it in one period in so-called blocked- or massed-practice sessions. Studying something in a few short sessions (e.g. four times 30 minutes) with a day or two between sessions works better than cramming on the night before a test for two hours. This is called the spacing effect (Cepeda et al., 2008). There is a caveat here: for immediate retention, cramming sometimes leads to equivalent or even slightly better learning, but for long-term retention spacing is significantly superior.

DISTRIBUTED AND SPACED PRACTICE
Highly effective methods of learning

CRAMMING
Good in the short-term, bad in the long-term

- For teachers: give small (homework) assignments that include both new and previously treated material frequently, give cumulative tests, plan short review sessions at the start of each lesson, implement a spiral curriculum, etc.
- For students: make exam schedules in which the study sessions are spread in time, practice basic skills repeatedly but in short intervals, etc.

The testing effect

Practice testing (retrieval practice) means that you are required to retrieve the information that was studied/learnt from long-term memory. This active recall/retrieval of information ensures that you remember this information better and for longer. This effect is called the testing effect (Roediger & Butler, 2011; Roediger & Karpicke, 2006).

- For teachers: use any instructional technique where your students are obliged to remember information such as quizzes, practice tests, and review questions.
- For students: use different forms of self-tests, such as flashcards, diagnostic exercises, quizzes. A great approach is what's known as Cornell notes (Pauk, 2001).

THE SPACING EFFECT

THE SPACING EFFECT is based upon what's known as the forgetting curve (see Figure 21.1), first discussed by Hermann Ebbinghaus in 1885! In essence, this means that we forget what we've read or learnt quickly and at a high rate (i.e. the curve is steep). By building retrieval moments into the learning process, we refresh what we know to 100% and also make the curve less steep.

THE SPACING EFFECT

The spacing effect is based upon what's known as the forgetting curve, first discussed by Hermann Ebbinghaus in 1885! In essence, this means that we forget what we've read or learned quickly and at a high rate (i.e., the curve is steep). By building retrieval moments into the learning process, we refresh what we know to 100% and also make the curve less steep.

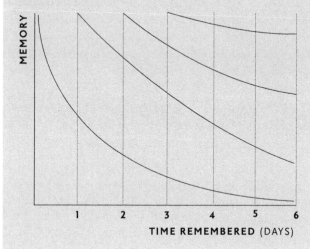

FIGURE 21.1
A TYPICAL FORGETTING CURVE (AFTER EBBINGHAUS, 1885)

How to use the work in your teaching

Effective learning techniques are not just for students

When making use of the learning techniques that have been shown to have a high utility, you need to remember a few things. First, it's important that you lead by example. It's not enough to teach your students the techniques and then to tell them to use them. You need to use them yourself. You need to give them assignments in such a way that they are spacing their practice. You need to plan your exams in such a way that there's enough time for the kids to space their practice. And here's a sticky point: you need to coordinate this with your fellow teachers (at least if you're a secondary school teacher) since students can't spread their learning moments if there are a series of exams in different subjects planned close to each other. No child will study Monday evening for a test on Friday if there's a test Tuesday in a different subject.

More frequent practice tests are more effective than one big one

Further, you need to make use of retrieval practice in your teaching. You can begin each lesson with a review in the form of a question, quiz, or whatever about what was studied or discussed the day before. In this way your students are required to retrieve what they have learnt. Barak Rosenshine (2010) moved this a step further saying that at the end of each week – or on the Monday of the new week – you should review in the form of a quiz the most important things that were handled the previous week and the same goes for each month. No big tests, just short quizzes to allow for retrieval. Finally, this also goes for starting a new unit: What was important in the previous unit for the new one?

And all of this means that you need to teach how to use the techniques properly. As stated, certain techniques such as highlighting/underlining and summarising have potential, but don't fulfil that potential because most students have never really learnt how to write a good summary or learnt how to discern what the main points of a paragraph of text are. If they think that everything is of equal importance, then nothing is actually important. And don't think that this is only the job of the English teacher. The learning and use of these techniques needs to be integrated into all subjects!

Takeaways

- Most students don't really know the best way to study. As a teacher you need to teach them this!
- Most teachers also don't know what the best learning techniques are and often use ones that don't work or don't work well.
- Teach your students those techniques that have been proven to be effective and explain why they work well; discourage techniques that don't work well and explain why they don't.
- Teach your students how to summarise, highlight, etc. so that these techniques have a chance at working.
- Repeat/review the material from the day(s) before and check what your students still know and what they do and don't understand.
- Use different types of practice tests such as quizzes, flashcards, and open ended questions, epistemic tasks, review questions, and so forth.
- It's better to give your students a number of small (homework) assignments distributed over time than one large assignment.

References

CEPEDA, N. J., VUL, E., ROHRER, D., WIXTED, J. T., & PASHLER, H. (2008). SPACING EFFECTS IN LEARNING: A TEMPORAL RIDGELINE OF OPTIMAL RETENTION. *PSYCHOLOGICAL SCIENCE, 19*, 1095–1102. AVAILABLE FROM HTTP://LAPLAB.UCSD.EDU/ARTICLES/CEPEDA%20ET%20AL%202008_PSYCHSCI.PDF.

DUNLOSKY, J., RAWSON, K. A., MARSH, E. J., NATHAN, M. J., & WILLINGHAM, D. T. (2013). IMPROVING STUDENTS' LEARNING WITH EFFECTIVE LEARNING TECHNIQUES: PROMISING DIRECTIONS FROM COGNITIVE AND EDUCATIONAL PSYCHOLOGY. *PSYCHOLOGICAL SCIENCE IN THE PUBLIC INTEREST, 14*, 4–58. AVAILABLE FROM WWW.INDIANA.EDU/~PCL/RGOLDSTO/COURSES/DUNLOSKYIMPROVINGLEARNING.PDF.

EBBINGHAUS, H. (1885). *ÜBER DAS GEDÄCHTNIS [ABOUT MEMORY]*. LEIPZIG: DUNKER.

PAUK, W. (2001). *HOW TO STUDY IN COLLEGE*. BOSTON, MA: HOUGHTON MIFFLIN COMPANY.

POMERANCE, L., GREENBERG, J., & WALSH, K. (2016). *LEARNING ABOUT LEARNING: WHAT EVERY TEACHER NEEDS TO KNOW*. AVAILABLE FROM HTTP://WWW.NCTQ.ORG/DMSVIEW/LEARNING_ABOUT_LEARNING_REPORT.

ROEDIGER, H. L. I. I. I., & BUTLER, A. C. (2011). THE CRITICAL ROLE OF RETRIEVAL PRACTICE IN LONG-TERM RETENTION. *TRENDS IN COGNITIVE SCIENCES, 15*(1), 20–27. AVAILABLE FROM HTTPS://READER.ELSEVIER.COM/READER/SD/PII/S1364661310002081?TOKEN=D5B516D6524C0607DCC7B71584FB21F927594D51DA984EC93543EC68A7D8C4AD60E12EDF1927B1EDE8B786BDD677378B.

ROEDIGER, H. L. I. I. I., & KARPICKE, J. D. (2006). THE POWER OF TESTING MEMORY: BASIC RESEARCH AND IMPLICATIONS FOR EDUCATIONAL PRACTICE. *PERSPECTIVES ON PSYCHOLOGICAL SCIENCE, 1*, 181–210.

ROSENSHINE, B. (2010). *PRINCIPLES OF INSTRUCTION. INTERNATIONAL ACADEMY OF EDUCATION, UNESCO*. GENEVA AND SWITZERLAND: INTERNATIONAL BUREAU OF EDUCATION. AVAILABLE FROM WWW.IBE.UNESCO.ORG/FILEADMIN/USER_UPLOAD/PUBLICATIONS/EDUCATIONAL_PRACTICES/EDPRACTICES_21.PDF.

SURMA, T., VANHOYWEGHEN, K, CAMP, G., & KIRSCHNER, P. A. (2018). DISTRIBUTED PRACTICE AND RETRIEVAL PRACTICE: THE COVERAGE OF LEARNING STRATEGIES IN FLEMISH AND DUTCH TEACHER EDUCATION TEXTBOOKS. *TEACHING AND TEACHER EDUCATION, 74*, 229-237. DOI:10.1016/J.TATE.2018.05.007

Suggested readings and links

PAUK, W. (2001). THE CORNELL NOTE-TAKING SYSTEM.

AVAILABLE FROM HTTP://LSC.CORNELL.EDU/NOTES.HTML.

POMERANCE, L., GREENBERG, J., & WALSH, K. (JANUARY 2016). *LEARNING ABOUT LEARNING: WHAT EVERY NEW TEACHER NEEDS TO KNOW.* **WASHINGTON, DC: NATIONAL COUNCIL ON TEACHER QUALITY.**

AVAILABLE FROM WWW.NCTQ.ORG/DMSVIEW/LEARNING_ABOUT_LEARNING_REPORT.

ROEDIGER, H. L. III, & PYC, M. A. (2012). INEXPENSIVE TECHNIQUES TO IMPROVE EDUCATION: APPLYING COGNITIVE PSYCHOLOGY TO ENHANCE EDUCATIONAL PRACTICE. *JOURNAL OF APPLIED RESEARCH IN MEMORY AND COGNITION, 1, 242–248.*

AVAILABLE FROM HTTPS://READER.ELSEVIER.COM/READER/SD/PII/S2211368112000915?TOKEN=4A00865C24695E0A291290C9AC347A64FC3655410FE8B6A68E13394031C1DE63A234D74F80637E591F926EA730E0F1EC.

SURMA, T., VANHOYWEGHEN, K, CAMP, G., & KIRSCHNER, P. A. (2018). DISTRIBUTED PRACTICE AND RETRIEVAL PRACTICE: THE COVERAGE OF LEARNING STRATEGIES IN FLEMISH AND DUTCH TEACHER EDUCATION TEXTBOOKS. *TEACHING AND TEACHER EDUCATION, 74, 229–237.*

AVAILABLE FROM HTTPS://READER.ELSEVIER. COM/READER/SD/PII/S074205IXI7320656?TOKEN=637A04F8CBDFC8I02B99 BA725A8IFB3I835A70E20DE3FAEI48I8E9CDFI8E06E89I2D8524BA9AI2EF88F 65758F8E2DC93.

DOWNLOADABLE MATERIALS (E.G. POSTERS AND INSTRUCTIONAL MATERIALS) BY THE LEARNING SCIENTISTS.

AVAILABLE FROM WWW.LEARNINGSCIENTISTS.ORG/ DOWNLOADABLE-MATERIALS/.

BLOG BY PAUL KIRSCHNER AND MIRJAM NEELEN ABOUT THE TESTING EFFECT.

AVAILABLE FROM HTTPS://3STARLEARNINGEXPERIENCES.WORDPRESS. COM/2018/06/19/AND-THE-WINNER-IS-TESTING/.

BLOG BY PAUL KIRSCHNER AND MIRJAM NEELEN ABOUT TOP AND FLOP LEARNING STRATEGIES.

AVAILABLE FROM HTTPS://3STARLEARNINGEXPERIENCES.WORDPRESS. COM/2015/07/14/LEARNING-THE-SMART-WAY-2/.

BLOG BY PAUL KIRSCHNER AND MIRJAM NEELEN ABOUT SPACED PRACTICE.

AVAILABLE FROM HTTPS://3STARLEARNINGEXPERIENCES.WORDPRESS. COM/2017/10/31/TIPS-AND-TRICKS-FOR-SPACED-LEARNING/.

BLOG BY PAUL KIRSCHNER AND MIRJAM NEELEN ABOUT HIGHLIGHTING.

AVAILABLE FROM HTTPS://3STARLEARNINGEXPERIENCES.WORDPRESS. COM/2019/01/08/LESS-IS-MORE-HIGHLIGHTING-AS-LEARNING-STRATEGY/.

POOJA AGARWAL'S GUIDES FOR RETRIEVAL PRACTICE AND SPACED RETRIEVAL PRACTICE ON *TRANSFORM TEACHING WITH THE SCIENCE OF LEARNING.*

AVAILABLE FROM WWW.RETRIEVALPRACTICE.ORG/LIBRARY/.

A VIDEO BY THE LEARNING SCIENTISTS ABOUT SPACED PRACTICE IS

AVAILABLE FROM WWW.YOUTUBE.COM/WATCH?V= 3WJYP98EYS8.

A VIDEO BY THE LEARNING SCIENTISTS ABOUT RETRIEVAL PRACTICE IS

AVAILABLE FROM WWW.YOUTUBE.COM/WATCH?V=PJRQC6UMDKM.

A VIDEO BY POOJA AGARWAL ABOUT MAKING THE MOST OF RETRIEVAL PRACTICE: SPACED PRACTICE IS

AVAILABLE FROM WWW.YOUTUBE.COM/WATCH?V=_V2Y0PLZVVO.

PART V

LEARNING IN CONTEXT

Learning is often seen as something cognitive, and that is definitely true. What we learn depends on how we process the information that we encounter and these processes take place in our brains. To learn, our brains must process new information and incorporate it into our existing knowledge or create new knowledge schemes. But this is not the whole story.

Learning is also a social event and thus the social environment – as with almost all our activities – also has a lot of influence on our learning. And that environment can greatly stimulate or stifle learning. Fellow students who do not participate in a group project can stand in the way of learning, while an expert teacher or classmates who cooperate constructively promote their own learning.

In this fifth part we deal with some aspects of that social learning environment. This section focuses on different social influences on learning such as situated cognition, cognitive apprenticeship, and communities of learners.

22

WHY CONTEXT IS EVERYTHING

CONTEXT

22 WHY CONTEXT IS EVERYTHING

PAPER   "Social learning theory: A contextualist account of cognitive functioning"[1]

QUOTE   *Learning is more than knowing what to do. It also involves knowing how to do it.*

Why you should read this chapter

If you walk around the streets of Amsterdam, you hear lots of different languages spoken. Of course, much of what you hear is standard language spoken either by Dutch people or by tourists and landed immigrants. But there's also a language that you hear that's spoken primarily by Dutch youths that seems to bear resemblance to many languages, but can't be pinned down to any one standard language: street language. As Amsterdam has a large population of residents from the Netherlands itself, first and second generation residents from former colonies (e.g. Aruba, Bonaire, Curacao, Suriname), and children of former economic "guest workers" from primarily Turkey or Morocco who've remained in the Netherlands, what you hear is a rich street language which is a strange cocktail of all of those. This language isn't spoken at home nor is it taught in school, but is rather an example of social learning. This language is acquired either in action or from observing peers. And this isn't only the case for "cognitive" learning. Social learning plays a role in acquiring attitudes, behaviours, and values and even in acquiring physical skills. When a child sees another child receive a treat, either as a reward for behaving politely or as a placation of a tantrum, then the child will possibly imitate the other child in the hope of also getting a treat. When a teenager sees a peer smoking a cigarette or

1   **ZIMMERMAN B. J.** (1983). SOCIAL LEARNING THEORY: A CONTEXTUALIST ACCOUNT OF COGNITIVE FUNCTIONING. IN: C. J. BRAINERD (SERIES ED.) *SPRINGER SERIES IN COGNITIVE DEVELOPMENT, RECENT ADVANCES IN COGNITIVE-DEVELOPMENTAL THEORY: PROGRESS IN COGNITIVE DEVELOPMENT RESEARCH* (PP. 1–50). NEW YORK, NY: SPRINGER.

Social context and
individual behaviours

consuming alcohol, (s)he might be tempted to do the same, especially if these behaviours are likely to gain them more social acceptance.

This chapter shows that learning occurs socially in terms of the modelling and imitation of specific tasks and behaviours but more importantly, it makes the claim that learning is highly contextual in nature (see also Chapter 23, The culture of learning) and is dependent largely on the prior knowledge of the learner and also on the way in which tasks are modelled. Put simply, social learning theory is the view that people learn by observing others. Though Albert Bandura published on social learning theory earlier than Barry Zimmerman, we chose his chapter as we feel it's more relevant to education. It was a toss-up and Barry won.

SOCIAL LEARNING
THEORY
We learn by
observing others

Abstract

Social learning theory grew out of the efforts of Bandura and Walters (1959, 1963) to explain how children acquired information and behavior by observing people in natural settings. Initially they investigated youngsters' simple imitation of common responses, such as aggression, by a model. Favorable results of this research prompted study of more complex classes of social learning, such as the development of emotional reactions (attraction and avoidance), cognitive and linguistic rules, self-regulating responses, personal standards, expectations, and self-efficacy judgments. This social interactionist approach to development revealed a distinctive but widely underestimated feature of children's knowledge: At all levels of complexity, it remained highly dependent on the social environmental context from which it sprang. This property of thought also became evident to other theorists as they began to study cognitive functioning in naturalistic settings. Several of these theorists have discussed the implications of their research on the basis of a general epistemology termed "contextualism".

Social interactionist
approach

CONTEXTUALISM
Viewing cognitive
processes in the real
world

The chapter

Zimmerman begins the chapter (p. 2) by stating that social learning theory "grew out of the efforts of Bandura and Walters to explain how children acquired information and behavior by observing people in natural settings". It's often seen as a bridge between behaviourist and cognitive learning theories encompassing attention, memory, and motivation. It can be seen as a reaction to the two prevalent – classical – explanations of learning, namely behaviourist models which saw behaviour as an internal mechanism which could be affected by classical conditioning and operant conditioning and cognitivist theories that saw learning as something that occurred in the brain. Both saw learning as

CLASSICAL
CONDITIONING
Involuntary stimulus
and response
OPERANT
CONDITIONING
Voluntary stimulus
and response

unrelated to its surroundings and independent of contextual factors. It also formed a shift away from studying cognition in laboratory settings to studying in more naturalistic settings broadly grouped under the category of "contextualism" (Jenkins, 1974; Labouvie-Vief & Chandler, 1978; Pepper, 1970). The central claims of contextualism are:

People interact with their environment

1. *Person–environment interaction.* Individuals make meaning through their interaction and relationship with the broader environment, where "environment" refers not just to the physical world but also the thoughts and actions of others (see Figure 22.1).

FIGURE 22.1
AN INTERA-
CTIONIST VIEW
OF SUBJECT AND
ENVIRONMENTAL
CONTRIBUTIONS
TO CAUSATION
OF EVENTS
(ZIMMERMAN,
1983, P. 8)

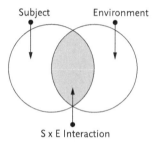

Events are made up of strands and textures

2. *Events as holistic phenomena.* Events in the world are not experienced by the individual as discrete episodes but rather as "cognitively unified phenomenon" (p. 8). An event is broken down into elements called *strands* and the relationships between those strands are called *textures*. An example of this is sentence comprehension (Jenkins, 1974) where the individual words in a sentence can be understood as strands and their relationships as textures. If one person asks another "when will it come?", the meaning of this question is dependent on a range of other factors such as intonation, facial expression, the individual character of the person, and the location of the individuals. In this case we're speaking about a bus stop where an agitated pedestrian who's late for an appointment (intonation, facial expressions) refers to "it" (the bus as he's standing at a bus stop).

3. *Contextualism is comprehensive and dynamic.* William James observed that it's almost impossible to analyse cognitive process in an elemental way because the human mind is always reacting to its environment. He suggested that "the human mind should be studied 'in motion' as a person adapted to changing environmental contexts" (p. 11). For the contextualist, the idea that psychological events can be reduced to a set of basic associations such as computer programs or logic, as early cognitivists did, needed to be rejected (Jenkins, 1974; Labouvie-Vief & Chandler, 1978; Neisser, 1976).

STAGE-THEORY
Belief that cognitive development is in stages and can be observed as such

Development is ongoing and diverse. Contextualists take issue with stage-theorists and their claims of the universal nature of cognitive development; that human development is universal, sequential and hierarchical. They claim that social developments such as entering school or changes in their home life affect performance shifts with a greater degree of accuracy than age or a stage of development.

Ecological validity

4. *Research methods and goals must be revised.* The contextualist view takes issue with traditional methods of research as "little attention is given to the confounding effects of historical and social context variables on age" (p. 14). Many researchers will compare research done in the laboratory with research done in the field, which raises the question of ecological validity or "the extent to which the environment experienced by the subjects in a scientific investigation has the properties it is supposed or assumed to have by the investigators" (Bronfenbrenner, 1979, p. 29).

According to Zimmerman, contextualists "assume that reality is dynamic and continuous in flow and that knowledge is the ever-changing cumulative product of one's personal transactions with the proximal and distal environment" (p. 17). This contextualist worldview is often contrasted with what is called the realist worldview which is often pejoratively characterised as a mechanistic, reductionist, or even cognitivist worldview. Table 22.1 summarises the differences between the two. We (the authors) must note here that a third worldview is often added here – the relativist worldview – but this falls outside of the scope of this chapter.

TABLE 22.1
A COMPARISON OF THREE BELIEFS ACROSS TWO EPISTEMOLOGICAL WORLDVIEWS (BASED ON SCHRAW & OLAFSON, 2002)

BELIEF	REALIST WORLDVIEW	CONTEXTUALIST WORLDVIEW
Ontological: Nature of reality and standards for judging truth	Reality is objective: Truth corresponds to external reality and universal standards.	There is no objective reality: Truth is consensual based on negotiated standards.
Epistemological: Nature of knowledge and knowing	Knowledge and knowing is: ■ Objective and universal ■ Independent of knower ■ Relatively unchanging	Knowledge and knowing is: ■ Situational ■ Adapted by knower to fit contextual demands ■ Changes consensually
Pedagogical: Nature of teaching and learning	Teaching and learning is: ■ Transmissive ■ Teacher-centred ■ Expert dissemination to passive but self-regulating recipients with little peer role	Teaching and learning is: ■ Transactional ■ Student and group-centred ■ Supportive co-collaborator and co-participant with self-regulating students and collaborative peers

Based on the contextualist view, it is argued that the beginning of social learning theory starts with Bandura's social learning formulation (Bandura & Walters, 1959, 1963) in which Bandura argued that social modelling and experience has a determining influence of child development. Bandura's theory (1971) claimed that there were four subprocesses in human learning behaviour; two which are cognitive (attention and retention) and two which are noncognitive (motivation and motoric). As Zimmerman notes "for children to learn from models, they must perceive and attend to such models" (p. 19). "Cognitive rule learning" refers to the fact that individuals will form a hierarchy of rules through the observation of others performing the task. Social learning theorists have noted that learning is possible without social models but that they are often inefficient as they depend on previous rule learning and naturalistic reinforcement.

COGNITIVE
FUNCTIONING
Specific knowledge
matters more than
age

In terms of cognitive functioning, social learning theorists take the view that a child's level of task-specific knowledge is a critical factor rather than their age, and that this knowledge is based on their prior experience with family members and peers. Physical maturation is believed to have a lesser role in development since experience is dependent on the child's physical capabilities at a certain age. In other words, it is not so much the age of the child which determines their cognitive functioning but rather the social conditions in which they have been. Critically, what is expected of them at that particular age will determine how an adult will relate to them. For example, you would not expect a 2-year-old to read a Modernist novel but you would expect them to "read" a picture book. Zimmerman notes that Myers and Perlmutter (1978) conducted a study on word recall by 2-year-olds and 4-year-olds and discovered that "age-related improvements in recall were uncorrelated with the use of such general strategies as rehearsal, elaboration, or organization. They concluded that age differences in recall were due to the older children's superior content knowledge" (p. 28).

EXPERIENCE
Degree of familiarity

Zimmerman puts forward the hypothesis that where experience is unrelated to someone's age, that variable of experience is a strong predictor of learning. "Experience" is more specifically defined as *familiarity* with a task or object" (p. 28). This was explored in a study by Micki Chi (1978) where adults and 10-year-olds were tested on their predictive skills on chess tasks with the "twist" being that the 10-year-olds were chess experts and the adults were novices. Both groups were asked to examine an arrangement of chess pieces for 10 seconds and then recall it from memory and they were also asked to predict how many trials they would need to get it correct. Not only were the children better in recalling the chess pieces but they were also better at predicting how many attempts they would need to get it correct. The conclusion was that "specific task-related knowledge outweighed all other factors (including information processing capacity measures) in explaining age differences in recall" (p. 28).

In linguistic acquisition, several social elements are reported to be highly salient factors such as parent facial cues and reinforcement (Brown, 1976), which indicated that comprehension and imitation were highly dependent on the "specific dynamic experience" (p. 35) of observing others. A final key point made by Zimmerman is that universal theories of learning have become increasingly unsatisfactory as "evidence of the contextual dependency of children's knowledge continues to mount" (p. 39).

UNIVERSAL
THEORIES OF
LEARNING
A problem when
context is taken into
account

Conclusions/implications of the work for educational practice

The central idea from this work is that people learn through observing others and so it's of vital importance to educators to consider exactly what students will be observing. Learners need not only to see tasks being performed but learners, particularly novices, need to see the performance and execution of those tasks broken down into constituent parts, which is where teachers need to consider how they are sequencing and modelling curriculum content (see also Chapter 24, Making things visible). This chapter also illustrates a common theme in this book, namely that most learning does not happen in a context-free way and that generic skill approaches to learning are often ineffective. It is particularly important that a requisite amount of context-specific knowledge is gained before attempting most tasks.

THE IMPORTANCE OF CONTEXT-SPECIFIC KNOWLEDGE

IN 1988, Donna Recht and Lauren Leslie did a study in which they asked seventh and eighth graders to read a passage about baseball. They used four groups: one group had kids who were strong readers (top 30%) who knew a lot about baseball, one had struggling readers (bottom 30%) who knew a lot about baseball, one had strong readers with who knew little about baseball, and one had struggling readers who knew little about baseball.

EXAMPLE
Importance of prior
knowledge

When, after reading a paragraph about baseball, the kids were asked a series of comprehension questions, Recht and Leslie saw results which they didn't really expect. Strong readers with a high knowledge of baseball performed best, but a close second were the struggling readers who knew a lot about baseball. These readers even outperformed their strong reading peers! The graph below shows how important context-specific knowledge is (see Figure 22.2).

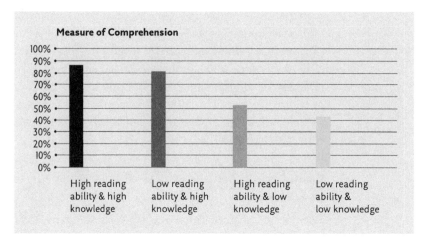

FIGURE 22.2
THE IMPORTANCE OF CONTEXT-SPECIFIC KNOWLEDGE FOR READING COMPREHENSION (RECHT & LESLIE, 1988)

Social learning is not as simple as it sounds

The term *social learning* implies that children learn in a social way as advocated by constructivists and while an element of this is true, an important factor often ignored is the previous knowledge of the child and the completeness of the modelled example. Social learning is not always positive; for example, unstructured experiences where children are engaging in low-level discussion about a play or even outright misconceptions of the parts of an atom are not useful at all. In that sense, it is vital that teachers consider the previous knowledge of the students and the types of modelling that is happening in their classroom; specifically whether real learning is actually happening or whether the students are just being busy. So the implication here is clear: children need clear modelled examples of how to succeed and secondly, they need a pre-requisite of specific knowledge in order to "unlock" the skills from the specific task.

How to use the work in your teaching

Modelling does not just refer to the teacher instructing a student. Other powerful ways of harnessing the tenets of social learning theory include peer teaching, where one student will instruct another student in an area in which they are particularly proficient. Setting up a mentorship programme where certain students are paired with others can have a powerful effect on learning as children are most likely to imitate the behaviour of their peers, particularly if the outcomes are seen as favourable. Possibly the most straightforward and powerful way of enacting social learning is to ask students to read out a piece of work that is an exemplar model of how to solve a problem or express an idea. If this becomes a regular part of class feedback on classroom assessments, the gains can be significant as peers can frame the steps to success in a way that teachers sometimes can't.

Students often pay more attention to peers than adults

One of the more subtle claims that this chapter makes is that modelling needs to be relatively complete in order to be effective and for children to learn the "rules" of a given task or objective. For example, Zimmerman (1974) instructed preschool children in a new method of grouping pictures that differed from a spontaneous method used by the children. The older children were able to switch back and forth between methods but the 3- and 4-year-olds were unable to until they were shown a method that flexibly used both methods together. In other words, these children needed to have explicit modelling not just of both methods but of using them *interchangeably* in order to be successful, and interestingly, individual differences between the children disappeared when this was done. The important point here is that when modelling something such as how to complete an equation or write an introduction to an essay, the crucial aspect is the *completeness* of the modelling. In cases where there are gaps in what is being modelled, the students with the stronger prior knowledge in these areas will be more successful. So, when teaching something (especially to novices) be as explicit as possible, otherwise you are just widening the gap between the students who have knowledge and those who don't.

Modelling needs to be a complete model to function well

A good example of this is in teaching students to write well. English teachers can be particularly effective if they model ways in which students can learn vicariously. They can do this in two ways: firstly by actually explicitly modelling to the class by writing a full essay or creative piece themselves "live" in front of the class, where they break down exactly what choices they have made and why, either by using a visualiser or simply typing on a screen. Secondly, as mentioned above, they can facilitate peer teaching by asking one of their students to model to their peers how they constructed a particular piece of writing by handing our copies of a particularly good piece of writing and having them break it down to the rest of the class step by step.

Takeaways

- Social learning is highly contextual in nature and this is often ignored.
- Universal accounts of cognitive functioning are problematic.
- It's not so much a child's age that determines performance but rather their previous knowledge based in their social experience.
- When learning rules to complete a task, the key element for novices is the *completeness* of the modelling.
- Carefully sequenced and explicit modelling of tasks is more effective than unstructured, naturalistic modelling experiences.
- Techniques such as peer teaching, imitation, role playing, and so forth are good examples of ways to facilitate social learning.

References

BANDURA, A. (1971). *PSYCHOLOGICAL MODELING – CONFLICTING THEORIES*. CHICAGO, IL: ATHERTON/ALDINE.

BANDURA, A., & WALTERS, R. (1963). *SOCIAL LEARNING AND PERSONALITY DEVELOPMENT*. NEW YORK, NY: HOLT.

BANDURA, A., & WALTERS, R. H. (1959). *ADOLESCENT AGGRESSION*. NEW YORK, NY: RONALD PRESS.

BRONFENBRENNER, U. (1979). *THE ECOLOGY OF HUMAN DEVELOPMENT*. CAMBRIDGE, MA: HARVARD UNIVERSITY PRESS.

BROWN, I., JR. (1976). ROLE OF REFERENT CONCRETENESS IN THE ACQUISITION OF PASSIVE SENTENCE COMPREHENSION THROUGH ABSTRACT MODELING. *JOURNAL OF EXPERIMENTAL CHILD PSYCHOLOGY, 22*, 185–199.

CHI, M. T. (1978). KNOWLEDGE STRUCTURES AND MEMORY DEVELOPMENT. IN R. S. SIEGLER (EDS.), *CHILDREN'S THINKING: WHAT DEVELOPS?*. HILLSDALE, NJ: ERLBAUM.

JENKINS, J. J. (1974). REMEMBER THAT OLD THEORY OF MEMORY? WELL, FORGET IT!. *AMERICAN PSYCHOLOGIST, 29*, 785–795.

LABOUVIE-VIEF, G., & CHANDLER, M. J. (1978). COGNITIVE DEVELOPMENT: IDEALISM VS. CONTEXTUALISM. IN P. B. BALTES (ED.), *LIFE SPAN DEVELOPMENT AND BEHAVIOR* (PP. 181–210). NEW YORK: ACADEMIC PRESS.

MYERS, N. A., & PERLMUTTER, M. (1978). MEMORY IN THE YEARS TWO TO FIVE. IN P. H. ORNSTEIN (ED.), *MEMORY DEVELOPMENT IN CHILDREN* (PP. 191–218). HILLSDALE, NJ: ERLBAUM.

NEISSER, U. (1976). *COGNITION AND REALITY*. SAN FRANCISCO, CA: W. H. FREEMAN.

PEPPER, S. C. (1970). *WORLD HYPOTHESES*. BERKELEY, CA: UNIVERSITY OF CALIFORNIA PRESS.

RECHT, D. R., & LESLIE, L. (1988). EFFECT OF PRIOR KNOWLEDGE ON GOOD AND POOR READERS' MEMORY OF TEXT. *JOURNAL OF EDUCATIONAL PSYCHOLOGY, 80*, 16–20.

SCHRAW, G., & OLAFSON, L. (2002) TEACHERS' EPISTEMOLOGICAL WORLDVIEWS AND EDUCATIONAL PRACTICES. *ISSUES IN EDUCATION, 8* (2), 99–149.

ZIMMERMAN, B. J. (1983). SOCIAL LEARNING THEORY: A CONTEXTUALIST ACCOUNT OF COGNITIVE FUNCTIONING. IN C. J. BRAINERD (SERIES ED.), *SPRINGER SERIES IN COGNITIVE DEVELOPMENT, RECENT ADVANCES IN COGNITIVE-DEVELOPMENTAL THEORY: PROGRESS IN COGNITIVE DEVELOPMENT RESEARCH* (PP. 1–50). NEW YORK, NY: SPRINGER.

ZIMMERMAN, B. J., & ROSENTHAL, T. L. (1974). CONSERVING AND RETAINING EQUALITIES AND INEQUALITIES THROUGH OBSERVATION AND CORRECTION. *DEVELOPMENTAL PSYCHOLOGY, 10*, 260–268.

Suggested readings and links

A SHORT VIDEO ON THE IMPORTANCE OF BANDURA'S BOBO DOLL EXPERIMENT WHERE SOCIAL LEARNING IS ACHIEVED VIA MODELLING OF BEHAVIOUR IS

AVAILABLE FROM HTTPS://YOUTU.BE/ZERCK0LRJP8.

BANDURA'S FOUR PRINCIPLES OF SOCIAL LEARNING THEORY.

AVAILABLE FROM WWW.TEACHTHOUGHT.COM/LEARNING/PRINCIPLES-OF-SOCIAL-LEARNING-THEORY/.

A VIDEO EXPLAINING RECHT AND LESLIE'S (1988) BASEBALL STUDY IS

AVAILABLE FROM WWW.YOUTUBE.COM/WATCH?V= QP6QPSRR3CG.

23 THE CULTURE OF LEARNING

CULTURE OF LEARNING

23 THE CULTURE OF LEARNING

PAPER   "Situated cognition and the culture of learning"[1]

QUOTE   *"The breach between learning and use, which is captured by the folk categories 'know what' and 'know how', may well be a product of the structure and practices of our education system".*

Why you should read this article

Biologically primary and secondary knowledge (see Chapter 4)

As we saw in the chapter discussing David Geary's biologically primary and biologically secondary learning, some things appear to be learnt almost "by themselves" without any real explicit instruction while other things take a lot of effort and are best learnt through proper instruction. Learning and communicating in our native language belongs to the former category. Children learn to communicate, first through simple sounds and gestures, and then through their native language by interacting – that is by listening and speaking with others in their direct environment. According to Miller and Gildea (1987), during their early years children acquire an average of 5000 new words per year (approximately 13 new words per day) by listening, speaking, and later reading. This process seems to be effortless and quick, especially if the child grows up in a rich linguistic environment. This is also the case for a second language, albeit to a lesser degree in families where multiple languages are spoken. But what happens when these same children go to school and try to learn new words in a foreign language there (or even new words in their own language from a vocabulary list)? Although we have no exact numbers here, we think that we can agree that the number is quite a bit lower and that it takes quite a lot of effort. Miller and Gildea put the number in the vicinity of 100 to 200 words. How does this happen? One would think that learning words in daily life doesn't differ

1   **BROWN, J. S., COLLINS, A., & DUGUID, P.** (1989). SITUATED COGNITION AND THE CULTURE OF LEARNING. *EDUCATIONAL RESEARCHER, 18*(1), 32–42.

that much from learning words at school. However, it does. As discussed in Chapter 2, one reason is that learning to communicate with others in our direct environment (let's call this our "culture") is an evolutionary necessity. In their article, John Seely Brown, Allan Collins, and Paul Duguid add a second dimension to this, namely that the context in which you learn makes a difference, and might even determine, what you learn.

Abstract of the article

Many teaching practices implicitly assume that conceptual knowledge can be abstracted from the situations in which it is learned and used. This article argues that this assumption inevitably limits the effectiveness of such practices. Drawing on recent research into cognition as it is manifested in everyday activity, the authors argue that knowledge is situated, being in part a product of the activity, context, and culture in which it is developed and used. They discuss how this view of knowledge affects our understanding of learning, and they note that conventional schooling too often ignores the influence of school culture on what is learned in school. As an alternative to conventional practices, they propose cognitive apprenticeship (Collins, Brown, & Newman, 1989), which honors the situated nature of knowledge. They examine two examples of mathematics instruction that exhibit certain key features of this approach to teaching.

Knowledge is situated

The article

John Seely Brown and his colleagues distinguish between how students learn at school, which focuses on context-free rules, algorithms, well-defined assignments and answers, and how people learn in their work and everyday life, which focuses on contextualised experiences bound to different situations (i.e. situated learning) and with real, vaguely defined problems with multiple solutions.

In both, the learner responds to things from the environment; in school it's a sum in a book or on the black, green, white, or interactive whiteboard, and in real life (e.g. a kitchen) on a recipe for four that needs to be expanded to seven people. In each of these situations, the person doing the calculations must solve the problem within these environments. The student writes down numbers and signs in a notebook or on an electronic device and carries out the solution algorithm or script, while the cook weighs the ingredients, judges the size of the eggs or broccoli, and chooses the proper pots, pans, and cooking times. For Brown et al., how they solve the problem depends greatly on the situation or context in which they find themselves. For example, a student is usually not allowed the freedom to approximate and the cook does not have an algorithm for calculating temperatures and cooking times for a recipe and choosing pots and pans for a 75% increase in dinner guests. What's common to both is that each knows what the authors call the "cultural rules" that apply to these situations. They know what materials they have at their disposal and what is expected of them. They have learnt that calculating a sum in school is different from resizing a recipe in a kitchen.

CULTURAL RULES
problem-solving is context specific

In contemporary education, the idea of situational or contextual learning is less earth-shattering than it was at the time this article was written. It has received much attention in schools, research, textbooks, and even standardised tests. More and more often, the material to be learnt is placed in an authentic context that pupils may also encounter in daily life. This, however, has also led to excesses. Realistic mathematics, discovery and enquiry learning, and so-called twenty-first century skills have focused so much on context and "realism" that some educators, schools, and even curricula have nearly banned the tuition and learning of facts, concepts, algorithms, heuristics, and the like.

ENCULTURATION
The gradual acquisition of cultural norms/ customs

According to the authors, learning is contextual and is a process of enculturation in which one makes the rules and culture of a certain setting their own. Learning is not merely context-sensitive but is actually context-dependent. In their view, "by ignoring the situated nature of cognition, education defeats its own goal of providing useable, robust knowledge" (p. 32) for applying what is learnt in real-life practice. As a new cook you learn how to deal with different ingredients, what you can and can't do, and how to handle a recipe in the "right way". As a student, you learn how to use an algorithm or a script that you have to use to carry out the tasks prescribed by the teacher or the textbook, and how to perform them. Viewed in this way, learning at school might look similar to learning in everyday situations, but the problem is that in school, we're trying to teach things that the learners can use outside of school, while this is not always the case in practice. According to Brown and colleagues, this is because school and life have become[2] two different cultures with different sets of rules, and this means that students cannot simply apply what they've learnt in one culture to another. For example, a student can get a very good score on her geography test, but sitting next to her parents in the car she may have no idea where the cities are in relation to each other and the mountains between them! The authors feel that

---

[2]   AS YOU WILL READ IN CHAPTER 24 (MAKING THINGS VISIBLE) ON COGNITIVE APPRENTICESHIP, WHAT YOU LEARNED YOU LEARNED IN THE REAL-LIFE SETTING.

we should abandon any notion that [concepts] are abstract, self-contained entities. Instead, it may be more useful to consider conceptual knowledge as, in some ways, similar to a set of tools... It is quite possible to acquire a tool but to be unable to use it.

(p. 33)

For Brown and his colleagues, the problem is that school learning has become divorced from the practice where it needs to be applied. Students learn to work with symbols and standardised strategies to gain abstract knowledge, based on the idea that they can then use it in other situations. According to them, nothing is less true. Because the cultural rules at school are so different from those in everyday contexts, transfer is problematic.

To solve this problem, they argue that school learning should look more like everyday learning. They call this *situated learning*. For them, knowing cannot be separated from doing because all knowledge is situated in activities that are bound to social, cultural, and physical contexts (i.e. all cognition is situated). To stimulate such learning in schools, they provide examples from arithmetic and vocabulary education. One example from Lampert (1986) concerns a math lesson on multiplication where students make use of coins. After mastering simple problems, the teacher then asks them to think of more maths money problems that deal with multiplication. Because the students think of and carry out many multiplication problems, they discover that multiplication happens in many different situations. Ultimately, the teacher teaches them the more abstract rules, concepts, and algorithms that are important in multiplication. In this way they also learn the "essence of multiplication", independently of a context, and they can also use this numeracy in new, unknown situations. First, a word of caution is needed here. Situated cognition isn't discovery learning. Instruction plays an important role here.

> Through this method, students develop a composite understanding of four different kinds of mathematical knowledge: (a) *intuitive knowledge*, the kind of short cuts people invent when doing multiplication problems in authentic settings; (b) *computational knowledge*, the basic algorithms that are usually taught; (c) *concrete knowledge*, the kind of concrete models of the algorithm associated with the stories the students created; and (d) *principled knowledge*, the principles such as associativity and commutativity that underlie the algorithmic manipulations of numbers.

(p. 38)

TRANSFER
The ability to use learning from one context in another

SITUATED LEARNING
Learning should be *situated* in the real-world

Instruction is an important part of situated cognition

Brown, Collins, & Duguid stress the use of authentic activities which they define as ordinary practices of the culture. These activities are framed by their culture and are meaningful, coherent, and purposeful. The parts are embedded in the whole activity so that the relationships are apparent. In this way it is very similar to what Van Merriënboer and Kirschner (2018) speak of when designing for complex learning.

FOUR COMPONENT INSTRUCTIONAL DESIGN AND COMPLEX LEARNING

JEROEN VAN MERRIËNBOER AND PAUL KIRSCHNER

(2018) present a teaching/training blueprint (see Figure 23.1) based upon four interrelated components, namely:

Four component
instructional design
(4C/ID)

1. *Learning tasks*: authentic whole-task experiences based on real-life tasks and situations that aim at integrating knowledge, skills, and attitudes.
2. *Supportive information*: information helpful for learning and performing the problem-solving, reasoning, and decision-making aspects of learning tasks, explaining how a domain is organised and how problems in that domain are (or should be) approached.
3. *Procedural information*: information prerequisite for learning and performing routine aspects of learning tasks. Procedural information specifies exactly how to perform the routine aspects of the task (i.e. how-to instructions) and is best presented just in time; precisely when learners need it.
4. *Part-task practice*: practice items provided to help learners reach a very high level of automaticity for selected routine aspects of a task.

This approach offers a solution for three problems, namely

- *compartmentalisation*: teaching knowledge, skills, and attitudes separately which hinders complex learning and competence development,
- *fragmentation*: splitting a complex learning domain in small pieces which often correspond with specific learning objectives, and then teaching the domain piece-by-piece without paying attention to the relationships between pieces, and
- the *transfer paradox*: using instructional methods that are highly efficient for achieving specific learning objectives (e.g. blocked practice), but that are not efficient for reaching transfer of learning.

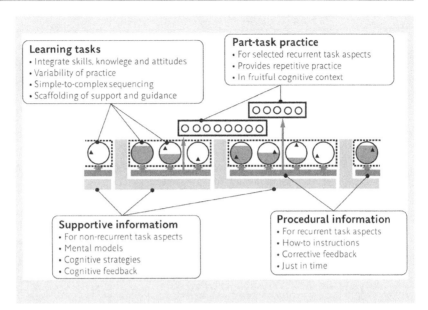

Within the figure:

Learning tasks
- Integrate skills, knowlege and attitudes
- Variability of practice
- Simple-to-complex sequencing
- Scaffolding of support and guidance

Part-task practice
- For selected recurrent task aspects
- Provides repetitive practice
- In fruitful cognitive context

Supportive informatiom
- For non-recurrent task aspects
- Mental models
- Cognitive strategies
- Cognitive feedback

Procedural information
- For recurrent task aspects
- How-to instructions
- Corrective feedback
- Just in time

Conclusions/implications of the work for educational practice

To make situated cognition and learning possible, learning experiences must become less abstract and more embedded in authentic tasks and contexts. To do this, you need to build your lessons, as in the maths lesson example, from authentic, context-specific practice to a more abstract level. In this context the authors speak of cognitive apprenticeship (see Chapter 24, Making things visible). In cognitive apprenticeship, the teacher is a (role) model who applies or uses what (s)he knows and can do to teach and guide students through authentic learning activities. If students have gained some confidence and have become somewhat familiar with the material, the teacher then challenges them to apply what they know and can do in different situations. This is often done in teams or in whole-class dialogues so that the students create a common language pertaining to the knowledge, skills, and attitudes to elevate it to a more abstract, conceptual level. To this end, collaboration is important. While working together, pupils must articulate their thinking and sense/meaning-making becomes social. After all, when they work together they have to look for a solution with each other and need to agree on what is needed to solve a particular problem in a particular situation. This is very similar to how people solve problems and gain knowledge in everyday situations, facilitating the transfer of school knowledge to everyday situations.

How to use the work in your teaching

Instruction, and especially direct instruction, has almost become a dirty word, which is not what Brown, Collins, and Duguid proposed. It has also led to standardised tests, for example in mathematics, that test reading and text-interpretation to the detriment of students from different cultures and/or with other first languages than the predominant language.

FUTUREPROOF LEARNING?

THERE'S A LIVELY DEBATE at the moment on twenty-first century skills. While many are finally aware of the fact that twenty-first century skills are the emperor's new clothes. First off, twenty-first century skills aren't twenty-first century; we've worked together, solved problems, been creative, and so forth since "the birth of civilization" in Mesopotamia around the sixtieth century BCE. They are presented as generic skills (like communication and problem-solving) which don't exist as all skills are domain specific. At best we can learn domain-general procedures (how to organise a report or article, the steps in dissecting a problem, etc.), but knowing the procedure for doing something isn't the same as having a skill to do it. Finally, many of the so-called twenty-first century skills are actually character traits and not skills (e.g. flexibility, leadership, perseverance) whose development can be stimulated or inhibited, but cannot be taught. Be this as it may, politicians, businesses, and worst of all eduquacks insist on building curricula around this myth. Kirschner and Stoyanov (2018) present a way to help students and workers to learn in a future-proof way so as to acquire the skills and attitudes necessary to continue to learn in a stable, lasting way in our rapidly changing world.

Twenty-first century skills aren't twenty-first century

Making your teaching more contextual is a good way to ensure that your students can use what they learn in your classroom in their daily lives. For example, in vocabulary education, don't offer single words, but teach in the context of a sentence or situation in which the words are often used. Then have the students practice the new words by inventing sentences and contexts themselves. With geography ask students to map out routes through the places they have learnt, and not only on traditional maps but also on maps where the terrain is visible (a mountain will add a lot of travel time if there's no tunnel). And so on.

Teaching in context

Finally, make good use of authentic whole tasks, but don't forget to present students with the necessary supportive and procedural information and knowledge needed to carry out those tasks. Don't make them discover it themselves as that doesn't work (see Chapter 2, Take a load off me and Chapter 17, Why discovery learning is a bad way to discover things/Why inquiry learning isn't). Only in this way can you guide students towards substantive understanding.

Takeaways

- Typical learning in schools is often devoid of the context (and thus the culture) in which the knowledge acquired is abstract and difficult for students to translate into everyday situations.
- Contextualised authentic learning environments help students translate what they are learning from school to the world.
- Authentic whole tasks allow for such contextualisation and, thus, help avoid compartmentalisation and fragmentation of learning.
- Discussion, collaboration, and extensive practice promote situational cognition and learning.
- Many so-called "twenty-first century skills" are actually traits that cannot be taught.

References

BROWN, J. S., COLLINS, A., & DUGUID, P. (1989). SITUATED COGNITION AND THE CULTURE OF LEARNING. *EDUCATIONAL RESEARCHER, 18*(1), 32–42. AVAILABLE FROM HTTPS://PEOPLE.UCSC. EDU/~GWELLS/FILES/COURSES_FOLDER/ED%20261%20PAPERS/SITUATED%20COGNITION.PDF.

COLLINS, A., BROWN, J. S., & NEWMAN, S. E. (1989). COGNITIVE APPRENTICESHIP: TEACHING THE CRAFTS OF READING, WRITING, AND MATHEMATICS. IN L. B. RESNICK (ED.), *KNOWING, LEARNING, AND INSTRUCTION: ESSAYS IN HONOR OF ROBERT GLASER* (PP. 453–494). HILLSDALE, NJ: ERLBAUM.

KIRSCHNER, P. A., & STOYANOV, S. (2018, ONLINE FIRST). EDUCATING YOUTH FOR NON-EXISTENT/NOT YET EXISTING PROFESSIONS. *EDUCATIONAL POLICY.* DOI: 10.1177/0895904818802086.

LAMPERT, M. (1986). KNOWING, DOING, AND TEACHING MULTIPLICATION. *COGNITION AND INSTRUCTION, 3,* 305–342. AVAILABLE FROM HTTP://EDUCATION.MSU.EDU/IRT/PDFS/OCCASIONALPAPERS/OP097.PDF.

MILLER, G. A., & GILDEA, P. M. (1987). HOW CHILDREN LEARN WORDS. *SCIENTIFIC AMERICAN, 257* (3), 94–99. AVAILABLE FROM HTTP://WEB.PDX.EDU/~FISCHERW/COURSES/ADVANCED/METHODS_DOCS/PDF_DOC/WBF_COLLECTION/0001_0050/0046_SA1987_HOWCHILDRENLEARNWORDS.PDF.

VAN MERRIËNBOER, J. J. G., & KIRSCHNER, P. A. (2018). *TEN STEPS TO COMPLEX LEARNING* (3RD ED.). NEW YORK, NY: ROUTLEDGE.

Suggested readings and links

SITUATED COGNITION. LEARNING THEORIES PROVIDES A SHORT SUMMARY OF SITUATED COGNITION.

AVAILABLE FROM WWW.LEARNING-THEORIES.COM/SITUATED-COGNITION-BROWN-COLLINS-DUGUID.HTML.

SITUATED COGNITION AND LEARNING ENVIRONMENTS: ROLES, STRUCTURES, AND IMPLICATIONS FOR DESIGN.

AVAILABLE FROM HTTP://TECFAETU.UNIGE.CH/STAF/STAF-E/PELLERIN/STAF15/SITUACOGN.HTM.

A PRESENTATION ON THE ESSENTIALS OF SITUATED COGNITION AND ITS RELATION TO OTHER LEARNING THEORIES IS

AVAILABLE FROM HTTPS://PREZI.COM/FHCFJSKNEMWA/SITUATED-COGNITION-AND-SITUATED-LEARNING-ACTIVITIES/.

24 MAKING THINGS VISIBLE

MAKING THINGS VISIBLE

24 MAKING THINGS VISIBLE

PAPER   "Cognitive apprenticeship: Making thinking visible"[1]

QUOTE   *"Cognitive apprenticeship is not a relevant model for all aspects of teaching ... [but rather] a useful instructional paradigm when a teacher needs to teach a fairly complex task to students".*

Why you should read this article

Beginning in the late Middle Ages and up through the beginning of the twentieth century, it was perfectly normal for children to get an education or be trained in a profession by being apprenticed to masters in their workplace. This was part of what is known as the guild system where experienced and confirmed experts in a field or craft (i.e. master craftsmen) hired new employees who began as apprentices and received their education or training in exchange for food, lodging, and, of course, work. The apprentice began by observing the master craftsman at work – for example a weaver, blacksmith, or printer – and learnt to look and practice under her or his (almost always his) tutelage. After a period of training under the eyes of the expert, the apprentice progressed to the level of journeyman who was considered to be competent and was authorised to work in that field. This journeyman could work for and with other master craftsmen within the guild. At a certain moment the journeyman would submit a master piece of work to the guild for evaluation which certified her or him as a master. The training was mostly about practical actions; the usefulness of what had to be learnt was clear, and there were clearly defined end products such as a cloth or tapestry, a knife, or a book. Also, the learning environment was social.

Today, most children learn in schools, with the teacher replacing the master craftsman, though some schools and professions still make use

THE GUILD SYSTEM
Experts overseeing their trade or craft

Apprentice, journeyman, master

I   **COLLINS, A., BROWN, J. S., & HOLUM, A.** (1991). COGNITIVE APPRENTICESHIP: MAKING THINKING VISIBLE. *AMERICAN EDUCATOR, 15*(3), 6–11, 38–46.

of at least part of this approach. An example of this is the vocational high school or even medical colleges where students spend a part of the week in the workplace or longer periods as interns there. Also, learning materials and assignments are now more abstract and independent of the context in which they'll ultimately be used. As a result, unless the teacher for example uses modelling as an educational approach, students may not have a good idea of how to carry out their assignments as they can no longer copy how an expert works and thinks. In their article, Allan Collins, John Seely Brown, and Ann Holum make a case for a form of instruction that resembles the former master–apprenticeship relationship. They call this method of instruction *cognitive apprenticeship*.

COGNITIVE
APPRENTICESHIP
A return to
the master–
apprenticeship
relationship

Abstract of the article

In ancient times, teaching and learning were accomplished through apprenticeship: We taught our children how to speak, grow crops, craft cabinets, or tailor clothes by showing them how and by helping them do it. Apprenticeship was the vehicle for transmitting the knowledge required for expert practice in fields from painting and sculpting to medicine and law. It was the natural way to learn. In modern times, apprenticeship has largely been replaced by formal schooling, except in children's learning of language, in some aspects of graduate education, and in on-the-job training. We propose an alternative model of instruction that is accessible within the framework of the typical American classroom. It is a model of instruction that goes back to apprenticeship but incorporates elements of schooling. We call this model "cognitive apprenticeship".

While there are many differences between schooling and apprenticeship methods, we will focus on one. In apprenticeship, students can see the processes of work: They watch a parent sow, plant, and harvest crops and help as they are able; they assist a tradesman as he crafts a cabinet; they piece together garments under the supervision of a more experienced tailor. Apprenticeship involves learning a physical, tangible activity. But in schooling, the "practice" of problem solving, reading comprehension, and writing is not at all obvious – it is not necessarily observable for the student. In apprenticeship, the processes of the activity are visible. In schooling, the processes of thinking are often invisible to both the students and the teacher. Cognitive apprenticeship is a model of instruction that works to make thinking visible.

The article

For learners to learn something, it's necessary for the teacher to make the reasoning and strategies needed to perform a task explicit. Otherwise, learners learn to solve these specific assignments, but they do this as a trick which they learn by heart. As a result, they won't get a grip on the required thinking processes and they'll have difficulty deploying what they have learnt, both with respect to content and strategies, in different contexts. The key to overcoming this is what Collins and his colleagues call *making thinking visible*.

MAKING
THINKING VISIBLE
Explicit modelling

But how do you make thinking visible? First, Collins, Brown, and Holum say we need to know what learners need to do a task and how we can transfer it. Cognitive strategies are central to the integration of skills and knowledge and certainly to abstract knowledge areas such as reading, writing, and arithmetic. These strategies are in their view best communicated through contemporary apprenticeship education: learners should see from an expert (teacher or more advanced fellow student) and hear how they solve the task, which strategies the expert uses and why. The student can then practice under supervision.

Learning as an apprentice

Collins et al. write that in "traditional apprenticeship, the expert shows the apprentice how to do a task, watches as the apprentice practices portions of the task, and then turns over more and more responsibility until the apprentice is proficient enough to accomplish the task independently" (p. 8). The authors see four important aspects of traditional apprenticeship namely modelling, scaffolding, fading, and coaching, which are also applicable to cognitive apprenticeship. In *modelling* an expert demonstrates the different parts of the to-be-learnt behaviour. In cognitive apprenticeship, this is accompanied by the expert explicitly explaining what (s)he is thinking and why (s)he doing certain things while carrying out a task (i.e. thinking aloud). *Scaffolding*, as we saw in Chapter 12, is the support and guidance the teacher provides while the students are carrying out the behaviour. As the student proceeds, the support and guidance is slowly removed – *faded* – as the student becomes able to carry out the task her-/himself. This increases the independence and responsibility of the student. Finally, *coaching* is the thread running through the entire apprenticeship experience; the expert diagnoses encountered problems, provides feedback, and generally oversees the learning.

MODELLING
Explicit
demonstration of a
skill or task
SCAFFOLDING
Support and
guidance that's
slowly removed

The interplay of all four of these aspects aids the student in developing self-monitoring and correction skills as well as in integrating the skills and conceptual knowledge needed to look critically at their own progress and learn further. In all of this, observation is critical. By seeing experts carrying out authentic whole tasks, students build conceptual models of the task: they see the entire task before getting started and follow the progress of all of its constituent parts through to its completion. As a result, they don't endlessly practice isolated skills without seeing the bigger picture. In this way, the four component instructional design model (4C/ID; Van Merriënboer, 1997; Van Merriënboer & Kirschner, 2018) can be seen as leaning on the idea of cognitive apprenticeship.

Since teaching and learning take place in schools and not in the real world with real tasks, the model of traditional apprenticeship needs to be translated to cognitive apprenticeship for three reasons. First, in traditional apprenticeship the process of carrying out a learning task is usually easily observable. In cognitive apprenticeship, however, we need to deliberately make the thinking involved in carrying out more abstract school tasks visible. "By bringing these tacit processes into the open, students can observe, enact, and practice them with help from the teacher and from other students" (p. 9). Second, in traditional apprenticeship, the tasks come up in the same way as they do in the real world while in the school, teachers are working with a curriculum which is "divorced from what students and most adults do in their lives. In cognitive apprenticeship, then, the challenge is to situate the abstract tasks of the school curriculum in contexts that make sense to students" (p. 9). Finally, in traditional apprenticeship, the skills to be learnt are specific to the tasks themselves. A carpenter learns to make a table leg, but doesn't need to learn to make a button hole or a bookbinding. This isn't the case in school where students need to be able to transfer what they learn to other tasks and areas. In cognitive apprenticeship, teachers need to "present a range of tasks, varying from systematic to diverse, and to encourage students to reflect on and articulate the elements that are common across tasks" (p. 9). To this end, Collins et al. note that for cognitive apprenticeship, teachers need to:

Learning in school is often not domain specific

- identify the processes of the task and make them visible to students;
- situate abstract tasks in authentic contexts, so that students understand the relevance of the work; and
- vary the diversity of situations and articulate the common aspects so that students can transfer what they learn.

IF EYES COULD TALK

A PROMISING FIELD with respect to making thinking visible is the field of eye tracking (sometimes also called gaze tracking). Halszka Jarodzka (2013) did research that builds on the work of Collins, Brown, and Holum, specifically with respect to identifying the processes of the task and making them visible (see Figure 24.1). She recorded the eye movements of experts

(Continued)

(Continued)

with an eye-tracker while they performed a task on a screen. Then she asked the experts to explain what they were doing, what they were looking at, and why. She then made instructional videos showing a model explaining and executing a task, while the attentional focus of the model is displayed in the form of her or his eye movements, which were presented to students as lessons. With these eye-movement modelling examples, students can gain insight into the actions and thinking of an expert, albeit through a slightly more modern approach than traditional apprenticeship.

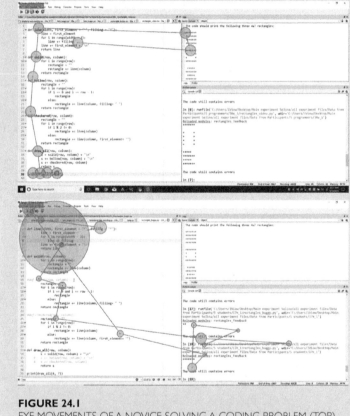

FIGURE 24.1
EYE MOVEMENTS OF A NOVICE SOLVING A CODING PROBLEM (TOP) AND AN EXPERT DOING THE SAME (BOTTOM). CIRCLES ARE FIXATIONS; THE SIZE OF THE CIRCLE REPRESENTS THEIR DURATION. THE LINES BETWEEN THE CIRCLES ARE SACCADES (I.E. THE JUMPS MADE BY THE EYES) (EMHARDT ET AL., JUNE 2019)

A social environment (i.e. the class) is an important aspect of cognitive apprenticeship. The class offers students continuous access to examples of others at varying degrees of expertise so that they can model their behaviour against those others and seek advice. This way they learn that more answers are often possible. After all, every expert will perform the task in his (or her) own way. Moreover, they see their peers at different levels of expertise, which "encourages them to view learning as an incrementally staged process, while providing them with concrete benchmarks for their own progress" (p. 9).

Switching roles/peer teaching and learning

The authors give expansive examples of cognitive apprenticeship in teaching reading, writing, and mathematics. For reading, they use Palincsar and Brown's (1984) reciprocal teaching of reading. This means that students in a class alternate in taking on the role of teacher. The procedure is as follows: the teacher and the students silently read a paragraph. The person who plays the role of teacher then summarises the paragraph, clarifies the text where necessary, formulates a question about the text, and then predicts what the next paragraph will be about. They do this after their real teacher has presented these four strategies and then practised them with the students with much guidance. Ultimately, the role of the actual teacher will become less visible and the students increasingly assume this role themselves. They then continue presenting an example of learning to write based on Marlene Scardamelia, Carl Bereiter, and Rosanne Steinbach (1984) who used contrasting models of novice and expert writing strategies to provide explicit procedural supports, in the form of prompts, to help students adopt more sophisticated writing strategies. Finally, they present an example of learning to solve maths problems based on Alan Schoenfeld's (1983, 1985) method for teaching mathematical problem solving.

Conclusions/implications of the work for educational practice

APPRENTICESHIP
FRAMEWORK
Content, method,
sequence, sociology

Collins, Brown, and Holum present a framework for designing cognitive apprenticeship learning environments. This framework (see Table 24.1) consists of four dimensions: content, method, sequence, and sociology.

The *content* should give learners a solid grounding in facts, concepts, and procedures. Having this they can learn to apply heuristics ("rules-of-thumb") making use of acquired control (i.e. metacognitive) strategies. Finally, students need to acquire learning strategies with which new concepts, facts, and procedures can be learnt. Cognitive apprenticeship teaching *methods* "should be designed to give students the opportunity to observe, engage in, and invent or discover expert strategies in context" (p. 43). The *sequencing* should structure learning but preserve the meaningfulness of what the learner is doing. Their ideas on sequencing are very similar to Reigeluth's elaboration theory (see Chapter 16, Zooming

PRINCIPLES FOR DESIGNING COGNITIVE APPRENTICESHIP ENVIRONMENTS

CONTENT Types of knowledge required for expertise

Domain knowledge Subject matter specific concepts, facts, and procedures

Heuristic strategies Generally applicable techniques for accomplishing tasks

Control strategies Generally approaches for directing one's solution process

Learning strategies Knowledge about how to learn new concepts, facts and procedures

METHOD Ways to promote the development of expertise

Modelling Teacher performs a task so students can observe

Coaching Teacher observes and facilitates while students perform a task

Scaffolding Teacher provides supports to help the student perform a task

Articulation Teacher encourages students to verbalise their knowledge and thinking

Reflection Teacher enables students to compare their performance with others

Exploration Teacher invites students to pose and solve their own problems

SEQUENCING Keys to ordering learning activities

Global before local skills Focus on conceptualising the whole task before executing the parts

Increasing complexity Meaningful tasks gradually increasing in difficulty

Increasing diversity Practice in a variety of situations to emphasise broad application

SOCIOLOGY Social characteristics of learning environments

Situated learning Students learn in the context of working on realistic tasks

Community of practice Communication about different ways to accomplish meaningful tasks

Intrinsic motivation Students set personal goals to seek skills and solutions

Cooperation Students work together to accomplish their goals

TABLE 24.1
PRINCIPLES FOR DESIGNING COGNITIVE APPRENTICESHIP ENVIRONMENTS
(COLLINS ET AL., 1991, P. 43)

out to zooming in). Finally, cognitive apprenticeship takes place in a *social* environment, situated in meaningful tasks, working with others. These methods come into their own in a class in which students work together with a teacher and with each other. By repeatedly articulating what they see, their thinking processes become visible, not only for themselves, but also for the teacher. In this way the teacher knows what students can do and where they still need guidance.

Finally, the authors also note that this model can be a useful tool at certain moments in the classroom, but it certainly does not suit all forms of instruction and learning. Reading a book or watching a documentary can also be very useful ways of learning, especially when it comes to learning factual knowledge.

How to use the work in your teaching

With cognitive apprenticeship it's important that you make your own thinking steps visible to your students and that you go from lots of guidance and support to minimal or even no guidance and support. Important rules of thumb for this are:

- List important thinking processes and procedures and make them transparent, for example by systematically thinking aloud when something happens.
- Show that a task is useful by placing it in an authentic context, for example, by linking it to the everyday environment of the students and making them clear on when they should apply this task.
- Apply the task in different contexts so that students discover what the underlying core is, for example, by showing that a certain strategy can be used in multiple situations.

First perform an entire task, supervise it, and then let the students do more and more themselves so that the students oversee the entire task and can safely try it themselves.

References

COLLINS, A., BROWN, J. S., & HOLUM, A. (1991). COGNITIVE APPRENTICESHIP MAKING THINKING VISIBLE. *AMERICAN EDUCATOR, 15* (3), 6–11, 38–39.

EMHARDT, S. N., JARODZKA, H., KOK, E. M., DRUMM, C., BRAND-GRUWEL, S., & VAN GOG, T. (JUNE 2019). KIJKGEDRAG VAN BEGINNERS EN ERVAREN PROGRAMMEURS EN HOE WIJ DIT VOOR INSTRUCTIE KUNNEN GEBRUIKEN [VIEWING BEHAVIOR OF BEGINNERS AND EXPERIENCED PROGRAMMERS AND HOW WE CAN USE THIS FOR INSTRUCTION]. SYMPOSIUM PRESENTATION AT THE ONDERWIJS RESEARCH DAGEN (ORD), HEERLEN, THE NETHERLANDS.

JARODZKA, H., VAN GOG, T., DORR, M., SCHEITER, K., & GERJETS, P. (2013). LEARNING TO SEE: GUIDING STUDENTS' ATTENTION VIA AN EXPERT'S EYE MOVEMENTS FOSTERS LEARNING. *LEARNING AND INSTRUCTION, 25,* 62–70.

PALINCSAR, A. S., & BROWN, A. L. (1984). RECIPROCAL TEACHING OF COMPREHENSION-FOSTERING AND COMPREHENSION-MONITORING ACTIVITIES. *COGNITION AND INSTRUCTION, 1,* 117–175. AVAILABLE FROM WWW.RESEARCHGATE.NET/PUBLICATION/200772570_RECIPROCAL_TEACHING_OF_COMPREHENSION-FOSTERING_AND_MONITORING_ACTIVITIES.

SCARDAMALIA, M., BEREITER, C., & STEINBACH, R. (1984). TEACHABILITY OF REFLECTIVE PROCESS IN WRITTEN COMPOSITION. *COGNITIVE SCIENCE, 8,* 173–190. AVAILABLE FROM HTTPS://PDFS.SEMANTICSCHOLAR.ORG/A895/BBB467B1DF55B0B238BDDBFF04F125EE1971.PDF.

SCHOENFELD, A. H. (1983). PROBLEM SOLVING IN THE MATHEMATICS CURRICULUM: A REPORT, RECOMMENDATIONS AND AN ANNOTATED BIBLIOGRAPHY. *THE MATHEMATICAL ASSOCIATION OF AMERICA, MAA NOTES,* NO. 1. WASHINGTON, DC: THE MATHEMATICAL ASSOCIATION OF AMERICA, COMMITTEE ON THE TEACHING OF UNDERGRADUATE MATHEMATICS.

SCHOENFELD, A. H. (1985). *MATHEMATICAL PROBLEM SOLVING.* NEW YORK, NY: ACADEMIC PRESS.

VAN MERRIËNBOER, J. J. G. (1997). *TRAINING COMPLEX COGNITIVE SKILLS: A FOUR-COMPONENT INSTRUCTIONAL DESIGN MODEL FOR TECHNICAL TRAINING.* ENGLEWOOD CLIFFS, NJ: EDUCATIONAL TECHNOLOGY PUBLICATIONS.

VAN MERRIËNBOER, J. J. G., & KIRSCHNER, P. A. (2018). *TEN STEPS TO COMPLEX LEARNING (THIRD EDITION).* NEW YORK, NY: ROUTLEDGE.

Suggested readings and links

JÄRVELÄ, S. (1995). THE COGNITIVE APPRENTICESHIP MODEL IN A TECHNOLOGICALLY RICH LEARNING ENVIRONMENT: INTERPRETING THE LEARNING INTERACTION. *LEARNING AND INSTRUCTION, 5*, 237–259.

AVAILABLE FROM WWW.SCIENCEDIRECT.COM/SCIENCE/ARTICLE/ PII/095947529500007P.

A NICE WEB SITE WITH A VERY UNDERSTANDABLE DISCUSSION OF COGNITIVE APPRENTICESHIP WITH LOTS OF LINKS TO OTHER SOURCES.

AVAILABLE FROM WWW.LEARNING-THEORIES.ORG/DOKU. PHP?ID=INSTRUCTIONAL_DESIGN:COGNITIVE_APPRENTICESHIP.

COGNITIVE APPRENTICESHIP. A WIKI ON COGNITIVE APPRENTICESHIP WITH EXPLANATIONS AND REFERENCES.

AVAILABLE FROM HTTP://EDUTECHWIKI.UNIGE.CH/EN/ COGNITIVE_APPRENTICESHIP.

A SHORT VIDEO LECTURE ON THE KEY POINTS IN SITUATED LEARNING THEORY AS PERTAINING TO COGNITIVE APPRENTICESHIP IS

AVAILABLE FROM HTTPS://SITES.GOOGLE.COM/SITE/ SOCIALAPPROACHESLEARNING/PROJECT-DEFINITION.

25 IT TAKES A COMMUNITY TO SAVE $100 MILLION

COMMUNITIES OF PRACTICE

25 IT TAKES A COMMUNITY TO SAVE $100 MILLION

PAPER   "Communities of Practice and Social Learning Systems"[1]

QUOTE   *"Since the beginning of history, human beings have formed communities that share cultural practices reflecting their collective learning: from a tribe around a cave fire, to a medieval guild, to a group of nurses in a ward, to a street gang, to a community of engineers interested in brake design. Participating in these 'communities of practice' is essential to our learning. It is at the very core of what makes us human beings capable of meaningful knowing."*

Why you should read this article

The Xerox corporation used to train their employees in a fairly orthodox way. They would provide manuals and training for their technicians who fixed the machines in order that they could meet the needs of the customer. Anyone having problems with their printer or photocopier would call a customer service rep who would send out a "trained" technician who would then fix the problem with the help of error codes. Sounds straightforward but in reality it didn't work like that.

First, the machines were highly unpredictable and often didn't malfunction in the way prescribed in the manual (anyone frantically flicking through the "troubleshooting" section of a computer manual will be familiar with this). There were usually a myriad of overlapping problems that were not covered by the manual or by training and the knowledge needed to fix them represented what Michal Polanyi (1958) refers to as "tacit knowledge", meaning things that we know, yet are difficult or that we are even unable to express. In other words, the way to fix the machines was not covered in manuals or training; it was often

TACIT
KNOWLEDGE
Implicit knowledge
that's hard to explain

---

1   **WENGER, E.** (2000). COMMUNITIES OF PRACTICE AND SOCIAL LEARNING SYSTEMS. *ORGANIZATION,* 7, 225–246.

contained in a collective wisdom about the machines that was borne out of direct experience in fixing them.

So how did they get anything done? Researcher Julian Orr spent time with the employees and noticed that many of them would meet for breakfast and discuss the problems they were facing while having coffee before work. They would share specialist knowledge of particular machines they had worked on and the various ways in which they could break down and the solutions they used to address the problem. He discovered that the employees would often share their stories and learn from each other in an informal way that the manuals and training did not cover.

Xerox then created a knowledge management system of this tacit knowledge called Eureka, which was initially rolled out in France and then worldwide, where workers would input problems and solutions to a database which other workers could then access and learn from. As one worker notes:

> Eureka isn't so much an end, as a beginning. Someone will call over the radio with a fault code like, 'I'm having 12–142s', and I can look it up in Eureka and scroll through common causes. It's faster to find it in Eureka than it is to go in and fire up the documentation CD for the repair procedures there.
>
> (Bobrow & Whalen, 2002, p. 55)

Eureka made its debut in 1994, and in 12 years of its implementation it saved Xerox over $100 million in service costs (Whalen & Bobrow, 2011). What they had created was a unique social learning system and a very good example of the power of a community of practice.

Abstract of the article

This essay argues that the success of organizations depends on their ability to design themselves as social learning systems and also to participate in broader learning systems such as an industry, a region, or a consortium. It explores the structure of these social learning systems. It proposes a social definition of learning and distinguishes between three "modes of belonging" by which we participate in social learning systems. Then it uses this framework to look at three constitutive elements of these systems: communities of practice, boundary processes among these communities, and identities as shaped by our participation in these systems.

The article

In 1991, Jean Lave and Etienne Wenger published a hugely influential book, claiming that learning is not a solitary enterprise but rather is formed through one's cultural and historical context (Lave & Wenger, 1991).

COMMUNITY OF
PRACTICE
A collective that
shares a profession
or craft

Three modes of
belonging

Communities of
practice are not
always positive

LIMINAL SPACE
A boundary or
threshold

Three elements need to be in place in order to be what they called a community of practice: the domain, the community, and the practice.

In this 2000 article, Wenger develops this idea and begins by making the case that learning is essentially "an interplay between social competence and personal experience" (p. 227), that is to say there are certain competencies or skills that are socially recognised, such as being a qualified plumber, and then there are the personal experiences of plumbers within that social structure. Wenger argues that whenever there is tension between the two and one starts to pull against the other, learning takes place.

What does it mean to "belong" to a community? There are three modes of belonging offered by the author: 1) *engagement*, where we do things together such as enter into dialogue or produce artefacts, 2) *imagination*, how we construct an image of ourselves; for example, conceiving of ourselves as a nation or that the earth is round are acts of imagination, and 3) *alignment,* where our activities chime with or are in sync with a broader set of processes such as the scientific method or obeying the law. These different modes help distinguish what a community is and how it functions in the sense that a community of imagination such as nation is very different from a community of engagement such as a team of electricians.

Communities of practice then are collectives which have a shared set joint enterprise, feature mutual engagement and will have produced a shared repertoire of resources such as language, artefacts, narratives etc. and have ready access to these. Communities of practice have been around for centuries in the form of medieval guilds and are now popular in the form of online communities, and although they are focused on learning, they are not always positive entities. For example, the Witch trials of the nineteenth century were a community of practice that had "learned not to learn" (p. 230) and had become more of a closed circuit fuelled by dogma and fear rather than a flourishing network informed by evidence and dialogue. We see this today on the Internet, where virulent dogmatic communities troll and threaten others who don't see the world as they do and dare to say so.

Boundaries are an important idea within communities of practice as they suggest a liminal space (what Turner (1969) calls a "betwixt and between space") where competence and experience converge and knowledge becomes expanded. For example, a group of educators who are largely concerned with philosophical aspects of education might come into contact with a community of cognitive scientists and learn more about the architecture of the brain, which might inform and even challenge preconceived ideas and thus expand their knowledge base, This process might even work the other way, with the cognitive scientists reconceiving their knowledge base and practice through the lens of various philosophical questions. In this way, a more cross-disciplinary approach can be enacted within organisations and institutions where different groups can meet, share, and exchange ideas with boundaries seen as a fruitful place of creation as opposed to rigid defensive boundaries to be protected.

Another key element of social learning systems is individual identities. Wenger claims that "we define ourselves by what we are not as well as by what we are, by the communities we do not belong to as well as by the ones we do" (p. 239). For example, we do not stop being a parent when we go to work or stop being a science teacher when we're not teaching science. We carry multiple identities as we move across boundaries from community to community, creating bridges as we do so. There are three elements to an identity: *connectedness*, *expansiveness*, and *effectiveness*. *Connectedness* refers to the kinds of enduring social relationships through which an identity gains depth. A robust identity has deep connections with others through shared history and experience and mutual commitments. *Expansiveness* refers to the fact that an identity will initially be defined in a local sense, but it will then cross multiple boundaries and will seek a range of experiences and direct participation in a range of other communities. *Effectiveness* asks whether an identity enables action and involvement and represents a vehicle for social participation. A healthy identity is empowering, not marginalising. Navigating the tensions between these different elements is a crucial aspect of forming a healthy identity within a social learning system.

ELEMENTS OF IDENTITY
Connectedness, expansiveness, and effectiveness

COMMUNITIES OF PRACTICE AND LEGITIMATE PERIPHERAL PARTICIPATION

For communities of practice, it requires a balance between core and boundary processes, so that the practice is both a strong node in the web of interconnections – an enabler of deep learning in a specific area – and, at the same time, highly linked with other parts of the system – a player in systemwide processes of knowledge production, exchange, and transformation.

(Wenger, 2000, p. 243).

Important here is the concept of *legitimate peripheral participation*, which describes how newcomers to a community of practice become experienced members and eventually old timers of

(Continued)

LEGITIMATE PERIPHERAL PARTICIPATION
Meaningful interaction between new and old members

(Continued)

that community. It sees learning as a social phenomenon that occurs in a context which is achieved through participation in a community. In this way we can see it as a form of situated learning (see Chapter 23, The culture of learning). Newcomers become community members by participating in simple, often low-risk tasks that are nevertheless both productive and necessary and which further the goals of the community. Through peripheral activities, novices become acquainted with the tasks, vocabulary, and organising principles of the community's practitioners. In time, as newcomers become old timers and gain a recognised level of mastery, their participation takes forms that are more and more central to the functioning of the community. Legitimate peripheral participation suggests that membership in a community of practice is mediated by the possible forms of participation to which newcomers have access, both physically and socially.[2]

Conclusions/implications of the work for educational practice

While all of the other articles in this book deal primarily with learning and teaching, this article possibly is more suited – in our opinion – to teachers and the community of practice that is the school.

In terms of how to use the ideas outlined on Wenger's article, he suggests that a community of practice should look at things like: events, leadership, connectivity, membership, projects, and artefacts (Table 25.1). Events bring together members of a community and must decide on the rhythm of these events; too many and members stop coming, too few and the community doesn't gain momentum. The community also needs internal leadership and multiple forms of active membership such as networkers, thought leaders, and administrative workers. It's also important for members of this community to be able to connect with each other through multiple forms of media (e.g. face-to-face, social media, computer-based environments)

Technology has afforded communities more opportunities

and to deepen their shared commitment by working on a range of projects together such as a literature review, empirical research, community projects, and so forth. Finally, a community should produce a set of artefacts such as documents, stories, tools, websites etc. which will remain practically useful as the community grows and evolves.

---

2 HTTPS://EN.WIKIPEDIA.ORG/WIKI/LEGITIMATE_PERIPHERAL_PARTICIPATION.

A good example of this in practice is the ways in which certain educators choose to engage with the wider research about their own practice in the form of journal reading groups where teachers will meet weekly or monthly to discuss a research paper they have read and then discuss how it applies to their own immediate context. In this way, these communities then act as a sort of "brokerage" between research and practice and create a more evidence informed community.

Enterprise: learning energy	Mutuality: social capital	Repertoire: self-awareness
Engagement		
What are the opportunities to negotiate a joint inquiry and important questions? Do members identify gaps in their knowledge and work together to address them?	What events and interactions weave the community and develop trust? Does this result in an ability to raise troubling issues during discussions?	To what extent have shared experience, language, artifacts, histories, and methods accumulated over time, and with what potential for further interactions and new meanings?
Imagination		
What visions of the potential of the community are guiding the thought leaders, inspiring participation, and defining a learning agenda? And what picture of the world serves as a context for such visions?	What do people know about each other and about the meanings that participation in the community takes in their lives more broadly?	Are there self-representations that would allow the community to see itself in new ways? Is there a language to talk about the community in a reflective mode?
Alignment		
Have members articulated a shared purpose? How widely do they subscribe to it? How accountable do they feel to it? And how distributed is leadership?	What definitions of roles, norms, codes of behaviour, shared principles, and negotiated commitments and expectations hold the community together?	What traditions, methods, standards, routines, and frameworks define the practice? Who upholds them? To what extent are they codified? How are they transmitted to new generations?

TABLE 25.1 COMMUNITY DIMENSIONS (ADAPTED FROM WENGER, 2000, P. 231)

How to use the work in your teaching

In many cases, communities of practice are typically used as a template for subject specific associations where groups of English or maths teachers will create a network to share domain-specific knowledge about teaching particular exam units or address changing requirements of exam boards and government policy changes. When teachers get together and share ideas and experiences in this way, the results are often profoundly useful to the members of that community and are far more practical than the "official" advice given by exam boards. Nuanced knowledge such as how to

COMMUNITIES OF PRACTICE IN ACTION

Using this book to
form a community
of practice

Traditional knowledge management approaches attempt to capture existing knowledge within formal systems, such as databases. Yet systematically addressing the kind of dynamic "knowing" that makes a difference in practice requires the participation of people who are fully engaged in the process of creating, refining, communicating, and using knowledge (Wenger, 1998, p. 2). In this respect, you as reader might consider using this book as a starting point for a community of knowledge and practice within your school or section. Each of the chapters could be the basis of thinking and discussion on the content, the theory, its use in the school and class, etc. Here's how: Every week or two one member of the community takes the time and makes the effort to thoroughly read a chapter (including some of the referenced materials); (s)he is the expert. The other teachers "just" read the chapter. Then, in a short (let's say one hour) meeting the expert presents the content, after which a discussion ensues about the research, its usefulness, and – probably most importantly – how the school or section can best implement it and where. Finally, this is all brought into a shared document, wiki, or whatever so that there is documentation where (1) new teachers can go to begin their membership in the community and (2) new thoughts, information, and uses can be added, growing the database. Kind of like Eureka, which was implemented at Xerox!

teach Shakespeare to specific age groups in specific contexts can provide powerful instances of professional development with huge benefits to not just teachers but the students in their charge.

In education we are currently seeing very far-reaching communities of practice form around education research, in the form of large networks such as researchED, but also more local ones in schools with the advent of research journal groups where teachers get together in their own time and read a particular article, literature review or book and then discuss ways in which that research is significant to their own context. The notion of communities of practice has particular resonance for all levels of educational institution, such as leadership for example, where head teachers often create networks to share and address specific problems that often only other school leaders can help with.

researchED
International
community sharing
education research
between researchers
and practitioners

By allowing communities of practice to not only form and collaborate but also to flourish beyond the borders of their own boundaries, educational institutions can harness a very powerful and old form of knowledge creation and also empower their own members at the same time. Unlike the Xerox corporation they may not save $100 million (impact is far more difficult to quantify in education) but the knowledge created can have far-researching benefits to both teachers and students alike.

Takeaways

- Communities of practice are systems of learning where participants come together in shared process of human endeavour.
- Communities of practice can create and share domain-specific knowledge that more formal systems cannot.
- The boundaries of such systems should not be closed and protected but rather should seek to connect with other communities to further knowledge.
- Communities of practice require three elements: domain, community, and practice.
- Belonging to a community of practice means having engagement, imagination and alignment.
- Communities of practice allow for legitimate peripheral participation where all members (newbies and old sods) can meaningfully participate.

References

BOBROW, D. G., & WHALEN, J. (2002). COMMUNITY KNOWLEDGE SHARING IN PRACTICE: THE EUREKA STORY. *REFLECTIONS, 4*, 47–59.

LAVE, J., & WENGER, E. (1991). *SITUATED LEARNING: LEGITIMATE PERIPHERAL PARTICIPATION.* CAMBRIDGE: CAMBRIDGE UNIVERSITY PRESS.

POLANYI, M. (1958). *PERSONAL KNOWLEDGE: TOWARDS A POST-CRITICAL PHILOSOPHY.* CHICAGO, IL: UNIVERSITY OF CHICAGO PRESS.

TURNER, V. (1969). *THE RITUAL PROCESS: STRUCTURE AND ANTI-STRUCTURE.* CHICAGO, IL: ALDINE PUBLISHING.

WENGER, E. (1998). COMMUNITIES OF PRACTICE LEARNING AS A SOCIAL SYSTEM. *SYSTEMS THINKER, 9*(5), NP.

WENGER, E. (2000). COMMUNITIES OF PRACTICE AND SOCIAL LEARNING SYSTEMS. *ORGANIZATION, 7*(2), 225–246.

WHALEN, J., & BOBROW, D. G. (2011). COMMUNAL KNOWLEDGE SHARING: THE EUREKA STORY. IN M. H. SZYMANSKI AND J. WHALEN (EDS.), *MAKING WORK VISIBLE: ETHNOGRAPHICALLY GROUNDED CASE STUDIES OF WORK PRACTICE* (PP. 257–284). CAMBRIDGE: CAMBRIDGE UNIVERSITY PRESS.

Suggested readings and links

FREQUENTLY ASKED QUESTIONS ABOUT COMMUNITIES OF PRACTICE, NETWORKS, AND SOCIAL LEARNING SET UP BY ETIENNE AND BEVERLY WENGER-TRAYNER ARE

AVAILABLE FROM HTTP://WENGERTRAYNER.COM/FAQS/.

A CHAPTER WRITTEN BY ETIENNE AND BEVERLY WENGER-TRAYNER: LEADERSHIP GROUPS, A PRACTICE FOR FOSTERING LEADERSHIP IN SOCIAL LEARNING CONTEXTS, IS

AVAILABLE FROM HTTPS://WENGER-TRAYNER.COM/WP-CONTENT/UPLOADS/2013/03/13-11-25-LEADERSHIP-GROUPS-V2.PDF.

 STRATEGIC EVALUATION OF NETWORK ACTIVITIES. HIGHLIGHTS OF THE DEVELOPMENT OF THE FRAMEWORK AND ITS APPLICATION TO A PROJECT.

AVAILABLE FROM HTTP://WENGER-TRAYNER.COM/RESOURCES/PUBLICATIONS/STRATEGICEVALUATION-OF-NETWORK-ACTIVITIES/.

 A RESOURCE FROM DURHAM UNIVERSITY ON HOW TO APPLY COMMUNITIES OF PRACTICE TO HIGHER EDUCATION WITH A FOCUS ON TECHNOLOGY IS

AVAILABLE FROM HTTP://COMMUNITY.DUR.AC.UK/LT.TEAM/?PORTFOLIO=COMMUNITIES-OF-PRACTICE.

 A GOOD DEFINITION OF LEGITIMATE PERIPHERAL PARTICIPATION IS

AVAILABLE FROM WWW.IGI-GLOBAL.COM/DICTIONARY/LEGITIMATE-PERIPHERAL-PARTICIPATION/17026.

PART VI

CAUTIONARY TALES

We close this book with four cautionary tales because, as they say in Dutch, a person forewarned counts double. We discuss whether learners really know what's best for them, when teaching kills learning, what are the ten dubious reasons for using multimedia, and what the ten deadly sins of education are.

26 DID YOU HEAR THE ONE ABOUT THE KINAESTHETIC LEARNER … ?

URBAN LEGENDS

26 DID YOU HEAR THE ONE ABOUT THE KINAESTHETIC LEARNER ... ?

PAPER "Do learners really know best? Urban legends in education"[1]

QUOTE *"The beliefs that a person holds persist in the face of data that disproves or even contradicts those beliefs"*

Why you should read this article

Did you hear the one about the little old lady (why is it always a little old lady?) who after walking her toy poodle in the rain wanted to dry it quickly? To this end, she put the poodle in the microwave oven – it used to be the clothes dryer – and mistakenly cooked it? Or how about the one about the grandparents who brought a cute little alligator home from their trip to Florida for their grandson [*sic*]? Well, as it grew the mother began to have qualms about it and flushed it down the toilet. Years later, a sewer worker in New York was killed and eaten by a 5 metre long alligator who flourished in the warm and food rich sewer system. Such stories are known as urban legends or myths; a story or description (often fictitious) that's broadly circulated, often told, seen by the narrator and listener as true, and that we want to believe but that there's no real proof for. Many books have been written about them. My favourite is *The vanishing hitchhiker: American urban legends and their meanings* by Jan Harold Brunvand. I read it when it first came out in 1981 and I was hooked.

URBAN LEGEND
Dubious story
widely circulated

You might think that such myths are harmless, but that's not always the case. The field of education is rife with myths which are undermining the learning of our children. There are so many myths in education that Paul, together with Pedro De Bruyckere and Casper Hulshof, has

[1] **KIRSCHNER, P. A., & VAN MERRIËNBOER, J. J. G.** (2013). DO LEARNERS REALLY KNOW BEST? URBAN LEGENDS IN EDUCATION. *EDUCATIONAL PSYCHOLOGIST*, 48(3), 169–183. DOI: 10.1080/00461520.2013.804395.

filled two complete books with them. Many myths can be dismissed as tangential or exotic (e.g. listening to Mozart makes you or your baby smarter), but there are quite a few pernicious ones. Take the idea that the brains of different generations are different and thus that teaching should accommodate this. The current generation is often referred to as *Generation Z, digital natives, homo zappiëns* ... because they grew up in a digital environment surrounded by the internet, smartphones, tablets, and the like. Playfully, without effort, they've been said to have acquired the ability to independently discover and learn, are knowledge builders and sharers, and so forth. In addition, as they're connected to all knowledge of the world via the internet they are assumed not to need to acquire factual and procedural knowledge or domain specific skills. Paul and Jeroen van Merriënboer make short work with these myths about this supposedly exceptional generation.

DIGITAL NATIVE
Incorrect claim that today's kids are different to previous generations

Abstract of the articles

This article takes a critical look at three pervasive urban legends in education about the nature of learners, learning, and teaching and looks at what educational and psychological research has to say about them. The three legends can be seen as variations on one central theme, namely, that it is the learner who knows best and that she or he should be the controlling force in her or his learning. The first legend is one of learners as *digital natives* who form a generation of students knowing by nature how to learn from new media, and for whom "old" media and methods used in teaching/learning no longer work. The second legend is the widespread belief that learners have *specific learning styles* and that education should be individualized to the extent that the pedagogy of teaching/learning is matched to the preferred style of the learner. The final legend is that learners ought to be seen as *self-educators* who should be given maximum control over what they are learning and their learning trajectory. It concludes with a possible reason why these legends have taken hold, are so pervasive, and are so difficult to eradicate.

LEARNING STYLES
Disproven theory that learners learn best in a particular style

The article

If you see kids with a tablet, you might think they really know what they're doing. They search for videos, effortlessly use all types of social media, and seem to remember passwords better than us. People call them digital natives and us (parents and teachers) digital immigrants. According to Marc Prensky (2001) who coined the term, these *digital natives* cannot learn in our present current educational system and thus should be taught in a different way because they think and process information fundamentally differently from their predecessors "as a result of this ubiquitous [digital] environment and the sheer volume of their interaction with it" (p. 1). Without ever making the effort to actually study this, he concluded that they (1) really understood what they were doing, (2) used their digital devices effectively and efficiently, and (3) needed a new type of education designed to accommodate this. Veen and Vrakking (2006) took this a step further and introduced the *homo zappiëns*; a new generation of learners who learn significantly differently from their predecessors who develop – on their own and without instruction – the metacognitive skills needed for inquiry-based learning, discovery-based learning, networked learning, experiential learning, collaborative learning, active learning, self-organisation and self-regulation, problem solving, and making their own implicit (i.e. tacit) and explicit knowledge explicit to others.

Kirschner and Van Merriënboer question this. Playing with tablets is different from learning via tablets and Instagramming each other is different from communicating and collaborating to learn. They question, thus, whether these children really know how to use the technology to learn. Along with this, they discuss two other things attributed to this generation, namely that children need instruction that caters to their specific learning styles and that they should have complete control over their own learning.

It's true that children can search for practically everything online, but there is also a lot of misinformation, disinformation, and even sheer nonsense online. They must therefore also be able to first formulate a proper search question and when the results are presented, they need to assess the information found with respect to its usefulness, reliability, truth, and so on. All of the hours children spend with new technology has not led to acquisition of these necessary skills (also known as *media literacy* or *information problem-solving skills*; Brand-Gruwel, Wopereis, & Walraven, 2009; see Figure 26.1).

Kirschner and Van Merriënboer also point to another risk of using such technology, namely that many researchers have found that children use the information they find very passively; mostly cutting and pasting, and fluttering via hyperlinks from one "interesting" piece of information to the next without understanding the underlying structure of the content. This is very similar to what is known as continuous partial attention (Stone, 2007) where we try to pay simultaneous attention to a number of sources of incoming information. When we try to do this, the result is paying attention at a superficial level with all of the consequences associated with this. They may remember some "interesting" facts, but don't really learn. Salomon (1998) called this the *butterfly defect*. An extra note here is that by simply cutting and pasting – and not even literally transcribing what is read with pen and paper or keyboard – learners don't process the information and, thus, don't learn from it!

"JUST GOOGLE IT"
A real problem without knowledge of what to trust

CONTINUOUS PARTIAL ATTENTION
Superficial focus through repeated distraction

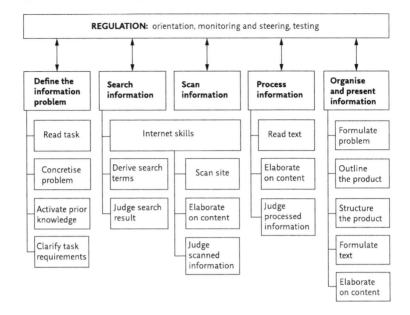

FIGURE 26.1
SKILLS NEEDED
TO SOLVE AN
INFORMATION
PROBLEM
(BRAND-GRUWEL,
WOPEREIS, &
WALRAVEN, 2009)

The second thing the authors warn of is differentiation based on the different learning styles. The idea is that in order to teach well, as a teacher, you need only determine the learning style of each pupil and then teach according to that style. This what people call the meshing hypothesis (Pashler et al., 2008). This means that you first need to determine what style each learner has. In the last half century, many different learning styles have been thought up. For example, we can use the VARK in which people are subdivided into four learning styles: visual, auditory, read/write, and kinaesthetic. On the other hand, you could use Kolb's four styles, where you divide learners into divergers, assimilators, convergers, and accommodators. Or you could choose to divide your students into holistic or analytical learners, impulsive or reflective learners, analytical, practical or creative learners, and so on. Frank Coffield and his colleagues investigated how many learning styles existed in the literature and came to no fewer than 71 different learning styles!

MESHING
HYPOTHESIS
Claim that
instruction should
match learning style

ONE LEARNING STYLE PER CHILD?

SUPPOSE YOU WANT TO USE learning styles to differentiate in your classroom. How would that work? First you test whether Mary is a diverger, assimilator, converger, or accommodator (Kolb). She appears to be a diverger (according to the test). Good start, but unfortunately you don't know if

(Continued)

she's visual, auditory, read/write, or kinaesthetic diverger. You now test her for this and she turns out to be a visual diverger, one of the now 16 possible styles (four Kolb times four VARK). But is she a holistic or an analytical visual diverger? You test her again and now we are on 32 different learning styles and she turns out to be an analytical visual diverger. Are you there yet? No! You don't know if she's an impulsive or reflective analytical visual diverger. Now we've reached 64 different learning styles and unfortunately you can continue for a while (remember, you've only tested for 4 of the 71). That's not only impossible, it also makes no sense at all.

And then a second, more serious problem. From overview studies of empirical studies of the effects of learning style on learning (e.g. Coffield, Moseley, Hall, & Ecclestone, 2004; Pashler et al., 2008) it appears that matching subject matter to learning style actually doesn't lead to better learning. If better learning was the case, pupils with an auditory learning style, for example, would learn better if allowed to listen to the instruction and less well or not at all if they had to read the instruction. This is the opposite for a pupil with a visual learning style (and we've purposely left out visual and kinaesthetic). This expected interaction between learning style and subject matter is shown in Figure 26.2. There has been a frantic search in the literature to confirm this interaction, but unfortunately none has been found.

Evidence for learning styles doesn't exist

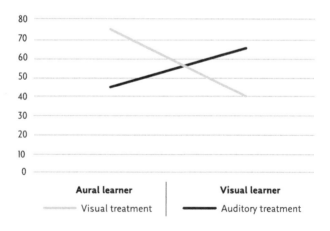

FIGURE 26.2
AN INTERACTION EFFECT AS ABOVE, ACCORDING TO PASHLER ET AL. (2008), IS THE ONLY ACCEPTABLE EVIDENCE FOR THE MESHING HYPOTHESIS

A third problem with learning styles is that most instruments used to determine learning styles (actually almost always self-response questionnaires) aren't reliable. One week, the person is classified as an assimilator and the next week as a converger. Allied to this problem is that the questions used are valid (i.e. do they measure what they purport to measure) for determining one's preference for a certain way of learning. But one's preference doesn't say anything about whether a person actually learns better using a preferred type of presentation. Do students really know what's good for them? Ask people about their favourite food and most tell you something that is fatty, and/or salty, and/or sweet. Is this eating preference (eating style) also the healthiest?

A final problem becomes clear with the following question: How do you explain to a pupil in an auditory way how crimson red and brick red look? Or how do you kinaesthetically explain how a blackbird sings? In other words, it's actually the subject matter and the learning goal that should determine how one teaches and not a preference or a non-existent learning style.

Content should be the determining factor in instructional design

So why are learning styles so popular? Part of the answer is psychological: every teacher would like to have a way to differentiate between pupils. Another reason is that there's good money in the learning style hype. Think about all of the providers of tests, materials, books, workshops, conferences, advice, and so on. Finally, it can be a welcome excuse for the child or parent to explain why the learning is not going well, and thus to tell the teacher or school that they are teaching wrong.

Third, Kirschner and Van Merriënboer discuss the often voiced idea – especially by those who are fans of Richard Ryan and Edward Deci (2000; self-determination theory) – that for students to learn best, they need control over their own learning process. In this way of thinking, they can make their own choices about what they want to learn, when they want to learn it, and how. By giving them control of (or autonomy with) their own learning process, they become more motivated and subsequently learn and perform better. A problem here is that students find it difficult to accurately estimate their own performance; they often think that they are better than in reality (see Chapter 7, Why independent learning is not a good way to become an independent learner). Also, we see that if pupils are given the opportunity to make their own choices, they often choose the things that they find easy. For example, they choose assignments that they already know they can do. In this way they do not challenge themselves, while this is exactly what we, as teachers, want them to do. They need our help. We have to support and guide them in making good choices and gradually reduce this support and guidance so that pupils can eventually do it by themselves (i.e. we must properly scaffold their learning choices; see Chapter 12, Why scaffolding is not as easy as it looks).

Learners are poor judges of their own learning

Conclusions/implications of the work for educational practice

The insights from this article help us to reflect on the role of digital technology in education, differentiation, and independent learning. We can't ignore the technology that surrounds us, but we can teach our students to actively and responsibly deal with digital information and make them media savvy. It's good to critically look at when and how to use a smartphone, tablet, or laptop; when it is effective and efficient for learning and when it isn't. Research will help us decide when and how technology will be of added-value in our teaching (see also Chapter 28, The medium is NOT the message).

As Kirschner and Van Merriënboer clearly show, learning styles don't exist. They therefore aren't a meaningful basis for differentiation. In fact, they are rather counter-productive because our memory benefits from instruction being presented in more than one modality and this applies to all pupils (see Chapter 5, One picture and one thousand words and Chapter 28, The medium is NOT the message). Teachers, thus, don't need to spend time determining each person's learning style and changing their teaching accordingly. There are many other, more effective ways to differentiate, but this falls outside of the scope of this book.

Finally, independent self-determined and directed learning is *not* something students can do spontaneously. They need support and guidance in making their choices and you, as teacher, are the perfect person to do this. You can't begin early enough with helping children to make good choices, but remember: it's not productive to do this too soon.

Self-determined and directed learning must be learnt!

How to use the work in your teaching

What about in your classroom and at your school? Do you and your colleagues believe in learning styles or even work with them? It's really hard to say goodbye to an idea that sounds so logical and even sympathetic; after all, aren't all human beings different and special? It's also hard to "reject" your own preferences when you may have elevated them to truths about how you learn best. But learning styles lack any scientific foundation and can even be counter-productive. Talk to colleagues who swear by learning styles. These kinds of conversations can be difficult, precisely because people have invested a lot in the method they use but in the end every teacher wants to do what is best for students.

Challenging established beliefs through evidence

Using technology can be very valuable for learning, after all most kids look like they're proficient in using it, but aren't. They're finger-fast but knowledge-poor. Don't be fooled into thinking that they possess the information problem-solving skills necessary for effectively using the internet. They need to learn to use it properly and you need to teach them/help them to learn to use it. Also remember that students can get distracted by working online. They are butterflies that flutter from link to link when they're not doing something else that's completely irrelevant to learning while online. Technology can be a blessing, but it's also a Pandora's box. Use it wisely.

From pre-school onwards, you can give children some control over their learning process. It starts with letting children choose in which corner of the room they want to work and play. Make sure they don't just choose to do what they know and can do; get them to try to do new things that challenge them. Of course the school is there to help children learn to better do that which they already can, but the primary job of the school should be to teach them to do things they can't! In higher grades you can continue to expand the choices they can make themselves, but under supervision. In maths, for example, first you determine how many addition problems and at what level they have to complete. Later you can slowly allow them to decide for themselves. You teach them not to look at what they like or dislike, but at what they themselves need to do to learn and achieve success. Let them see the effect of their choices on their learning and achievement.

Effective learning means taking on challenge

Takeaways

- Stop propagating the myths of learning styles and *digital natives*. Both don't exist and teaching according to them is a waste of time and is often bad for the student!
- Be careful with self-determination, including self-directed and self-determined learning. Students must acquire these skills with your support and under your guidance.
- Work with students when searching for information on the web and teach them how to judge the reliability and validity of what they find.
- Learners are often the worst judges of how they "learn best".
- Schools should consider the role of a "research lead" to act as a buffer against urban myths in education.

References

BRAND-GRUWEL, S., WOPEREIS, I., & WALRAVEN, A. (2009). A DESCRIPTIVE MODEL OF INFORMATION PROBLEM SOLVING WHILE USING INTERNET. *COMPUTERS & EDUCATION, 52*, 1207–1217. AVAILABLE FROM WWW.SCIENCEDIRECT.COM/SCIENCE/ARTICLE/PII/S0360131509001511?VIA%3DIHUB.

COFFIELD, F., MOSELEY, D., HALL, E., & ECCLESTONE, K. (2004). *LEARNING STYLES AND PEDAGOGY IN POST-16 LEARNING. A SYSTEMATIC AND CRITICAL REVIEW.* LONDON: LEARNING AND SKILLS RESEARCH CENTRE. AVAILABLE FROM WWW.LEERBELEVING.NL/WP-CONTENT/UPLOADS/2011/09/LEARNING-STYLES.PDF.

PASHLER, H., MCDANIEL, M., ROHRER, D., & BJORK, R. (2008). LEARNING STYLES: CONCEPTS AND EVIDENCE. *PSYCHOLOGICAL SCIENCE IN THE PUBLIC INTEREST, 9*(3), 105–119.

PRENSKY, M. (2001). DIGITAL NATIVES, DIGITAL IMMIGRANTS PART 1. *ON THE HORIZON, 9*(5), 1–6. AVAILABLE FROM WWW.MARCPRENSKY.COM/WRITING/PRENSKY%20-%20DIGITAL%20NATIVES,%20 DIGITAL%20IMMIGRANTS%20-%20PART1.PDF.

RYAN, R. M., & DECI, E. L. (2000). SELF-DETERMINATION THEORY AND THE FACILITATION OF INTRINSIC MOTIVATION, SOCIAL DEVELOPMENT, AND WELL-BEING. *AMERICAN PSYCHOLOGIST, 55*(1), 68–78. AVAILABLE FROM HTTPS://SELFDETERMINATIONTHEORY.ORG/SDT/DOCUMENTS/2000_ RYANDECI_SDT.PDF.

SALOMON, G. (1998). *NOVEL CONSTRUCTIVIST LEARNING ENVIRONMENTS AND NOVEL TECHNOLOGIES: SOME ISSUES TO BE CONCERNED WITH.* KEYNOTE ADDRESS PRESENTED AT THE EARLI MEETING, ATHENS, GREECE, AUGUST 1997. AVAILABLE AT WWW.SCIENCEDIRECT.COM/SCIENCE/ARTICLE/PII/ S0959475298000073.

STONE, L. (2007). *CONTINUOUS PARTIAL ATTENTION* [BLOG POST]. AVAILABLE FROM: HTTPS:// LINDASTONE.NET/QA/CONTINUOUS-PARTIAL-ATTENTION/.

VEEN, W., & VRAKKING, B. (2006). *HOMO ZAPPIENS, GROWING UP IN A DIGITAL AGE.* LONDON: NETWORK CONTINUUM EDUCATION.

Suggested readings and links

DANIEL WILLINGHAM'S FAQ ON LEARNING STYLES ARE

AVAILABLE FROM WWW.DANIELWILLINGHAM.COM/LEARNING-STYLES-FAQ.HTML.

KIRSCHNER, P. A., & DE BRUYCKERE, P. (2017). THE MYTHS OF THE DIGITAL NATIVE AND THE MULTITASKER. *TEACHER AND TEACHER EDUCATION, 67,* 135–142. DOI: 10.1016/J.TATE.2017.06.001

AVAILABLE FROM WWW.SCIENCEDIRECT.COM/SCIENCE/ARTICLE/PII/ S0742051X16306692.

PROFESSOR DANIEL WILLINGHAM DESCRIBES RESEARCH SHOWING THAT LEARNING STYLES ARE A MYTH.

AVAILABLE FROM WWW.YOUTUBE.COM/WATCH?V=SIV9RZ2NTUK.

LEO LAPORTE AND DANAH BOYD, AUTHORS OF *IT'S COMPLICATED: THE SOCIAL LIVES OF NETWORKED TEENS,* **TALK ABOUT HOW THE IDEA OF "***DIGITAL NATIVES***" IS A MISNOMER.**

AVAILABLE FROM WWW.YOUTUBE.COM/WATCH?V=S0K-RX4SHT8.

27 WHEN TEACHING KILLS LEARNING

WHAT DOESN'T WORK

27 WHEN TEACHING KILLS LEARNING

PAPER   "When teaching kills learning: Research on
            mathemathantics"[1]

QUOTE   *"A central objective of educational research is to identify 'mathema-*
            genic' instructional methods (i.e. those that 'give birth' to learning).
            Yet there has been increasing evidence for 'mathemathantic' effects
            in instructional research (i.e. where instruction 'kills' learning)"

Why you should read this article

Nothing ventured, nothing gained. There's no harm in trying. What
doesn't kill me makes me stronger.[2] How often have you heard these
maxims? But is this really the case? As far as Richard Clark is concerned,
with respect to education, the answer is *no*. Sometimes, research shows
that a certain classroom intervention, no matter how well-intentioned,
didn't have the intended effect. This is somewhat similar to the *cobra*

THE COBRA
EFFECT
Law of unintended
consequences

effect[3] in policy and/or economics where an attempted solution to a
problem makes the problem worse. What is often the case is that there
was no effect for the intervention in comparison to the control condition;
usually the "standard" teaching practice. It may have taken more effort
by the teacher or learner or required more resources, but the kids learnt
as well as the control, so no harm done; in any event with respect to
learning. If we know this, then we don't have to spend the extra time,
effort, and/or money on something that doesn't work. But sometimes

1   **CLARK, R. E.** (1989) WHEN TEACHING KILLS LEARNING: RESEARCH ON MATHEMATHANTICS. IN
    H. MANDL, E. DE CORTE, N. BENNETT, & H. F. FRIEDRICH (EDS.), *LEARNING AND INSTRUCTION. EUROPEAN*
    RESEARCH IN AN INTERNATIONAL CONTEXT (VOL. II). OXFORD, UK: PERGAMON.
2   THE GERMAN PHILOSOPHER FRIEDRICH NIETZSCHE'S WROTE *"WAS MICH NICHT UMBRINGT MACHT*
    MICH STÄRKER". IT COMES FROM THE "MAXIMS AND ARROWS" SECTION OF NIETZSCHE'S BOOK,
    TWILIGHT OF THE IDOLS (1888).
3   THE BRITISH GOVERNMENT IN INDIA OFFERED A BOUNTY FOR DEAD COBRAS TO DECREASE
    THEIR NUMBERS. SOME PEOPLE SAW A CHANCE AND BEGAN BREEDING COBRAS TO MAKE MONEY.
    WHEN THE BRITS REALISED THIS AND SCRAPPED THE PROGRAMME, THE BREEDERS SET THE NOW-
    WORTHLESS SNAKES FREE, RESULTING IN AN INCREASE IN THE COBRA POPULATION.

something else happens. Sometimes, the students who received the new approach actually performed worse than the students in the control group and/or performed worse after the intervention than before. In educational research we find few publications about these types of results (i.e. what doesn't work or works worse) because many people think that the goal of educational research is only to discover robust instructional methods that do work. This so-called publication bias (the distortion that arises when only positive results are published, but not the negative results) is a shame because we can also learn a lot from what doesn't work. In this article, Clark draws attention to the fact that what doesn't work also tells us something about the relationship between learning and instruction. He shows how certain learning activities can be counter-productive to learning. These so-called "mathemathantic activities" (cf. mathemagenic, Chapter 15; *manthanein* = learning + *thanatos* = death), a term first used by Richard Snow in an address to the American Educational Research Association in 1972, are instructional methods that unintentionally create conditions whereby pupils learn less well or even lose knowledge through the offered material (Snow, 1972). The theory of mathemathantic activities clearly shows why differentiation is also important for the more gifted pupils; after all, these students have something to lose, their existing knowledge.

MATHEMATHANTIC
ACTIVITIES
Activities that kill
learning

Abstract of the article

Instructional research is reviewed where teaching failures have produced students who are less able to use learning skills or had less access to knowledge than before they were taught. Three general types of "mathemathantic" (i.e. where instruction "kills" learning) effects are hypothesized, theoretical explanations for each effect are examined and representative studies in each area are described. The three types of effects described are where instruction serves to: 1) substitute learning procedures (e.g. novel learning strategies are hypothesized to interfere with the learning of higher general ability learners and inadequate learning strategies are provided to those with lower general ability); 2) impose less desirable motivational goals on learners (e.g. when teaching methods lead constructively motivated learners to believe that failure avoidance has replaced achievement directed goals and, conversely, when defensively motivated students believe that achievement directed goals have replaced the opportunity to avoid failure); and 3) substitute student control for system control over instructional method (e.g. by allowing lower cognitive load instructional methods to be chosen by high general ability, constructive students and/or by allowing higher cognitive load methods to be chosen by defensive students who have low general ability).

The article

The holy grail of educational research is to invent and/or identify instructional methods that are *mathemagenic* (see Chapter 15, Activities that give birth to learning). If the idea, theory, or hypothesis fails, they generally expect that the achievement or skills of the participants either remain at pre-experiment levels or are the same as those who didn't take part in the study. Clark was triggered to write this article by what he called "increasing evidence for 'mathemathantic' effects in instructional research" (p. 1).

MATHEMAGENIC ACTIVITIES
Activities that give birth to learning

He operationally defined a mathemathantic effect as when an intervention has one of four different effects. First, we see such an effect when the control group – the group of students that doesn't receive the intervention – significantly outperforms the experimental group that did. That is to say, instruction without the intervention led to more learning than with. The second is when pre-test scores for the intervention group are significantly higher than their post-test scores. Here, the intervention led to a loss of knowledge or skill. The third is when there are "significant disordinal interactions between student's aptitudes and instructional treatments" (p. 2); that is, an aptitude-treatment interaction (Cronbach & Snow, 1977) is observed. In plain terms, this is when one intervention leads to better learning in a certain type of learner but to poorer results for another. In Figure 27.1, a contrast of student-centred (i.e. unstructured, discovery) and teacher-centred (i.e. directed, monitored) instruction with students with different levels of anxiety is shown. Higher anxiety students profited from the greater structure provided by a teacher-centred approach while lower anxiety students profited more from a student-centred approach. Finally, we see a mathemathantic effect when increasing amounts of some approach to instruction produces significantly negative correlations with learning; that is "more is worse".

Aptitude-treatment interaction is similar to learning styles

In Clark's view, the interpretation of negative research results (i.e. mathemathantic effects) requires analysing the role that individual differences play in learning from instruction. "What is mathemathantic for

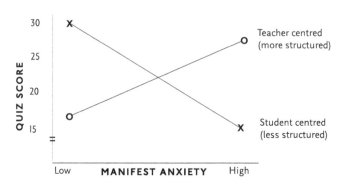

FIGURE 27.1
DISORDINAL INTERACTION WITH ANXIETY PREDICTING QUIZ SCORES UNDER MORE AND LESS STRUCTURED TREATMENTS FOLLOWING DOWALIBY AND SCHUMER (1973)

one aptitude level may be mathemagenic for another" (p. 2). This means that when offering instruction, we must take a good look at the match or possible mismatch between the instruction and individual learner. Clark focuses on two possible areas where a mismatch can arise, namely learning strategies and learning environments. What the mismatch looks like depends on the prior knowledge and abilities of the learner.

Learning strategies mismatch

When implementing an instructional treatment where the learner replaces an effective strategy that (s)he already uses with a new and often unfamiliar one, learning is often depressed. This *strategy substitution* can take two forms. First, substituting an existing strategy with a novel strategy mainly affects higher aptitude students as they often replace an automated effective strategy with a less familiar one. These novel strategies interfere with these learners' existing skill repertoires. However, the same strategies that are mathemathantic for higher aptitude learners often benefit low aptitude students who lack an effective approach (see below).

STRATEGY
SUBSTITUTION
Effective methods
for ineffective ones

The second is where inadequate strategies are introduced that provide learners with unsuccessful and/or incomplete learning procedures. This is, for example, the case for discovery learning which might work by experts but not by novices (see Chapter 1, A novice is not a little expert). Such strategies negatively affect lower aptitude students as they're often too abstract and are based on partly automated knowledge which beginners don't possess. He gives an example where math teachers discourage using concrete "finger counting", a strategy that slower math learners use while performing arithmetic operations, and encouraging more "abstract" learning strategies was mathemathantic for lower aptitude or younger learners. These inexperienced learners not only know less, but their cognitive schemata – how their knowledge, skills, and strategies are stored in their brains – are also very different from experienced ones. As a result, the information they receive isn't complete and their learning process falters.

EXAMPLE
Introducing an
inadequate strategy

PRIOR KNOWLEDGE AND EXPERTISE REVERSAL

IF THE INSTRUCTION WORKS BETTER for more expert learners than for beginners – or vice versa – we speak of an "expertise reversal effect", a concept introduced by Kalyuga, Ayres, Chandler, and Sweller (2003), and Kalyuga (2007).

(continued)

(continued)

As prior knowledge is the most important factor in learning (see Chapter 6, What you know determines what you learn), it's clear that instruction should take the learners' prior knowledge into account. Instruction and/or guidance that's essential for beginners (for example what is given in worked examples) can hamper learning in more experienced learners by making them do things that are contrary to what they already can effectively do, especially if these learners can't ignore or otherwise avoid the redundant information and guidance. In the same way, what works for more experienced learners hampers beginners who need the explicit support and guidance. To optimise cognitive load in each student (see Chapter 2, Take the load off me), suitable instruction and support should be given to novice learners, while unnecessary guidance and instruction should be removed or remembered as pupils acquire higher levels of competence in a specific domain.

Instruction must consider learner prior knowledge

Learning environment mismatch

Learning strategy substitution only partly explains the mathemathantic effects of certain forms of instruction. A second source lies in motivational variables affecting learners. For example, a learning environment can be very structured and guiding, limiting learner choice, or more open and less structured, giving more choice. Research shows that learners have different goals in learning, for example some learners do their best to be successful while others do their best because they fear failing (i.e. failure avoidance). Learners who fear failure are better served by structured and guiding environments where they feel safe and do their best. Learners focused on success work better in less structured environments where they can show what they're worth and later thank their success to themselves. For both groups, if they have to perform in an environment that does not fit well with their, say, motivational style, they won't perform well. The learning environment can then be counter-productive for learning.

LEARNING ENVIRONMENT MISMATCH
The same classroom can have very different outcomes

Does this mean that we should differentiate by giving in to learner preferences for a learning environment so that each learner can choose something that suits her or him? No! Students do not make good choices. Those with little prior knowledge or who experience *performance anxiety* often opt for an unstructured environment where they can make many choices with little support. In such an environment, they can discreetly fail. Also, learners with little prior knowledge also tend to overestimate themselves. We see this when students are asked to evaluate their own learning (judgements of learning). This is close to the Dunning–Kruger effect; a psychological phenomenon where people who are less competent in a certain area assess themselves too positively. On the other hand, better learners who would like to experience success often opt for the structured environment, because they expect to score better there. In addition, they sometimes have the tendency to underestimate themselves (also part of the Dunning–Kruger effect), in order to secure success. These choices are the exact opposite of what both groups need. It is therefore up to the teacher to properly align both the instruction and the learning environment with each learner.

THE DUNNING–
KRUGER EFFECT
Mistakenly predicting
your ability as better
than it is

Conclusions/implications of the work for educational practice

Teachers should take into account the different levels of knowledge and skills of individual students when teaching. This also includes attending to their levels of strategy use, such that experienced (i.e. more expert) learners are allowed to use their existing strategies when carrying out a task while beginners (i.e. novices) are given step-by-step support and guidance. In addition, teachers must motivate their students in a "prescriptive" way so that learners who are afraid of failure aren't put under too much pressure while learners who go for high grades are challenged. Finally, learners need to be guided in the choice of assignments. Good pupils who don't want to fail need to be inhibited in their tendency to opt for easier assignments. The table below shows the most common mathemathantic effects. In these cases instruction fails or is even harmful.

How to use the work in your teaching

This chapter makes clear what you intuitively already knew: what works for one student can be counter-productive to the other. Clark gives some rules of thumb that provide guidance in tailoring your instruction and teaching activities to the needs of individual students. Students with little prior knowledge benefit from small concrete steps, while pupils with a lot of prior knowledge actually thrive in a setting in which they can use this knowledge. They must be given the opportunity to use their strategies and automated knowledge. In addition, help learners with a fear of failure by providing structure and support. Learners who want to and can perform on their own, thrive better in an open learning environment. Remember that you often know better what a student needs than himself. Students often underestimate or overestimate themselves.

Students with
greater knowledge
benefit from more
independence

Knowing what doesn't work (i.e. approaches that are mathemathantic) is just as important as knowing what works (i.e. approaches that are mathemagenic). That's why we conclude this chapter with an overview of the most common mathemathantic effects; that is where instruction fails or is counter-productive.

TABLE 27.1
WHEN
MATHEMATHANTIC
EFFECTS OCCUR

Mathemathantic effects occur if learners…	
learning strategies	
… have little prior knowledge	but are given strategies which assume the availability of (partially) automated strategies, knowledge, and skills
… have much prior knowledge	but are given strategies which interfere with already available and automated strategies, knowledge, and skills
motivational goals	
… are afraid of failing	but are placed / allowed to learn in minimally structured and guided environments
… want to achieve success	but are placed / allowed to learn in highly structured environments with much support and guidance
learning environments	
… need a lot of support and guidance	but are made to work in an open environment that asks a lot of them
… need little support and guidance	but are made to work in a highly structured and controlled environment

Takeaways

- What works for one learner doesn't work for the other, or even worse it can be counter-productive and hurt learning.
- Beginners benefit from a great deal of structure and guidance, while more experienced learners benefit from more space and independence.
- You know best what your students need – they often over- or underestimate themselves; catering to their preferences – often seen as learning styles – is not the way to go because they usually do not know what's best for them.
- There are ways to avoid the expertise reversal effect such as gradually reducing support (so-called fading of scaffolding) as learners progress.
- When designing your instruction, make sure what you do adhere to the medical-ethical maxim "to do no harm".[4] This means that it's sometimes better not to do something, or even to do nothing, than to do more harm than good.

---

4   THIS PHRASE IS OFTEN ATTRIBUTED TO THE HIPPOCRATIC OATH, BUT IT ACTUALLY DOESN'T APPEAR IN THE OATH ITSELF.

References

CLARK, R. E. (1989). WHEN TEACHING KILLS LEARNING: RESEARCH ON MATHEMATHANTICS. *LEARNING AND INSTRUCTION: EUROPEAN RESEARCH IN AN INTERNATIONAL CONTEXT, 2*, 1–22. AVAILABLE FROM WWW.RESEARCHGATE.NET/PROFILE/RICHARD_CLARK3/ PUBLICATION/234744652_WHEN_TEACHING_KILLS_LEARNING_TYPES_OF_MATHEMATHANTIC_ EFFECTS/LINKS/56DEFD8608AEC8C022CF35ED/WHEN-TEACHING-KILLS-LEARNING-TYPES-OF-MATHEMATHANTIC-EFFECTS.PDF.

CRONBACH, L., & SNOW, R. (1977). *APTITUDES AND INSTRUCTIONAL METHODS: A HANDBOOK FOR RESEARCH ON INTERACTIONS.* NEW YORK, NY: IRVINGTON.

DOWALIBY, F. J., & SCHUMER, H. (1973). TEACHER-CENTERED VS. STUDENT-CENTERED MODE OF COLLEGE CLASSROOM INSTRUCTION AS RELATED TO MANIFEST ANXIETY. *JOURNAL OF EDUCATIONAL PSYCHOLOGY, 64*, 125–132. THESIS AVAILABLE FROM HTTPS://SCHOLARWORKS.UMASS. EDU/CGI/VIEWCONTENT.CGI?ARTICLE=2602&CONTEXT=THESES.

KALYUGA, S. (2007). EXPERTISE REVERSAL EFFECT AND ITS IMPLICATIONS FOR LEARNER-TAILORED INSTRUCTION. *EDUCATIONAL PSYCHOLOGY REVIEW, 19*, 509–539.

KALYUGA, S., AYRES, P., CHANDLER, P., & SWELLER, J. (2003). THE EXPERTISE REVERSAL EFFECT. *EDUCATIONAL PSYCHOLOGIST, 38*, 23–31. AVAILABLE FROM HTTP://RO.UOW.EDU.AU/ EDUPAPERS/136/.

SNOW, R. E. (APRIL 1972). INDIVIDUAL DIFFERENCES IN LEARNING-RELATED PROCESSES. *PAPER PRESENTED AT THE ANNUAL MEETING OF THE AMERICAN EDUCATIONAL RESEARCH ASSOCIATION,* CHICAGO, IL..

Suggested readings and links

PRINCIPLE TO PRACTICE 3: EXPERTISE REVERSAL EFFECT AND WORKED EXAMPLES.

AVAILABLE FROM HTTPS://FURTHEREDAGOGY.WORDPRESS. COM/2018/07/21/PRINCIPLE-TO-PRACTICE-3-EXPERTISE-REVERSAL-EFFECT-AND-WORKED-EXAMPLES/.

THE DUNNING–KRUGER EFFECT: A POISONOUS PARADOX.

AVAILABLE FROM HTTPS://3STARLEARNINGEXPERIENCES.WORDPRESS. COM/2016/09/06/DE-DUNNING-KRUGER-EFFECT-A-POISONOUS-PARADOX/.

Psychologists Justin Kruger and David Dunning published an article in 1999; *Unskilled and unaware of it: How difficulties in recognizing one's own incompetence lead to inflated self-assessments.* The Dunning-Kruger effect means that incompetent people (in this case, people with little to no knowledge on the topic at hand) are not capable – because of their incompetency – to see that their reasoning, choices and/or conclusions are just plain wrong.

LEARNING ORIENTATION RESEARCH: INDIVIDUAL DIFFERENCES IN LEARNING.
LEE CRONBACH'S AND RICHARD SNOW'S IMPORTANT LESSONS FROM THE PAST: HISTORICAL PERSPECTIVE.

AVAILABLE FROM WWW.TRAININGPLACE.COM/SOURCE/RESEARCH/ CRONBACH.HTM.

THE COBRA EFFECT – PREFERABLY APA6.

AVAILABLE FROM WWW.YOUTUBE.COM/WATCH?V=F0Y79KUEVXQ.

28 THE MEDIUM IS NOT THE MESSAGE

MEDIUM NOT THE MESSAGE

28 THE MEDIUM IS NOT THE MESSAGE

PAPER   "Reconsidering research on learning from media"[1]

QUOTE   *"The best current evidence is that media are mere vehicles that deliver instruction but do not influence student achievement any more than the truck that delivers our groceries causes changes in our nutrition".*[1]

Why you should read this article

Every new medium that has been "invented" seems to also have been touted as being a revolutionary educational change-maker. Each invention, followed by its general availability, has seen this hype, be it the phonograph, radio, film strip, movies, television, computer, or internet. Thomas Alva Edison (1878, 1888) claimed, for example, that the phonograph would allow for preserving the explanations given by teachers so that pupils would be able to refer to them at any moment. He also said that lessons could be placed on the phonograph for convenience in committing them to memory and would also become the primary teacher for children. In 1913[2] he stated "Books will soon be obsolete in the public schools. Scholars will be instructed through the eye. Our school system will be completely changed inside of ten years". And in 1922[3] he said

> I believe that the motion picture is destined to revolutionize our educational system and that in a few years it will supplant largely, if not entirely, the use of textbooks. I should say that on average we get about two percent efficiency out of school books as they are written

---

1   **CLARK, R. E.** (1983). RECONSIDERING RESEARCH ON LEARNING FROM MEDIA. *REVIEW OF EDUCATIONAL RESEARCH, 53*, 445–459.

2   **SMITH, F, J,** (JULY 9, 1913). THE EVOLUTION OF THE MOTION PICTURE: VI – LOOKING INTO THE FUTURE WITH THOMAS A. EDISON. *THE NEW YORK DRAMATIC MIRROR*, P. 24.

3   THE QUOTATION IS TAKEN FROM HENRY A. WISE'S (1939, P. 1) BOOK *MOTION PICTURES AS AN AID IN TEACHING AMERICAN HISTORY* (HARTFORD, CN: YALE UNIVERSITY PRESS).

today. The education of the future, as I see it, will be conducted through the medium of the motion picture ... where it should be possible to obtain one hundred percent efficiency.

With the introduction of each new medium, people in and around education (e.g. parents, teachers, researchers, administrators, politicians, and of course commercial companies) expected that each would revolutionise education, lead to amazing improvements in learning performance, and unalterably change the world of the teacher. But is any one medium really better than any other medium? And is that even the right question to ask? Richard Clark (1983) answered this question in a ground-breaking article and it still stands: It's not the medium that determines if teaching/learning is effective or efficient but, rather, the method.

How you teach is more important than the medium used

Abstract of the article

Recent meta-analyses and other studies of media's influence on learning are reviewed. Consistent evidence is found for the generalization that there are no learning benefits to be gained from employing any specific medium to deliver instruction. Research showing performance or time-saving gains from one or another medium are shown to be vulnerable to compelling rival hypotheses concerning the uncontrolled effects of instructional method and novelty. Problems with current media attribute and symbol system theories are described and suggestions made for more promising research directions.

The articles

This chapter is actually about two articles. The first is "Reconsidering research on learning from media" in which Clark looks back on earlier research into the effect of different types of media (i.e. "mechanical instruments, such as television and computers" (p. 445) used as delivery devices for instruction) on learning. In the article's introduction, he presents the spoiler when he says that:

> most current summaries and meta-analyses of media comparison studies clearly suggest that media do not influence learning under any conditions. Even in the few cases where dramatic changes in achievement or ability have followed the introduction of a medium ... it was not the medium that caused the change but rather a curricular reform that accompanied the change.

Technology is not a form of pedagogy

(p. 445)

AS OLD AS …

IN 1924, RÉVÉSZ AND HAZEWINKEL working at the Psychological and Paedagogical [sic] Laboratory in Amsterdam, published "The didactic value of lantern slides and films" in the *British Journal of Psychology*.[4] In that article, they studied the value of films versus slides for educational purposes. They wrote,

> No reasonable objection can be raised against the cinematograph as a means of spreading knowledge, or as an auxiliary in scientific research and instruction. About its usefulness in these fields all are agreed, but there is no consensus of opinion, when the merits of the film are weighed against those of the camera, and when the question is put whether the film is in every way to be preferred to the lantern-slide and can entirely replace it. This question can not [sic] be answered off-hand, but only after a thorough experimental investigation.
>
> (p. 184).

They conclude, "Our investigations have shown that the energetic propaganda made for the film on the strength of its alleged didactic importance is not well-founded. On the other hand, its educational importance has not been disproved" (p. 197).

What did Clark actually do? His article is an overview study (today we might call it a meta-analysis) in which he took a close look at research – both empirical studies and previous review studies – on media use in the classroom and their effects on learning. Most studies sought to answer the question of what the best medium was for offering learning material. Clark called such research *media comparison studies*: researchers compared one group that was taught with the new medium to another group that was offered the same material in a "regular" way. In general, these studies found no differences and he concluded that offering lessons via different types of media has no influence on learning. In that article he also noted that comparative studies suffered from three problems.

META-ANALYSIS
Analysis of many studies in a particular area

The research was contaminated

He noted that in the studies that did show a positive effect of the new medium there were more differences between the two groups than just the medium used. The method of teaching also differed. We all know,

---

4 THIS WAS A SHORTENED VERSION OF THEIR ORIGINAL 1923 ARTICLE, PUBLISHED IN DUTCH IN *PAEDIGOGISCHE STUDIËN*.

or at least should know, that to draw valid conclusions from a piece of research it's imperative that all aspects of the intervention and the control groups are exactly the same except for the one being studied. This means that if one were to compare the effects of television to the effects of a live lecture, then everything in the two conditions must be the same except for the media involved (live versus televised lecture). If the television lecture also includes illustrations of a concept using moving pictures or animations while the teacher in the classroom only uses a chalkboard and/or static images (i.e. the method used to teach the concept), then it's not possible to determine if any difference found is due to the medium or the method. In this example, the teacher should also have used animations or moving images to illustrate the concept in class or the TV lecture should have shown her/him in front of the chalkboard or using the static images. Clark noted that the differences in effects between the experimental and the control groups become smaller as researchers put more effort into keeping the groups as equal as possible. His conclusion: *There's no specific effect of any medium on learning, but that the (small) effects found can easily be explained differently.*

Education research is messy

New is interesting and sexy

The second problem with research on the effect of media on learning is the *novelty effect*; the increased effort and attention that participants in such studies tend to give to media that are novel to them. After all, it's often about new (and sexy) media, and introducing new things in the classroom often ensures enthusiastic students, which can cause them to work harder. While this novelty of the medium leads to a learning effect, it's short-lived. As soon as the medium becomes "normal", the effect decreases and dies away. When the iPad was first used in education, students became very enthusiastic about it; now the novelty is gone. Clark also found evidence for the novelty effect in the overview studies; the longer the interventions lasted, the smaller the effects became.

*NOVELTY EFFECT
When participants in a study respond 'differently' to something new*

Publication bias

The third problem is that studies with significant effects are more likely to be published than studies with no difference between experimental and control groups. That is what's known as *publication bias*. Clark explains that scientific journals want the most notable studies which makes the scientific evidence for media effects appear larger than it actually is. Research showing no differences or even the reverse are often shunned by journals.

*PUBLICATION BIAS
Tendency to only publish positive results*

Conclusion

Clark comes to this conclusion: It may seem that (new) media have positive effects on student learning, but these effects can largely be explained by things other than the characteristics of that medium.

He cites Glaser and Cooley (1973) who recommended using any acceptable medium as "a vehicle for making available to schools what psychologists have learned about learning" (p. 855). And that is the crux of the matter. It's the instruction (i.e. the method) and not the carrier of that instruction (i.e. the medium) that leads to a learning effect. According to Clark, researchers can therefore focus better on effective instruction.

The second publication is a chapter by Richard Clark and Dave Feldon in the second revised edition of the *Cambridge handbook of multimedia learning* (2014). There, they raise questions with respect to ten commonly espoused reasons that people give for implementing multimedia in education. They discussed five reasons in a chapter in the first edition of the book (2005) on the basis of strong empirical research. In the second edition they did the same for five new positively perceived learning benefits of multimedia (in addition to the original five that were in the first edition of the book). The first five were that people felt that multimedia instruction should be used because it:

1. *Leads to more learning.* Clark and Feldon show that there's no convincing or plausible proof that one medium or a combination of various media, including multimedia, lead to better learning. If there is proof of better learning then this can be explained by "non-media" factors such as instructional theory (e.g. the method/pedagogy), intelligence, social economic status, ability level of the learner, teacher quality, etc.

2. *Is more motivating.* It's possible that multimedia instruction seems more attractive for learners and that they'll prefer this type of learning approach if available, however this interest doesn't equal motivation for learning nor does it lead to better achievement.

   > Motivation doesn't lead to achievement

3. *Uses pedagogical agents that support learning.* The idea is that agents make learning more personal, though what they actually do is provide just-in-time scaffolding (e.g. hints, procedures, feedback, instruction). Designing, developing, and implementing such agents requires more time and is more expensive. They're often also, according to the authors, quite silly and learners get bored with them fairly quickly (remember "Clippy", Microsoft's paperclip agent?).

4. *Adapts to various learning styles and thus optimises learning for more learners.* First, learning styles don't exist (Kirschner, 2017). Clark and Feldon explain that multimedia make it possible to map the differences between learners with regard to *what* they learn and perhaps also to offer various versions of instructional material. However, there's no such thing as interaction between multimedia and non-existing learning styles, except for mathemathantic interactions (activities that kill learning – see Chapter 27, When teaching kills learning).

What methods
of instruction are
effective in the first
place?

5. *Facilitates learner-directed, constructivistic, and discovery learning approaches*. The question shouldn't be if multimedia learning facilitates these types of learning, it should be if constructivistic and discovery learning facilitate learning in the first place (see Chapter 17, Why discovery learning is a bad way to discover things/Why inquiry learning isn't). Interestingly, PISA 2015 makes clear that on the one hand teacher directed instruction has a strong positive effect on achievement while on the other hand enquiry learning has a medium to strong negative effect on achievement.

Clark and Feldon show that guided instruction is more effective and that the only types of learners who are good at discovery or inquiry-based learning are experts (also see the next principle).

The next (new) five focus on the *expectation* that multimedia instruction is *good for learning* because it provides:

AUTONOMY
Most learners aren't
equipped to direct
their own learning

6. *Autonomy and control over the sequence of instruction*. Although many multimedia environments allow for this, there are two challenges associated with learner control. First, learners typically don't have the required cognitive or metacognitive knowledge to effectively and efficiently determine their own learning sequence (see Chapter 26, Did you hear the one about the kinaesthetic learner … ?). When allowed this type of control, they usually achieve less. Second, experts would be really good at controlling their own learning sequence but experts usually don't require instruction.

7. *Higher order thinking skills*. There's limited evidence that multimedia instruction supports these skills, but even if it does, we encounter the same challenges as with the previous principle. It's more likely that the instructional approach is supporting the increase in higher order thinking skills and not the multimedia.

INCIDENTAL
LEARNING
Not all learning is
useful

8. *Incidental learning of enriching information*. Incidental learning takes place when you learn more than planned for in the instruction. Multimedia research shows that if you emphasise something in instruction, this will be learned (i.e. intentional learning) and all remaining points (i.e. incidental learning) are at a disadvantage. This goes for all types of instruction and not just for multimedia instruction. Think here of learning prompts, adjunct questions, stated learning goals, etc.).

9. *Interactivity*. This refers to, for example, accessing content through hyperlinks. This, unfortunately, doesn't actually add to learning but rather distracts from it. Gavriel Solomon called this the butterfly defect (learners fluttering like a butterfly from one piece of seemingly interesting information to another without actually learning). Linda Stone (2014) referred to this as *continuous partial attention* where a person pays simultaneous attention to a number of different sources of

BUTTERFLY
DEFECT
Flittering from
hyperlink to
hyperlink

incoming information, but at a superficial level. Furthermore, proponents of multimedia instruction seem to forget that the instructor is actually the most interactive medium and an intelligent one as well.

10. *Authentic learning environments and activities.* The idea here is that the advantage of multimedia lies in increasing motivation (see the principle 2) and/or facilitating transfer. However, according to Clark and Feldon, there's hardly any evidence that this is actually the case.

Just to make it clear: Clark and Feldon are not against using multimedia in education! They're only saying that 1) multimedia aren't a panacea, 2) multimedia itself achieve nothing, 3) using multimedia wrongly does more harm than good (i.e. is mathemathantic; see Chapter 27, When teaching kills learning), and 4) the instructional method used is the most critical factor for learning. And this last one is and remains the learning professional's – the teacher's – expertise!

Conclusions/implications of the work for educational practice

As stated, Clark doesn't say that media can't contribute to learning. Remember, it's not the vehicle, but the instructional method used that influences achievement. In other words, it doesn't matter whether the vegetables that you eat come to the store via plane, train, or truck, you become healthier because of the vegetables you eat (and the way you prepare them) and not because of the means of transporting them. That's why, according to Clark, we shouldn't carry out simple media comparison studies, but rather view media as tools that we can use properly and improperly. We also need to see how the tools can be improved.

This perspective has led to fruitful research into general principles for designing, developing, and implementing multimedia learning material. Richard Mayer is an important name here. His cognitive theory or multimedia learning – based on a combination of information processing theory, cognitive load theory, and dual coding theory (see Chapter 2, Take a load off me and Chapter 5, One picture and one thousand words) – is a useful guide for using multimedia in class (see Figure 28.1).

Cognitive theory of multimedia learning

Mayer formulated 12 design principles based on these three constituent theories (an overview can be found via the link at the end of this chapter). The most famous is probably the *multimedia principle,* which states that people learn better from words and pictures than from words alone (again, see Chapter 5, One picture and one thousand words). Many teachers and makers of instructional materials try to do this, but according to a second principle – the *redundancy principle* – using visual material plus audio is better than the use of visual material plus audio with written text (think about the teacher that reads her/his PowerPoint®

MULTIMEDIA PRINCIPLE
See dual-coding theory

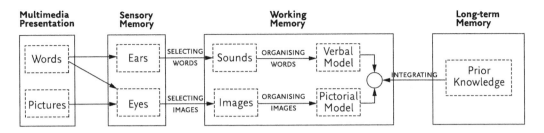

FIGURE 28.1
COGNITIVE
THEORY OF
MULTIMEDIA
LEARNING
(MAYER, 2005)

COHERENCE
PRINCIPLE
Keep it simple

slides to the class) care is needed. The latter is too much of a good thing and can lead to cognitive overload and poorer learning. A third important principle is the *coherence principle*, namely that people learn better when extraneous words, pictures and sounds are excluded rather than included. These extraneous, often eye-catching or sexy, artefacts distract learners. With Mayer's design principles in hand, we can effectively choose or design multimedia teaching materials.

How to use the work in your teaching

The first rule here is to choose media carefully. The media that you choose should make your teaching more efficient, more effective and more enjoyable, both for you and your students. To do this, you need to know the characteristics of the different media and what the best educational uses of them are.

What media can and cannot do

Thanks to Clark and Feldon, we know the ten things that media doesn't do. For example, media doesn't motivate, doesn't increase learning, doesn't facilitate construction of new knowledge, and so forth. Thanks to Mayer we know that you shouldn't include seductive or superficial elements that merely "engage" students as they are often counterproductive and can distract students. Also you need to take care that you don't overload students when using (multi)media and thus that you should use the media's possibilities to help them focus their attention on what's important. From this chapter, but also from Chapters 2 and 5, you now know that if you want to explain something with written text and images, you must make sure you integrate them properly. Either present a figure showing the steps in a process with their description in the figure (i.e. create spatial contiguity) or verbally describe the steps without the accompanying written text (i.e. avoid redundancy).

Takeaways

- No one medium is better than any other medium.
- It's not the medium, but the instructional method that makes the difference.

- Don't fall prey to the hypes around using media in the classroom.
- For meaningful use of (multi)media in your teaching you need knowledge of characteristics of the media and their educational uses.
- More media is not always better.
- If you use PowerPoint® or another presentation programme, make sure that what you say and what you project complement each other; *do not* read your slides.
- Just because students are "engaged", it doesn't mean they are learning anything. The call for new forms of media in education goes back over 150 years despite a distinct lack of evidence to back its use.
- The content and learning goals should determine the choice of media, not the other way around. Technology for the sake of technology is bad practice.

References

CLARK, R. E. (1983). RECONSIDERING THE RESEARCH ON LEARNING FROM MEDIA. *REVIEW OF EDUCATIONAL RESEARCH*, 53, 445–459. AVAILABLE FROM WWW.UKY.EDU/~GMSWAN3/609/CLARK_1983.PDF.

CLARK, R. E., & FELDON, D. F. (2014). TEN COMMON BUT QUESTIONABLE PRINCIPLES OF MULTIMEDIA LEARNING. IN R. E. MAYER (ED.), *THE CAMBRIDGE HANDBOOK OF MULTIMEDIA LEARNING* (2ND ED.) (PP. 151–173). CAMBRIDGE, MA: CAMBRIDGE UNIVERSITY PRESS.

EDISON, T. (1878). THE PHONOGRAPH AND ITS FUTURE. *THE NORTH AMERICAN REVIEW*, 126(262), 527–536. AVAILABLE FROM HTTP://EDISON.RUTGERS.EDU/YEAROFINNO/DEC13/EDISON_PHONOGRAPH%20AND%20IT%27S%20FUTURE_NORTH%20AMERICAN%20REVIEW_1878.PDF.

EDISON, T. (1888). THE PERFECTED PHONOGRAPH. *THE NORTH AMERICAN REVIEW*, 146(379), 641–650.

GLASER, R., & COOLEY, W. W. (1973). INSTRUMENTATION FOR TEACHING AND INSTRUCTIONAL MANAGEMENT. IN R. TRAVERS (ED.). *SECOND HANDBOOK OF RESEARCH ON TEACHING* (PP. 832–857). CHICAGO, IL: RAND MCNALLY COLLEGE PUBLISHING.

KIRSCHNER, P. A. (2017). STOP PROPAGATING THE LEARNING STYLES MYTH. *COMPUTERS AND EDUCATION*, 106, 166–171. AVAILABLE FROM WWW.SCIENCEDIRECT.COM/SCIENCE/ARTICLE/PII/S0360131516302482.

OECD (2016). *PISA 2015 RESULTS (VOLUME II): POLICIES AND PRACTICES FOR SUCCESSFUL SCHOOLS.* PARIS, FRANCE: OECD PUBLISHING.

RÉVÉSZ, G., & HAZEWINKEL, J. F. (1923). OVER DE DIDACTISCHE WAARDE VAN DE PROJECTIELANTAARN EN DE BIOSKOOP. *PEDAGOGISCHE STUDIËN*, 4, 33–67.

RÉVÉSZ, G., & HAZEWINKEL, J. F. (1924). THE DIDACTIC VALUE OF LANTERN SLIDES AND FILMS. *BRITISH JOURNAL OF PSYCHOLOGY*, 15, 184–197.

STONE, L. (2014). *CONTINUOUS PARTIAL ATTENTION.* RETRIEVED FROM HTTPS://LINDASTONE.NET/QA/CONTINUOUS-PARTIAL-ATTENTION/.

Suggested readings and links

HARTFORD UNIVERSITY, FACULTY CENTER FOR LEARNING DEVELOPMENT, 12 PRINCIPLES OF MULTIMEDIA LEARNING,

AVAILABLE FROM HTTP://HARTFORD.EDU/ACADEMICS/FACULTY/FCLD/DATA/DOCUMENTATION/TECHNOLOGY/PRESENTATION/POWERPOINT/12_PRINCIPLES_MULTIMEDIA.PDF.

HENDRICK, C. (JULY 6, 2018). CHALLENGING THE "EDUCATION IS BROKEN" AND SILICON VALLEY NARRATIVES.
AVAILABLE FROM HTTPS://RESEARCHED.ORG.UK/CHALLENGING-THE-EDUCATION-IS-BROKEN-AND-SILICON-VALLEY-NARRATIVES/.

 CLARK, R. E. (1994). MEDIA WILL NEVER INFLUENCE LEARNING. *EDUCATIONAL TECHNOLOGY RESEARCH & DEVELOPMENT 42(2), 21–29.*
AVAILABLE FROM WWW.EMPORIA.EDU/~HOLLANDJ/IT810/CLARK.PDF.

 KOZMA, R. B. (1994). WILL MEDIA INFLUENCE LEARNING? REFRAMING THE DEBATE. *EDUCATIONAL TECHNOLOGY RESEARCH & DEVELOPMENT 42(2), 7–19.*
AVAILABLE FROM WWW.EMPORIA.EDU/~HOLLANDJ/IT810/KOZMA.PDF.

 AN INTERVIEW WITH RICARD E. CLARK – HPT LEGACY SERIES 2012.
AVAILABLE FROM WWW.YOUTUBE.COM/WATCH?V=0YF0JJBWNNU.

 TECHNOLOGY CAN HELP LEARNING WHEN INSPIRED BY PEDAGOGY AND SOUND INSTRUCTIONAL DESIGN PRINCIPLES, RICHARD CLARK ON MEDIA VS. METHODS.
AVAILABLE FROM WWW.YOUTUBE.COM/WATCH?V=DPKCCNVJL20.

29 THE TEN DEADLY SINS IN EDUCATION

TEN DEADLY SINS

29 THE TEN DEADLY SINS IN EDUCATION

QUOTE *"This isn't right. This isn't even wrong".*[1]

This book is about a particular tradition, a tradition which focuses on how to cultivate the best conditions which foster learning. By "learning" we mean a change in long-term memory (Kirschner, Sweller, & Clarke, 2006). Any attempt to do this which ignores the cognitive architecture of the brain is unlikely to be successful and may even hinder long-term learning. For many teachers on the frontline, the advice they have been given has been based on folk wisdom, vague abstract theory and approaches that conform to Wolfgang Pauli's famous quip: "This isn't right. This isn't even wrong". One aim of this book is to empower teachers to be able to not only evaluate what they are advised to do but to provide a strong evidence base from which they can refine and reflect on their own practice and create the best conditions under which their students can flourish.

The Christian teaching, attributed to the Desert Fathers, speaks of seven cardinal or deadly sins that we need to overcome to live a virtuous life: pride, greed, lust, envy, gluttony, wrath, and sloth. In this final chapter we very briefly describe what we feel are the ten deadly sins of education. Giving in to those sins is often tempting, but if you do you'll be guilty of implementing evidence-uninformed education and flying in the face of evidence.

1. The learning pyramid

The learning pyramid (see Figure 29.1) is a seemingly useful model that reflects the effectiveness of different forms of teaching. According to the pyramid, pupils only remember 5% of a classroom lesson (what the teacher says), 10% of what they read, 20% of an audio-visual

---

[1] WOLFGANG PAULI WAS AN AUSTRIAN BORN PHYSICIST. HE IS REPORTED TO HAVE SAID THIS AFTER READING A COLLEAGUE'S PAPER. IT IS QUOTED IN *THE SUCCESSFUL TOASTMASTER: A TREASURE CHEST OF INTRODUCTIONS, EPIGRAMS, HUMOR, AND QUOTATIONS* (1966, P. 350) BY PROCHNOW AND IN *MATHEMATICAL APOCRYPHA REDUX: MORE STORIES AND ANECDOTES OF MATHEMATICIANS AND THE MATHEMATICAL* (2005, P. 194) BY KRANTZ.

presentation, 30% of a demonstration, 50% of a discussion, 75% of what they do themselves and 80–90% of what they explain to others. The percentages vary in different sources, but that's not important. What is important is that it's nonsense that you shouldn't fall for.

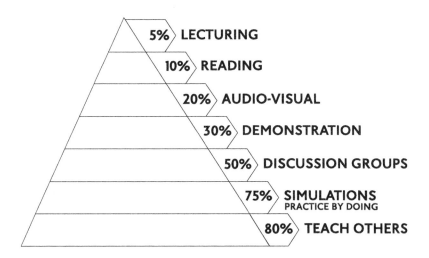

FIGURE 29.1
THE LEARNING
PYRAMID

First, there is no basis for such percentages. Even the institution that everyone quotes (National Training Laboratories in Bethel, Maine, USA) says they don't have data to support them. Furthermore, the pyramid is simply a corruption of Edgar Dale's cone of experience (1954), in which he indicated how different media differ along a continuum from abstract (language, letters) to concrete (direct experience). Finally, even if the percentages were correct, you can't do anything with it. A teacher standing in front of the class and teaching about electricity (5%) can write the main points and principles on the whiteboard or show them in a PowerPoint® presentation (+10%), show a video clip about circuits (+20%), give a small demonstration of a battery or lamps in series and in parallel (+30%) and then discuss the results of the demonstration with the students (+50%), etc. No lesson is purely one or the other and just adding these percentages up teaches us that you could learn more than 100%!

2. Learning styles

People are all different and just as they may prefer different foods, they also may prefer different ways of learning. One prefers pictures while the other prefers words. While it sounds and even feels logical that there are children who are visual learners (learn best when information is presented as pictures, diagrams, and charts), while others are auditory (learn best in a lecture or group discussion) readers/writers (learn best through reading and writing) or kinesthetic (hands-on learners who learn best through physical experience), there's no evidence whatsoever for this. And this is just one of the 72 different learning styles (the so-called VARK) that Coffield and colleagues (2004) found when they went through the literature.

Unfortunately, all that glitters is not gold. This way of looking at how children learn, and therefore how the teacher should teach, has at least three problems, as we have already described in Chapter 26, Did you hear the one about the kinaesthetic learner … ?. First, in most studies learning styles are determined based on what people say they prefer. It's therefore about learning *preferences* and not learning *styles*. Second, there's a big difference between these and what leads to better learning. I think we all can agree that if we ask people what they prefer to eat, many if not most will say fatty things and/or salty things and/or sugary things. I think that we can also all agree that these preferences are not the constituents of a healthy diet. That you prefer it doesn't make it good for you, both in food and learning. Finally, most so-called learning styles are based on specific types: people are classified into different groups. However, there's no evidence for the existence of these groups. And this discounts the fact that even if they all did exist, if the 72 types of learning styles were simply dichotomous (e.g. concrete versus abstract thinkers), which they aren't as we saw with VARK, there would be 2^{72} different combinations of learning styles, or 4,722,366,482,869,669,245,213,696 different combinations – more than the number of people who have ever lived on earth – so good luck tailoring your teaching to them!

But possibly the most important problem is that if we put learners in different boxes and teach accordingly (i.e. pigeonhole them), we create situations that instead of promoting learning, hinder it (see Chapter 27, When teaching kills learning).

3. Children are digital natives and think differently from previous generations

We have to radically change education! We're teaching a new type of learner with specific competencies that enable them to use ICT effectively and efficiently. This new learner is the *digital native*. Marc Prensky introduced this term in 2001: the idea of a generation that has never lived without digital technologies and therefore has exceptional and unique characteristics that distinguish it from all previous generations with respect to thinking and learning (Prensky, 2001). He concluded that we must design and introduce new forms of education that focus on the special gifts of these digital natives. Unfortunately, he based all of this on simple personal observations of young people and not on any research.

Wim Veen and Ben Vrakking (2006) followed suit, introducing the term *homo zappiëns* to describe a new generation of students who learned significantly differently from their predecessors. They claim that *homos zappiëns* independently and without instruction develop the metacognitive skills needed for discovery learning, networked learning, experimentation, collaborative learning, active learning, self-directed learning, and problem-based learning. Based on these claims (again acquired through personal observation and not research) a growing group of people, including politicians and administrators, believe that education should respond to this. We hear things like "Let's Googlify education", "Knowledge acquisition isn't necessary", and "We need to harness the cognitive and metacognitive skills of this technology-savvy generation!"

Don't! There's no evidence that young people today have any special skills (other than very fast-moving thumbs) that would allow them to learn differently. The proponents of these ideas based this purely on their own experiences and anecdotal evidence.

4. Children can multitask

One of the competencies that people attribute to the non-existent digital native is that of multitasking. There's much confusion about this concept. Multitasking is the ability to simultaneously perform two or more tasks that require thinking (or information processing) without a loss of speed or accuracy. To really multitask you need two or more separate processing units (think of a multicore computer with two, four, eight, or even more CPUs). The problem is that people only have one CPU, namely their brains. When it comes to automated tasks that don't require thinking, we can easily do two or more things at the same time.

What we actually do is switch between tasks (i.e. task switching). But when we switch between tasks, we lose time and we make mistakes. If we switch tasks, we (unconsciously) make a "decision" to shift our attention from one task to another. Our brain then activates a rule to end the processing of one task whereby you leave the cognitive schema that you were using, and initiates another rule to enable the processing of the other task with its concomitant schema. Switching between tasks takes time and distributing attention between these two tasks requires space in our working memory. The two tasks therefore interfere with each other. In short, we simply can't multitask. If we try to do two or more things at the same time that require thought, we do things worse and it takes more time in total than if we had done them one after the other (i.e. serially monotask).

5. With Google, knowledge is no longer important

We hear that just about all the "knowledge" we need can be found on the internet via Google or other search engines and, thus, that we no longer need to know as much as we used to, as long as we can look it up. But there are problems here, First, there's no knowledge on the internet; only information, of which a great deal is non-information or outright nonsense from questionable sources. Without a solid knowledge base we can do little with what we find on the internet. In an interview with a Dutch quality newspaper, two women who run a nutrition website propagating a healthy lifestyle stated in 2016 that eggs are the menstruation of chickens and are, therefore, bad for you. The two are registered dietitians and therefore you might conclude that this is true.[2] But mammals menstruate and chickens aren't mammals! In other words, nonsense. But how could you know that without basic knowledge of biology?

So what we read, see, and understand is determined by what we already know and not the other way around (see Chapter 6; What you know determines what you learn). Our prior knowledge and experiences determine how we see, understand, and interpret the world around us. It also determines how well we can look up, find, select, and process (or evaluate) the information available on the internet. Unfortunately, in the best case, students only have minimal prior knowledge of a subject (after all, they are students; if they already had the knowledge, they would be experts).

Related to this is the myth that knowledge has a limited expiration date (as perishable as fresh fish is sometimes said). This is nonsense too. The vast majority of what we have learned is still correct. There is a huge increase in information. But as said, without knowledge we can do little with it.

6. You learn to solve problems by solving problems

Problem-based learning is quite popular. One of its premises is that the best way to learn to solve problems is to solve them. Unfortunately this isn't the case (see Chapter 2; Take a load off me). To solve problems, we must first have knowledge of and skills in the domain in which we must solve that problem. We can't solve a chess problem without being able to play chess (knowing how the pieces move, what the rules are, what the common strategies and tactics are, etc.), just as we cannot solve a math problem without math knowledge. In other words, skills are domain specific.

Also, it helps enormously if we have a set of possible solution strategies plus knowledge of when we can best use each one. This is

---

2   THE DUTCH NUTRITION CENTRE WARNS THAT FOLLOWING THE ADVICE OF THESE TWO WOMEN CAN LEAD TO A WEAKENED IMMUNE SYSTEM, BONE LOSS, AND WEAKENED MUSCLES.

called procedural knowledge (knowing what the steps are) and is very similar to the so-called twenty-first century computational thinking skill, which means that you can analyse a problem in smaller steps so that you can solve it. But again, without knowledge you can't carry out the procedure and so you cannot acquire this domain-general twenty-first century skill.

Finally, without domain-specific and procedural knowledge, problem-solving becomes an exercise in trial and error. This is neither effective nor efficient, especially since we're constantly hitting walls because we're doing it wrong (which can be quite frustrating). And then, should we happen to solve the problem, we usually don't know why we've succeeded and it's therefore difficult to repeat and apply in other situations. And finally there's a good chance that we'll teach ourselves a wrong approach that we'll have to unlearn in the future.

7. Discovery learning is the best way to learn

Jerome Bruner introduced discovery learning as a research-based instructional form in 1967 (Bruner, 1967). He assumed that it would be better for students to discover facts and the connections between them than to provide them as a teacher. But if we use such an approach with starting students, we do not take into account the limitations of their working memory (see Chapter 1, A novice is not a little expert). During discovery learning, we must always look for links between things and the principles that apply in the domain. Beginners, however, hardly have any domain knowledge and also have no systematic approach to finding it. This therefore requires a great deal of their working memory, all the more because inexperienced students are capable of connecting any and all elements in the domain through ignorance. They're faced with an explosion of combinations without knowledge to keep them under control. Moreover, this load on working memory doesn't result in more knowledge in long-term memory as it was used to discover and not to learn.

In addition, this approach is based on the idea that a child is a kind of miniature scientist. But children not only have less knowledge than a scientist (who can use discovery as a way to move forward; it's their epistemology), they also see and interpret the world differently (much more naively), think differently (concretely and not abstract) and therefore experience the world differently. That is why we shouldn't use the working method of the scientist as an educational approach for the inexperienced student!

8. Motivation leads to learning

A frequently heard statement from parents, teachers, politicians, and even scientists is that the problem with contemporary education is that pupils find it boring and unattractive and therefore don't learn well. People often use concepts such as motivation and engagement as keys to better education and as proxies for learning; as if being hyped about or engaged with something means that you've also learned something. The idea is that the more we motivate learners, the better they'll learn. Unfortunately this isn't the case. Don't get us wrong. Of course motivation is great and motivated students will start on something sooner than if they aren't motivated, but this is no guarantee for learning. In fact, if a student starts out motivated but doesn't succeed, that motivation fades away very quickly and we're worse off than if the learner was only lukewarm to begin with.

What we know from research is this: there's neither a causal relationship (motivation does not lead to better learning and performance) nor a reciprocal relationship (in the sense that motivation leads to learning and learning leads to motivation) between motivation and learning. It's learning that leads to motivation. When we experience success, no matter how small that success is, it feeds our motivation to continue (as we saw in Chapter 8, Beliefs about intelligence can affect intelligence). For example, good maths performance has a significant positive effect on the intrinsic motivation of students for maths, but motivation for maths doesn't lead to better math performance (Garon-Carrier et al., 2016; McConney et al., 2014). And that applies to both boys and girls.

9. Non-existent grit

It's weird. On the one hand, we hear that learning is boring and hard and should be fun, but on the other hand, everyone is talking about grit. Grit is putting your shoulders to the wheel and noses to the grindstone. According to the creator of the term, Angela Lee Duckworth, grit is the passion and perseverance to achieve long-term goals combined with interest, practice, purpose, and hope. For her, grit is being so driven to reach your goal that you never ever give up – even in the face of adversity – and do everything you can to achieve it. In short, perseverance, dedication, efficacy, and resilience.

Marcus Credé and his colleagues (2016) have shown that grit is just old wine in new bottles and is actually nothing more than perseverance. In addition, they looked at, among other things, the relationship between grit and both learning performance and remembering what was learned, and that was also disappointing. Researchers found poor correlations between grit and learning performance and grit and remembering, while there are strong correlations between, for example, learning and cognitive ability (IQ), study habits, and skills. Even perseverance alone, without all the extra trimmings from Duckworth, was more strongly correlated with learning than grit!

10. School kills creativity

Ever heard of a straw man? According to Wikipedia, a straw man is a type of fallacy – reasoning that is wrong, but seems plausible – whereby the actual position of an opponent isn't refuted, but a caricature thereof. The man who claimed that schools kill creativity – Sir Ken Robinson – was guilty of this. He presented the school as a place where teachers do nothing but preach from the pulpit and where students do nothing but listen obediently and do their homework. We don't know of any such teachers or schools; do you?

Strange here is that Sir Ken defines creativity as "the process of having/coming up with original ideas that have value – usually the result of the interaction of different disciplinary ways of seeing things".[3] In other words, based on domain-specific knowledge! Without knowledge and skills which we acquire at school it's impossible – except in the case of luck – to come up with something of value. The most creative painters, even surrealists, first learned how to paint. Therefore, we suggest that you quote Keith Sawyer rather than Ken Robinson. Sawyer (Sawyer, 2012) says that "creativity is largely domain specific – that the ability to be creative in any given domain, whether physics, painting, or musical performance, is based on long years of study and mastery of a domain-specific set of cognitive structures" (pp. 11–12).

This idea that everything has to be "relevant" to children is a debased view of the profession. The notion that children can only learn things through the prism of their own interests and that to ask them to consider things outside of that is somehow beating a love of learning out of them is demeaning, not just to teachers but to students themselves. Possibly the greatest thing a teacher can do is to introduce students to wondrous worlds beyond the limited borders of their own experience, to allow them to see the previously unseen and to make new and enriching connections that were hitherto unavailable to them.

Takeaway

- If you want to teach well, avoid these ten deadly sins!

---

3 WWW.TED.COM/TALKS/KEN_ROBINSON_SAYS_SCHOOLS_KILL_CREATIVITY/TRANSCRIPT?LANGUAGE=EN

References

BRUNER, J. S. (1967). *ON KNOWING: ESSAYS FOR THE LEFT HAND.* NEW YORK: ATHENEUM.

COFFIELD, F., MOSELEY, D., HALL, E., & ECCLESTONE, K. (2004). *LEARNING STYLES AND PEDAGOGY IN POST-16 LEARNING. A SYSTEMATIC AND CRITICAL REVIEW.* LONDON: LEARNING AND SKILLS RESEARCH CENTRE. AVAILABLE FROM WWW.RESEARCHGATE.NET/PUBLICATION/232929341_LEARNING_STYLES_AND_PEDAGOGY_IN_POST_16_EDUCATION_A_CRITICAL_AND_SYSTEMATIC_REVIEW.

CREDÉ, M., TYNAN, M. C., & HARMS, P. D. (2016). MUCH ADO ABOUT GRIT: A META-ANALYTIC SYNTHESIS OF THE GRIT LITERATURE. *JOURNAL OF PERSONALITY AND SOCIAL PSYCHOLOGY.* AVAILABLE FROM WWW.ACADEMIA.EDU/25397556/MUCH_ADO_ABOUT_GRIT_A_META-ANALYTIC_SYNTHESIS_OF_THE_GRIT_LITERATURE

DALE, E. (1954). *AUDIO-VISUAL METHODS IN TEACHING* (2ND ED. ORIGINALLY PUBLISHED 1946). NEW YORK: THE DRYDEN PRESS.

GARON-CARRIER, G., BOIVIN, M., GUAY, F., KOVAS, Y., DIONNE, G., LEMELIN, J.-P., SÉGUIN, J., VITARO, F., & TREMBLAY, R. (2016). INTRINSIC MOTIVATION AND ACHIEVEMENT IN MATHEMATICS IN ELEMENTARY SCHOOL: A LONGITUDINAL INVESTIGATION OF THEIR ASSOCIATION. *CHILD DEVELOPMENT, 87* (1), 165–175. AVAILABLE FROM WWW.RESEARCHGATE.NET/PUBLICATION/282135309_INTRINSIC_MOTIVATION_AND_ACHIEVEMENT_IN_MATHEMATICS_IN_ELEMENTARY_SCHOOL_A_LONGITUDINAL_INVESTIGATION_OF_THEIR_ASSOCIATION

KIRSCHNER, P. A., SWELLER, J., & CLARK, R. E. (2006). WHY MINIMAL GUIDANCE DURING INSTRUCTION DOES NOT WORK: AN ANALYSIS OF THE FAILURE OF CONSTRUCTIVIST, DISCOVERY, PROBLEM-BASED, EXPERIENTIAL, AND INQUIRY-BASED TEACHING. *EDUCATIONAL PSYCHOLOGIST, 46* (2), 75–86. DOI:10.1207/S15326985EP4102_1.

MCCONNEY, A., OLIVER, M. C., WOODS-MCCONNEY, A., SCHIBECI, R., & MAOR, D. (2014). INQUIRY, ENGAGEMENT, AND LITERACY IN SCIENCE: A RETROSPECTIVE, CROSS-NATIONAL ANALYSIS USING PISA 2006. *SCIENCE EDUCATION, 98,* 963–980. AVAILABLE FROM HTTP://EPRINTS.NOTTINGHAM.AC.UK/27768/1/INQUIRYENGAGEMENT%26LITERACYINSCIENCE-REVISEDMAR2014.PDF.

PRENSKY, M. (2001). DIGITAL NATIVES, DIGITAL IMMIGRANTS. ON THE HORIZON. *NCB UNIVERSITY PRESS, 9,* 1–6. AVAILABLE FROM WWW.MARCPRENSKY.COM/WRITING/PRENSKY%20-%20DIGITAL%20NATIVES,%20DIGITAL%20IMMIGRANTS%20-%20PART1.PDF.

SAWYER, R. K. (2012). A CALL TO ACTION: THE CHALLENGES OF CREATIVE TEACHING AND LEARNING. *TEACHERS COLLEGE RECORD, 117* (10), 1–34. AVAILABLE FROM HTTP://KEITHSAWYER.COM/PDFS/SAWYER%202015%20TCR.PDF.

VEEN, W., & VRAKKING, B. (2006). *HOMO ZAPPIENS: GROWING UP IN A DIGITAL AGE.* LONDON: NETWORK CONTINUUM EDUCATION. THE ACCOMPANYING POWERPOINT IS AVAILABLE FROM WWW.SCRIBD.COM/DOC/2578647/WIM-VEEN – NO LONGER AVAILABLE ONLINE.

Further reading and links

BLOG GRIT: TO GRIT OR NOT TO GRIT: THAT'S THE QUESTION.

AVAILABLE FROM HTTPS://3STARLEARNINGEXPERIENCES.WORDPRESS.COM/2016/07/05/TO-GRIT-OR-NOT-TO-GRIT-THATS-THE-QUESTION/.

BLOG MOTIVATION: CLOSE THE STABLE DOORS: EFFECTS OF MOTIVATION AND ENGAGEMENT ON LEARNER ACHIEVEMENT?

AVAILABLE FROM HTTPS://3STARLEARNINGEXPERIENCES.WORDPRESS.COM/2016/05/17/CLOSE-THE-STABLE-DOORS-EFFECTS-OF-MOTIVATION-ANENGAGEMENT-ON-LEARNER-ACHIEVEMENT/.

BLOG DIGITAL NATIVES: THE DISTURBING FACTS ABOUT DIGITAL NATIVES.

AVAILABLE FROM HTTPS://3STARLEARNINGEXPERIENCES.WORDPRESS.COM/2015/10/20/THE-DISTURBING-FACTS-ABOUT-DIGITAL-NATIVES/.

LEARNING STYLES: IS WHAT LEARNERS SAY THAT THEY PREFER GOOD FOR THEM? [BLOG]

AVAILABLE FROM HTTPS://3STARLEARNINGEXPERIENCES.WORDPRESS.COM/PAGE/11/?S=LEARNING+STYLES.

LEARNING PYRAMID: AN UPDATE TO THE LEARNING PYRAMID [BLOG].

AVAILABLE FROM HTTPS://THEECONOMYOFMEANING.COM/2016/07/08/AN-UPDATE-TO-THE-LEARNING-PYRAMID/.

LEARNING PYRAMID: A NEW STUDY ON THE DIFFUSION OF THAT *%*§§§ LEARNING PYRAMID [BLOG].

AVAILABLE FROM HTTPS://THEECONOMYOFMEANING.COM/2015/10/19/A-NEW-STUDY-ON-THE-DIFFUSION-OF-THAT-%C2%A7%C2%A7%C2%A7-LEARNING-PYRAMID/.

SOME EXCELLENT PIECES ON WHY SIR KEN ROBINSON'S ARGUMENTS ARE PROBLEMATIC ARE

AVAILABLE FROM CRISPIN WESTON: HTTPS://EDTECHNOW.NET/GUEST-POSTS/KEN-ROBINSON-REBUTTAL.

JOE KIRBY: HTTPS://PRAGMATICREFORM.WORDPRESS.COM/2013/10/12/WHAT-SIR-KEN-GOT-WRONG

CARL HENDRICK: WWW.TES.COM/NEWS/KEN-ROBINSON-TEACHER-BASHER-SCHOOLS-MUST-STOP-LISTENING-HIS-PANGLOSSIAN-IDEAS

Index

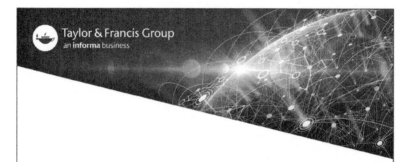